Construction Drawings

electrical training ALLIANCE
IBEW · NECA

TABLE OF CONTENTS

TABLE OF CONTENTS

INTRODUCTION

The *Construction Drawings* textbook was developed by the *electrical training ALLIANCE* to aid field workers in the electrical industry in properly interpreting the drawings and documentation created to convey the design intent of a building prior to its construction. The knowledge, skills, and abilities required to demonstrate proficiency in accurately interpreting construction drawings will be relied upon each day in the career of a tradesperson.

The textbook systematically explores deepening levels of construction drawing beginning with the conceptual purpose of the drawing. Next, the content explores the need for and use of scales in construction drawings. After the groundwork and necessary preparation has been completed to begin the study of construction drawings, the textbook explores one-by-one the need and use for each type of common drawing used on most construction drawing blueprint sets.

The plan view, a horizontal view of a building, is followed by the elevation view, a vertical view of the building's features. Following the most used drawings, the textbook explores deepening levels of interpretation of detail about the building utilizing section and detail views. The final piece of the most commonly used construction drawings is information that is not as easily conveyed via a drawing, but through the use of text- and table-based information. The specifications and schedules provide the finishing touches on a set of construction drawings in order to ensure that no detail is left to chance.

ABOUT THIS BOOK

This process of acquiring the skills required to read construction drawings has been reimagined and relies heavily on the use of ancillary visual content far beyond the printed pages of the textbook or pixels on the screen in an eBook. The new features include three-dimensional and layered image information to augment and enhance the learning process. At the center of the ancillary visual content is the *Construction Viewer* online content presentation software. This software allows for a consistent, easy-to-use presentation of pertinent reinforcing material to each concept presented in the textbook.

In addition to the visual augmentation of the construction drawings content is the inclusion of additional resources for remediation. The new feature "For More Information" allows the student to review additional methods of content presentation via text, images, and animations. This additional content allows the user to experience new concepts from multiple perspectives to allow for greater depth in the understanding of the most important content.

This text was developed by blending up-to-date practices with long-lived theories to help tradespersons learn how to better perform on the job. It is written at a level that invites further discussion beyond its pages while clearly and succinctly answering the questions of how and why.

ACKNOWLEDGMENTS

TECHNICAL INFORMATION AND ASSISTANCE

Autodesk, Inc.

Calculated Industries

Klein Tools, Inc.

National Institute of Standards and
Technology (NIST)

NECA 100-2013 NEIS Symbols for
Electrical Construction Drawings
(ANSI)

Procore

TECHNICAL REVIEWERS

Fred Meeske, E.E.T
Vice President
Rosendin

John Simmons
Training Director Emeritus
Florida East Coast Electrical JATC

Ian Warner
Building Construction Consultant
Trimble Buildings Construction Field
Systems

Tyler Westfall
Arizona BIM Manager
Rosendin

Michael Zapp
BIM Coordinator III
Rosendin

FEATURES

Figures, including photographs and artwork, clearly illustrate concepts from the text.

The **Construction Viewer** is available for figures with the Viewer icon and QR code.

When **Remediation** is available for the student, the Viewer icon will be **red** to indicate that the student will see a "For More Information" tab in the Construction Drawings Viewer.

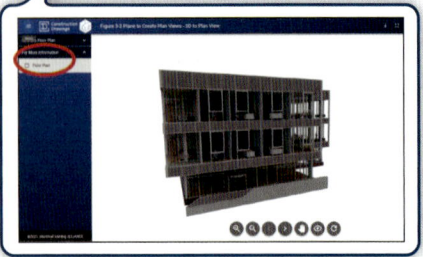

For additional information related to QR codes, visit qr.njatcdb.org Item #1079

Quick Response Codes (QR Codes) create a link between the textbook and the Internet. They can be scanned using Smartphone applications to obtain additional information online. (To access the information without using a Smartphone, visit qr.njatcdb.org and enter the referenced Item #.)

FEATURES

The **Construction Viewer** provides additional visual content to enhance the text via 360° images, 3D models, and layered images.

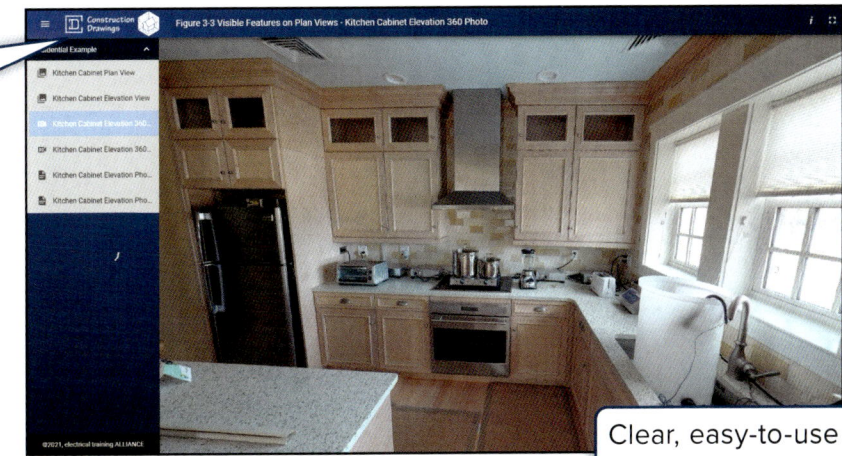

Clear, easy-to-use **Contents** pages in the front of the text-book and inside each chapter enable the reader to quickly find important *Construction Drawings* concepts.

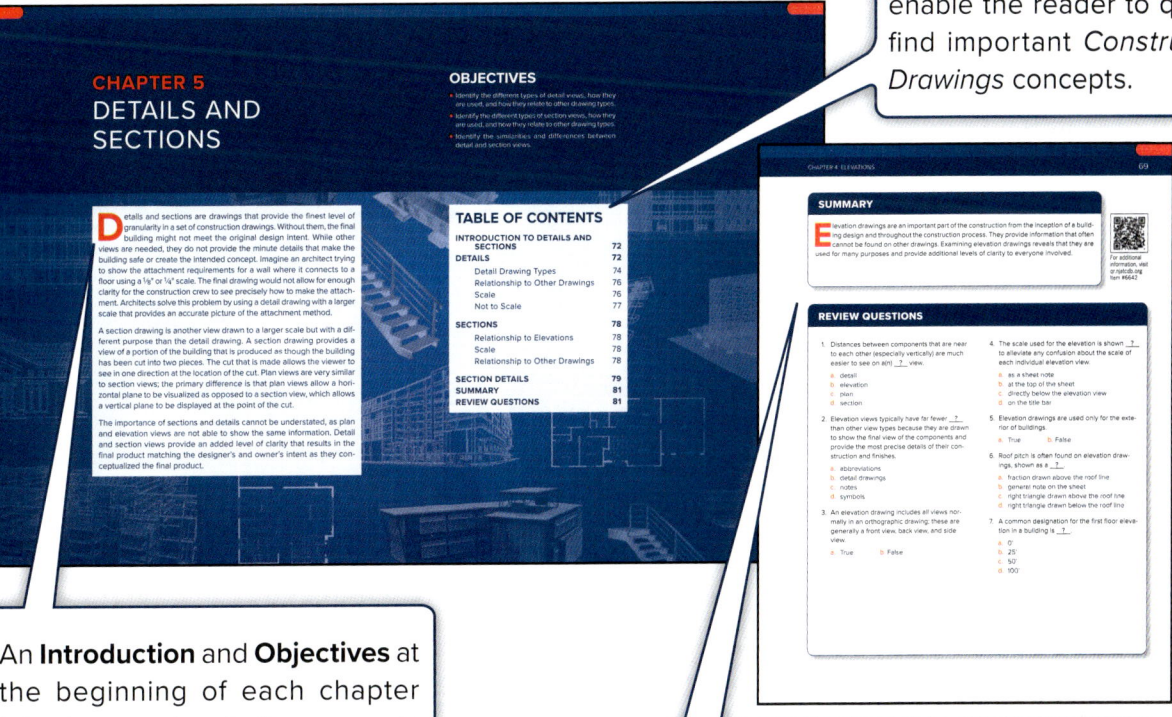

An **Introduction** and **Objectives** at the beginning of each chapter introduce readers to the concepts to be learned in the chapter.

At the conclusion of each chapter, a concise chapter **Summary** and **Review Questions** reinforce the most important concepts included in the chapter.

CHAPTER 1
INTRODUCTION TO BLUEPRINTS AND THE DESIGN PROCESS

Imagine a master craftsperson, without any knowledge about how construction drawings are assembled or interpreted, is given a set of blueprints for a NASA space shuttle. Although the craftsperson has all the requisite skills to build the spacecraft, building the intended vehicle will be a struggle. The confusion will be evident from the outset, and the project will be in trouble. It would be almost impossible for the craftsperson to complete the job without being trained to understand the drawings.

Blueprint reading for the construction trades is remarkably similar to this scenario. A person cannot simply view a set of construction drawings and construct a building without knowing how to read and use the information contained within the drawings and documentation. Because the drawings and documentation are structured in a standardized and consistent format, novices can learn the necessary reading skills. An understanding of industry practices will allow construction drawings to be accurately interpreted, resulting in a building constructed by skilled tradespeople that matches the architect's vision.

Gaining an understanding of types of drawings, varieties of views, their purpose, and written documentation that accompany the drawings provides the foundational information necessary to understand the designer's intent.

OBJECTIVES

- Recognize the conceptual design process and its importance to the construction process.
- Review the evolution of construction and introduce the documentation process.
- List the standards used for design professionals.
- Identify the standard components used in construction documentation.

TABLE OF CONTENTS

CONCEPTUAL DESIGN PROCESS

The construction of a building begins long before any action takes place on the parcel of land. The process starts when property owners, developers, or a group of people interested in building space communicate their desires to an architect or architectural firm. The initial step in the process involves meetings where the ownership conveys their needs to the design team. Discussions include their space needs, the use of the space (residential, commercial, or industrial), the proposed building's location, and their vision of the building's appearance. **See Figure 1-1.**

Once the wishes and concerns of ownership are conveyed to the design team, the creation of the construction documents begins. Elevation drawings are usually the first plans created by the design team to show their vision of the intended concepts. These drawings provide a view of each side of the building's exterior as it should appear after completion. In many cases, the architectural team will create more than one set of elevation drawings for the building. Each set of elevations shows a different aesthetic view of the building each with varying costs to construct the included features.

The design team will present their drawings to the ownership with estimated construction costs associated with each set. When one of the designs is approved, the architectural team creates a complete set of drawings. The amount of work required to complete the construction drawings depends on many factors, including the building size, its use, the type of equipment used, and trade-specific enhancements.

The approved set of elevation drawings sets the stage for creating site plans, landscape drawings, various plan views, interior elevations, sections, and details. In some cases, the design team may include drawings with other titles in their construction drawings. The

PRELIMINARY BUILDING SKETCH

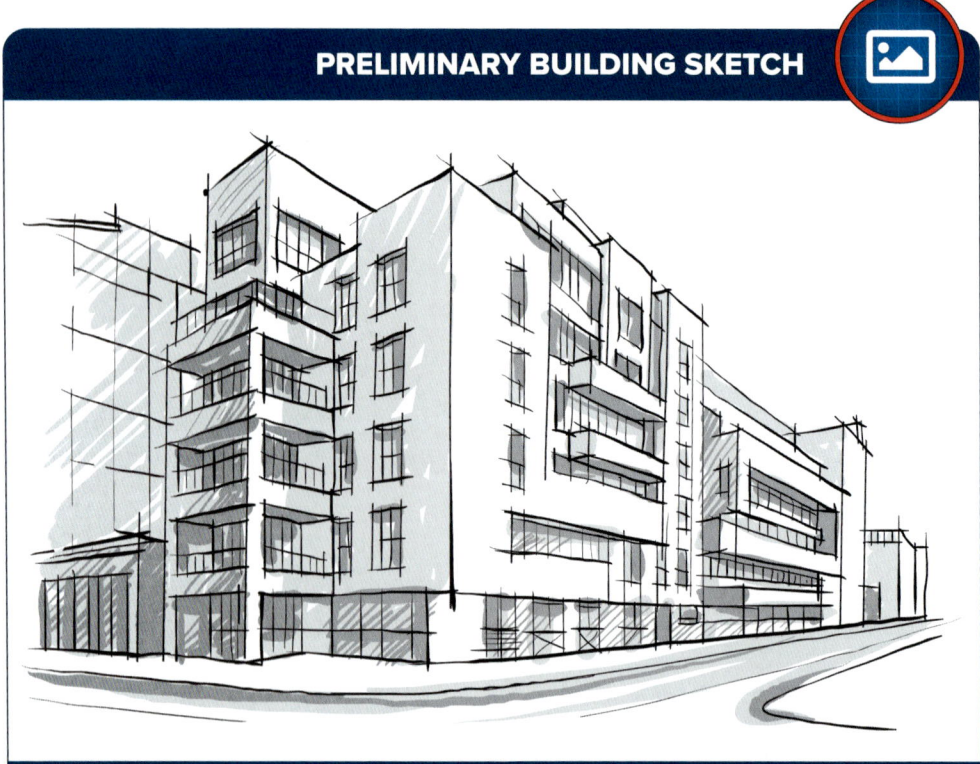

Figure 1-1. *The process of building design starts with preliminary sketches that are continually refined and eventually integrated into the construction drawings and blueprints.*

design team will also create specifications for the job with detailed requirements for everything involved with the building's construction, including materials, equipment, and contractor/subcontractor responsibilities.

Most large buildings require a team of design professionals to draw a complete set of construction drawings. Usually, the architectural firm will take the lead since they created the original vision of the building. The firm will employ the services of other design professionals, including civil, electrical, fire, mechanical, structural, and chemical engineers. The architect will assemble the various drawings provided by each professional, and the review process will begin.

After the architectural firm finishes the final review, the plans are submitted to ownership for their comments and to the building department for final approval and construction permits. The building department process usually involves several reviews. Most projects are traditionally reviewed and must be approved by the local governmental body after the zoning department has given its approval. The building department review process includes

several stops, including structural, electrical, fire, mechanical, and plumbing. Permits will not be issued until the plans meet the required codes and standards and are approved by each examiner.

It is only after the plans have received the final blessing that construction can begin. While the architect's vision has been placed on paper or in the hard drive of a computer and has reached the final goal of being approved, the vision is not complete. The final test comes when the construction team opens the plans and constructs the building. If the construction plans provide adequate detail and are accurately interpreted, the building will mirror the architect's vision.

THE EVOLUTION OF BUILDINGS AND CONSTRUCTION DOCUMENTATION

Construction of buildings and structures and the drawings used to create them have evolved and helped to shape the tools that we use today.

The primitive cave-like structures from centuries ago have developed into

A Picture is Worth a Thousand Words

To ensure that all involved in a project are in agreement about what is to be built, a set of construction drawings, commonly referred to as blueprints, provides the clarity needed. Visual information provides additional clarification to even the most basic items that most everyone is familiar with. The pictures on the construction drawings clarify exact types, sizes, and proportions to move from a general level of understanding about a project to a minute level of detail in which there is no ambiguity. **See Figure 1-2.**

Figure 1-2. Visual communication aids in providing the clarity needed to ensure that a project is built in the manner that it is intended.

For additional information, visit qr.njatcdb.org Item #6650

the highly automated buildings constructed today. **See Figure 1-3.** One of the factors that helped structures change is the structured and repeatable process for documenting ideas about buildings into a cohesive, understandable, and

CONSTRUCTION DRAWING EVOLUTION

The Egyptians are believed by many historians to be the first builders. Their construction process included a period of planning in which the project design was developed. Construction drawings and details were drawn on papyrus or limestone slabs. An archaeological dig discovered a limestone model of a section of a pyramid. The discovery indicates that the Egyptians may have been the first to create models of their construction projects.

Skarae Brae, a 10-house complex in Scotland, was built around 3500 BC. The ceilings are 5.25 feet high.

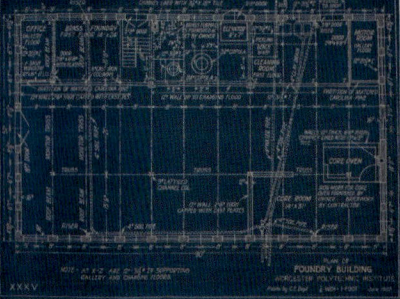

Blueprint from 1902

Architectural drawings moved from drawings on papyrus to hand-drawn ink drawings on sheets of paper. The process remained relatively unchanged until the nineteenth century. The blueprint process was invented in 1842, using a dye developed in Germany around 1704.

Architectural plans continue to evolve with the computer age. Scanners allow plans to be copied and printed. They can be stored on computers. Plans are now being drawn on a computer, stored on a computer, and shared over the Internet.

Figure 1-3. *Construction drawings have evolved from very basic sketches in difficult mediums to more modern formats created on a computer.*

consistent set of information. The documentation process has also evolved and continues evolving toward an electronic means of information transfer. There will be a time soon when a structure is built twice, once on a computer (sometimes called a digital twin) and again on the building's proposed site.

Design Professional Standards

A building's design and construction require designers and constructors to be well versed in the building codes applicable to the construction type and the jurisdiction where the structure will be built. The earliest known building code is part of the Hammurabi Code created by King Hammurabi (1792-1750 BC) of Mesopotamia. The code has 282 provisions, with 6 dedicated to construction. For example, Rule 229 states, "If a builder has built a house for a man and has not made his work sound, and the house he built has fallen and caused the death of its owner, that builder shall be put to death." Luckily, today's building codes are not as severe as they once were.

Architects design buildings and place their visions on a set of drawings that enable a construction team to turn the idea into reality. The design process has loose guidelines to add consistency to the final product used for construction. They are not so strict, however, that they would impede the creativity of the individual designers. Each set of drawings reflects the designer's vision, as influenced by the building owner, making it important to create a functional building and add aesthetic value to the community.

Although there is flexibility in the guidelines used in creating construction documentation, all applicable codes, standards, and regulations must be strictly followed to create a safe structure. Structural drawings must comply with building codes and strict design guidelines. Trade-specific drawings, such as electrical, mechanical, and plumbing, must comply with all applicable codes, standards, and laws within the local jurisdiction. **See Figure 1-4.**

In most cases, state statutes or local government regulations require engineering and architectural professional licensing and define each scope of work. The parameters for the scope of work often change depending on the size of the project. More extensive projects usually have a design team consisting of an architect, a civil engineer, a structural engineer, an electrical engineer, and a mechanical engineer.

A trade-specific engineer creates plans for their scope of work: the structural engineer is responsible for designing the structural components of the building; the civil engineer is responsible for the site plans, grading, drainage, and other site elements to prepare the site for construction; and the architect usually controls the project's overall design, including its size, appearance, final plans package, and specifications.

It is crucial for everyone involved in the construction process to know how to interpret blueprints and apply the information correctly. These skills will position anyone associated with the construction process to grasp the design intent for any residential, commercial, or industrial project.

APPLICABLE REGULATIONS

Figure 1-4. The building process is driven by many codes and standards to ensure occupant and structure safety. These regulations are taken into account at the earliest stages of the design process.

COMMON COMPONENTS OF CONSTRUCTION DOCUMENTATION

The primary function of construction documentation is presenting information needed to create a building or structure on a plot of land. This information is required from the start of construction until a building's completion when the certificate of occupancy (CO) is issued. Architects achieve success by creating construction documentation that lays out the entire construction process from start to finish. Each component of the documentation has a specific purpose and is used to provide needed information for the construction process. A common approach is used to create each of the set's parts allowing this documentation to remain clear and easy to use.

Drawings

Common parts associated with construction documentation include specific drawing types and written documentation to show everything needed for the accurate "description" of the design intent. The most frequently used component of construction documentation is the drawing. **See Figure 1-5.** Most drawings included in construction documentation are two-dimensional. Two-dimensional drawings create an inherent obstacle because almost

For additional information, visit qr.njatcdb.org
Item #6651

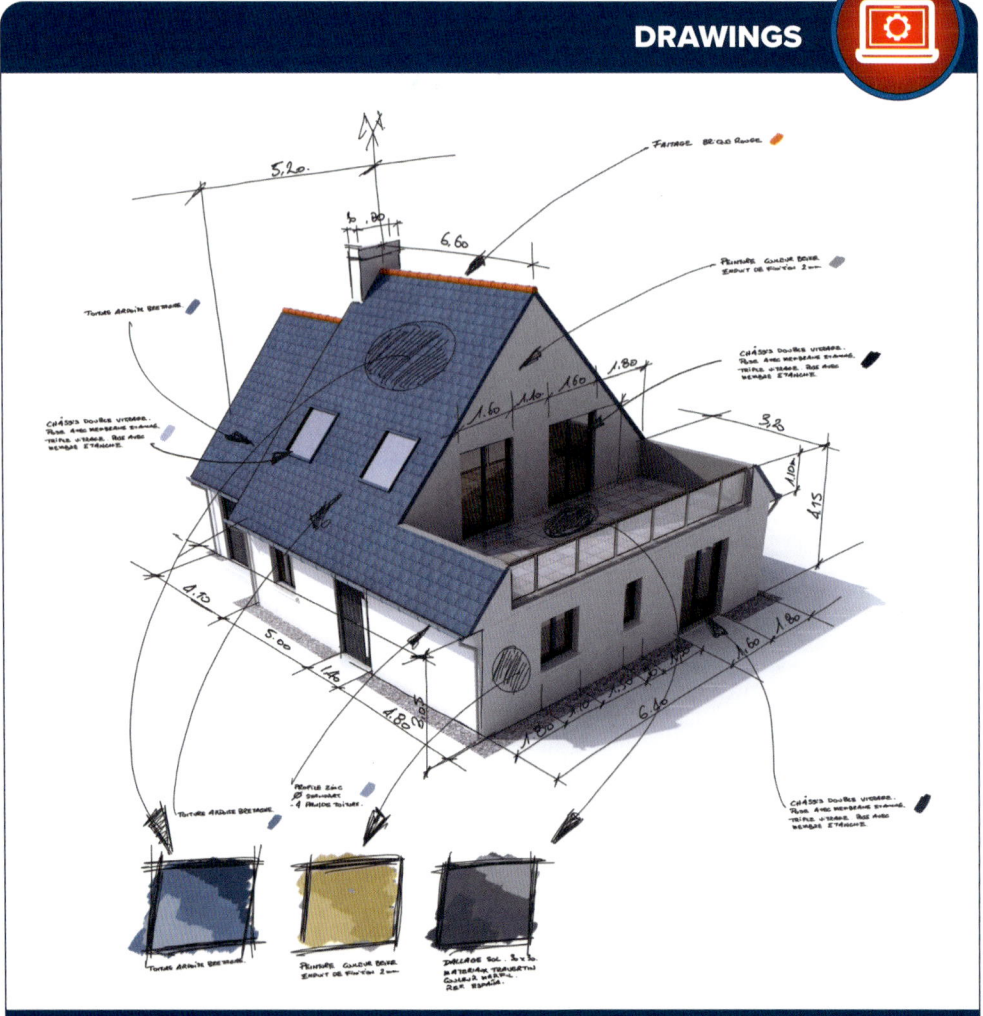

DRAWINGS

Figure 1-5. *Visual communication in the form of drawings provide clarity to the description of the intended final product.*

everything involved with construction is three-dimensional. It is not easy to understand the intricate details of a three-dimensional object using two-dimensional drawings. Using two-dimensional drawings to display three-dimensional objects is a difficult task for a designer or a blueprint creator. For this reason, it is crucial designers use standard views that are easy to interpret. The two most common types of views are orthographic and isometric.

Orthographic Drawing

Orthographic drawings, also called orthographic projections, are two-dimensional drawings used to represent three-dimensional objects. **See Figure 1-6.** Most orthographic views contain at least three separate scaled drawings of an object. The standard views in an orthographic projection include the top view, the front view, and the side view (most often the right-side view). However, most drawings on blueprints do not show three-dimensional representations of objects, but instead show only one of the standard three views represented in an orthographic projection. Individual views within a print set use one of the three most common orthographic views to depict almost everything within a building. Architectural plans generally provide four two-dimensional elevations, with each drawing showing the exterior side of the building.

Isometric Drawing

Since it is difficult to visualize a three-dimensional object's construction using orthographical drawings, architects often include a perspective view or an isometric drawing in the plans. An isometric projection is a method of visually representing two-dimensional objects in technical drawings. While perspective drawings have all the horizontal lines of an object converging on a focal point, an isometric drawing has lines parallel to each other and not converging. Horizontal lines of an isometric drawing are drawn at a 30° angle to the horizontal plane, while vertical lines are drawn vertically. **See Figure 1-7.**

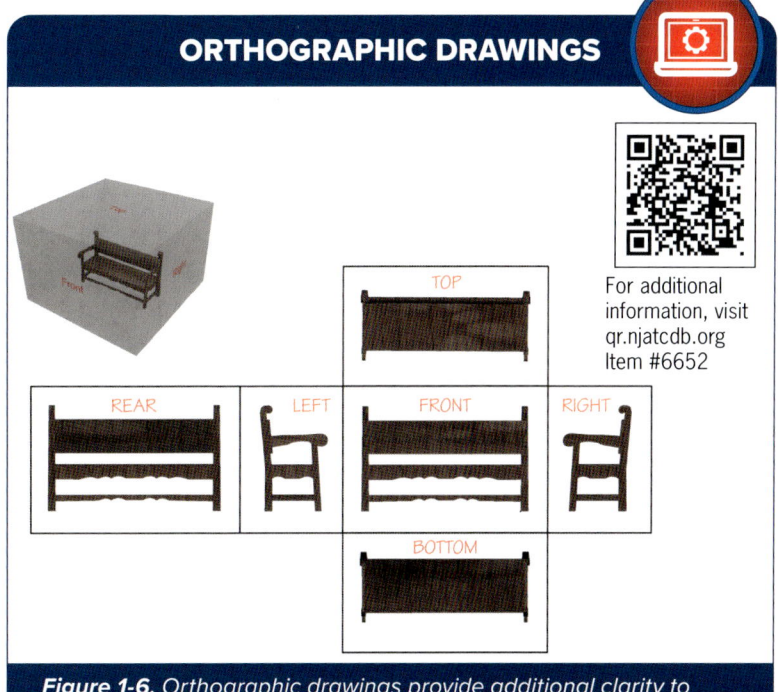

ORTHOGRAPHIC DRAWINGS

For additional information, visit qr.njatcdb.org Item #6652

Figure 1-6. Orthographic drawings provide additional clarity to three-dimensional objects by including multiple views of the object from different sides.

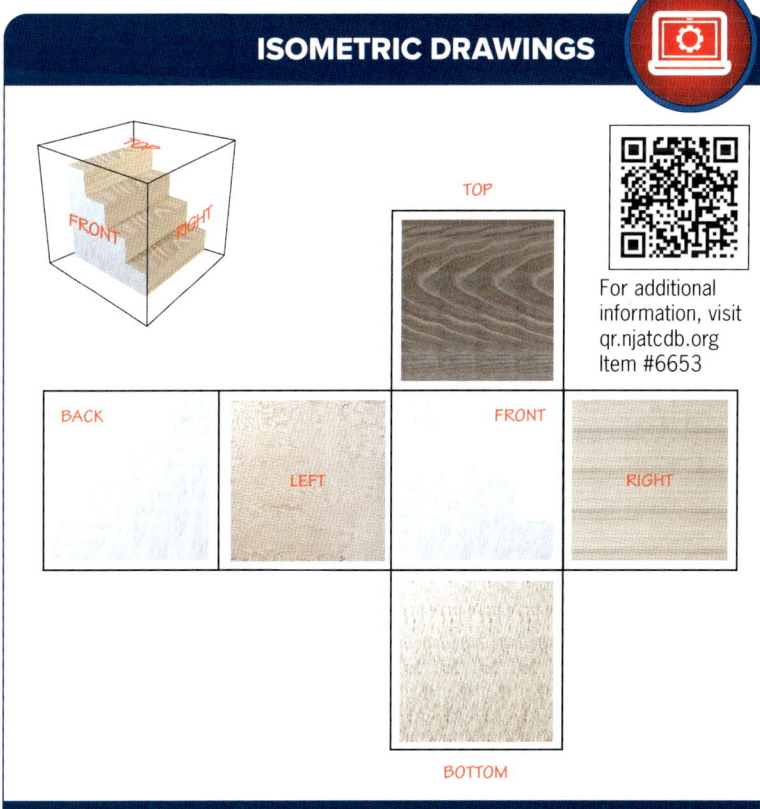

ISOMETRIC DRAWINGS

For additional information, visit qr.njatcdb.org Item #6653

Figure 1-7. Isometric drawings help to provide a three-dimensional type of view that is not possible in many other drawing types that are viewed from a flat plane.

Common Architectural Views

Most views of a building or structure in a set of construction drawings, such as orthographic views, are seen from a set plane. A plane is an imaginary, flat, two-dimensional surface extending infinitely in every direction, that wholly contains a line between two points. When used on a set of construction drawings, planes are usually drawn either parallel to the earth at that point (level) or perpendicular to the earth, at the same point (plumb) 90° from a level plane. **See Figure 1-8.** Using planes allows for an accurate and consistent representation of specific parts of a structure that are usually constructed to be either level or plumb. The use of specific planes for some of the standard views in a set of construction drawings makes them easier to read and understand.

The plan view is the most common drawing in a set of construction drawings. The plan view is a top-down view of the building's layout based on a horizontal plane that is approximately four feet above the finished floor level. Another standard view is an elevation drawing, which is a representation of a part of a structure on a vertical plane. The most common types of elevation views are the interior and exterior elevations. Detail views show smaller pieces of a structure to provide details and additional insights into their construction.

Written Documentation

Although drawings are the most common construction documentation method, many details are not well suited to conveyance through drawings. In these cases, architects provide written documentation to augment the drawings and bring additional clarity. Written documentation includes specifications, contractor and subcontractor responsibilities, and other construction-related details that a drawing cannot provide.

For additional information, visit qr.njatcdb.org Item #6654

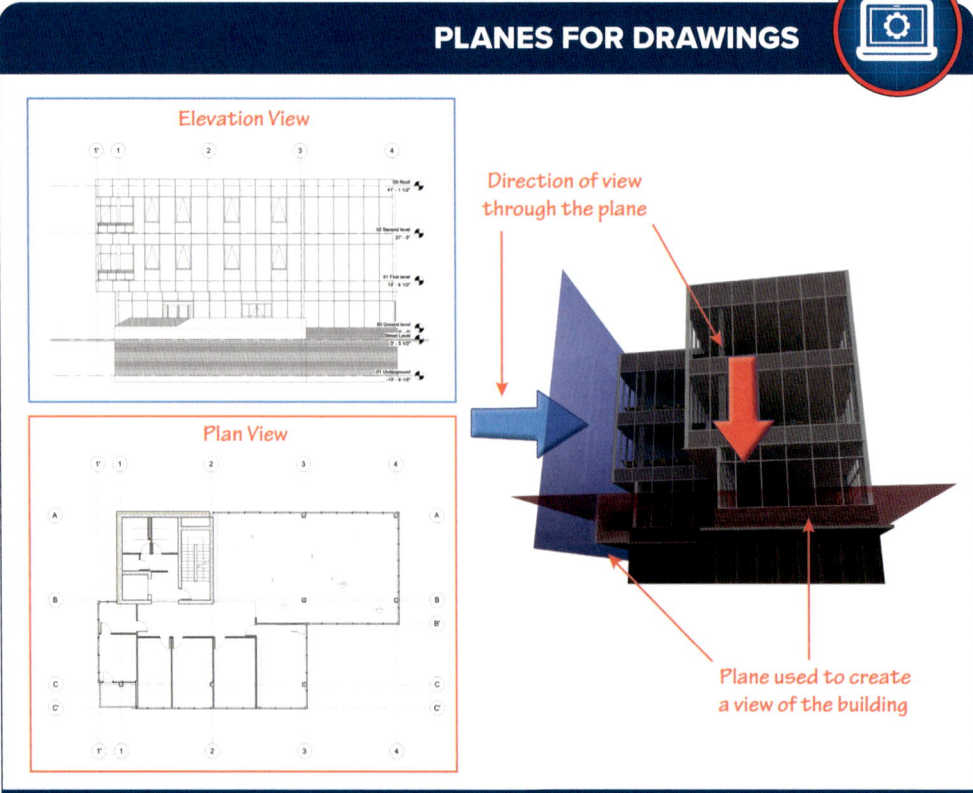

PLANES FOR DRAWINGS

Elevation View

Plan View

Direction of view through the plane

Plane used to create a view of the building

Figure 1-8. *Planes are utilized to create vantage points within a building, usually viewed from a level or plumb orientation.*

Specifications

Architects include required construction methods and materials for constructing a building in a written format, which is a better form of communication than placing the information on a drawing. Specifications, written in a component format, are the documents used to present the information. **See Figure 1-9.** The documents included in structured specifications add to the plans' design intent by containing detailed requirements for the building's materials and processes broken down by product and trade types. For example, the specifications also provide separate sections for concrete, windows, doors, mechanical systems, and electrical systems.

Abbreviations and Notes

Many drawings within a set of blueprints require additional information to understand the feature's construction thoroughly. Notes provide additional information needed to build a feature according to the intended design and convey a complete understanding of the construction methods used to construct it. Many times, construction drawings will include a schedule of abbreviations used throughout the drawings. It is also essential to look for notes on each sheet that address specific requirements for items like doors and windows. Some notes and abbreviations may apply to the complete set of drawings, while others only apply to the sheet they are on.

ADDITIONAL CONSTRUCTION DOCUMENTATION ITEMS

In addition to the common drawing types, views, and written methods of communicating the design intent for a building, designers use standard representations of items and traditional drawing methods to ensure construction documentation is consistent from project to project and easy to interpret.

Symbols

Most architectural drawings need to convey a great deal of information,

SPECIFICATIONS

Figure 1-9. Specifications provide supplemental information to augment the drawings in a construction drawing set.

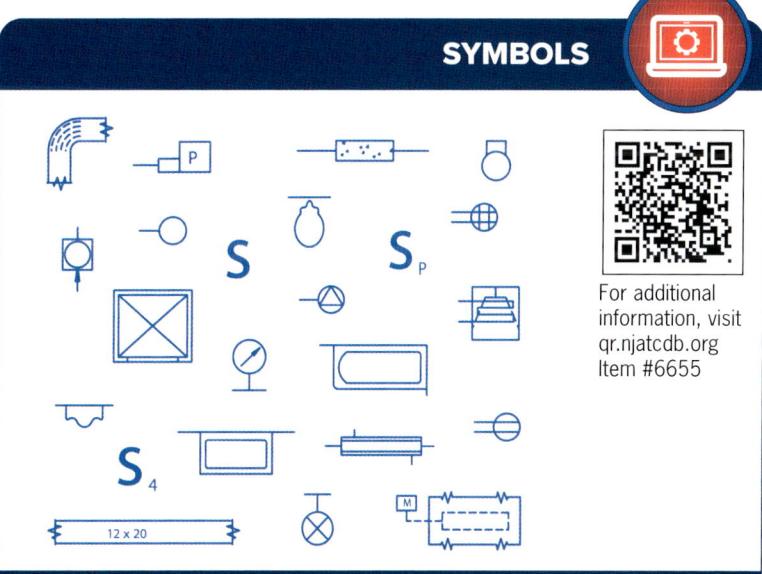

SYMBOLS

For additional information, visit qr.njatcdb.org Item #6655

Figure 1-10. Symbols help to keep construction drawings clean by providing information in a clear concise manner without the need to include an excess of either visual or text.

which can create clutter and make them unreadable. Designers correct this problem by using symbols to represent many building components. The use of symbols keeps the drawing clear, concise, and easy to read. **See Figure 1-10.**

LINES

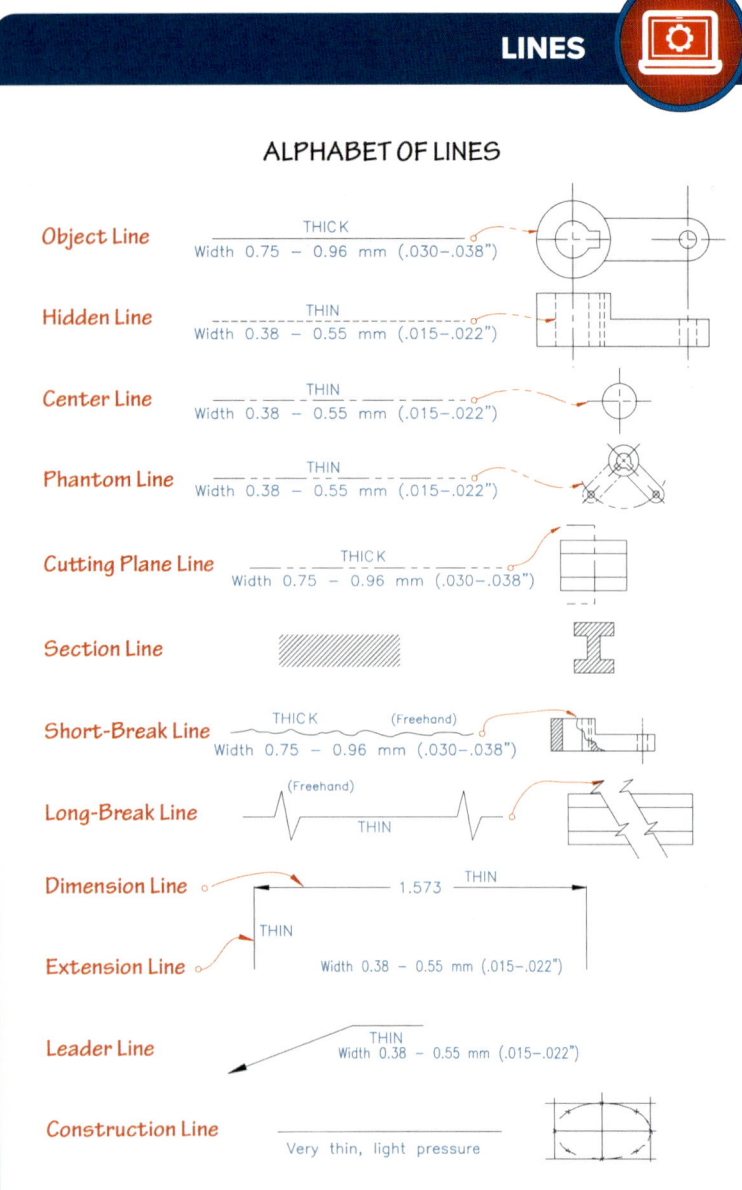

ALPHABET OF LINES

Object Line — THICK — Width 0.75 – 0.96 mm (.030–.038")

Hidden Line — THIN — Width 0.38 – 0.55 mm (.015–.022")

Center Line — THIN — Width 0.38 – 0.55 mm (.015–.022")

Phantom Line — THIN — Width 0.38 – 0.55 mm (.015–.022")

Cutting Plane Line — THICK — Width 0.75 – 0.96 mm (.030–.038")

Section Line

Short-Break Line — THICK (Freehand) — Width 0.75 – 0.96 mm (.030–.038")

Long-Break Line — (Freehand) — THIN

Dimension Line — 1.573 — THIN

Extension Line — THIN — Width 0.38 – 0.55 mm (.015–.022")

Leader Line — THIN — Width 0.38 – 0.55 mm (.015–.022")

Construction Line — Very thin, light pressure

Figure 1-11. Various lines and types of lines are used to represent specific meanings on construction drawings.

Most sets of construction drawings include a symbol schedule that provides common symbols used on the drawings. Typically, the schedule is located on a sheet near or at the beginning of the set of drawings. On larger projects, where engineers draw the plans for only their work scope, the symbols for that scope may be found on one of their discipline-specific sheets. It is essential to see all the symbol schedules to fully understand the architect's design intent. It is additionally vital to pay particular attention to any notes attached to the symbol schedule as they may modify one or more of the symbols.

Lines

Architects use several types of lines to create construction drawings. The lines define and convey the design intent to the construction team. Each type of line used has an intended application. **See Figure 1-11.** The most crucial aspect of interpreting line types on a drawing is to note the variations in each line's appearance. Different designers use line types in various manners, but they only vary the types used where there is a specific reason to do so. Explore the variations carefully.

For additional information, visit qr.njatcdb.org
Item #6656

SUMMARY

Consistent use of construction documents ensures designers will provide information to skilled trades document interpreters allowing everyone to share the owner's design vision. A standard industry method addresses the problem by allowing large objects to be drawn on a much smaller scale while providing accurate dimensions required to construct a building. The addition of horizontal plan views and vertical elevations begin to paint the final picture. They are the glue that holds construction drawings together; without them, the designer's vision would not manifest a final product matching that vision.

The finest level of detail is reached by added text documents that enhance the pictorial drawings provided. These documents, including legal language, tables, material lists, specifications, schedules, and contractor responsibilities, ensure that the construction documentation package is complete. The design process results in consistent and accurate communication of the design intent conveyed from the owner to the architect and ultimately to the skilled workers who build the structures that the drawings represent. The quality of communication in this very specialized process allows the owner's original concept to result in an envisioned building at the project's end.

For additional information, visit qr.njatcdb.org Item #6640

REVIEW QUESTIONS

1. The first plans usually created by the design team are __?__.

   a. elevation drawings
   b. plan views
   c. section views
   d. site plans

2. One of the factors that helped structures change is the structured and repeatable process for documenting ideas about buildings into a cohesive, __?__, and consistent set of information.

   a. accurate
   b. organized
   c. precise
   d. understandable

3. The most frequently used component of construction documentation is/are the __?__.

   a. construction contracts
   b. construction schedule
   c. drawings
   d. specifications

4. Most orthographic views contain at least three separate __?__ drawings of an object.

   a. detailed
   b. enlarged
   c. isometric
   d. scaled

5. Using __?__ allows for an accurate and consistent representation of specific parts of a structure that are usually constructed to be either level or plumb.

   a. accurate measurements
   b. levels
   c. planes
   d. scales

CHAPTER 2
SCALING AND DIMENSIONS

The practice of measuring the length of objects has existed since the beginning of history. The first measurements were based on parts of the body: fingers, hands, and arms. These measures were not consistent, varying from region to region and country to country.

Measurement types have evolved over time. The cubit, a common measurement defined as the distance between the elbow and the middle finger's tip, appeared in Egypt around 3,000 BC. The problem of inconsistency remained until the Egyptians and the Mesopotamians created standard rods for the cubit. The two nations' rods were not identical, but they were among the first attempts to develop standard measurements. For more information on the history of measurement open the online resource.

For additional information, visit qr.njatcdb.org Item #6709

Measurements are critical to construction, but the plans that make it possible to build them would never exist without scaling. The use of scales to create drawings allows architects to draw large buildings on standard architectural sized sheets of paper while maintaining desired proportions and providing accurate measurements needed to construct the building according to the design. A thorough understanding of the application of scales on building projects will provide a firm foundation for the accurate interpretation of construction documentation and drawings.

OBJECTIVES

- Interpret the principles of standardized scaling and dimensioning, and the clarity they bring to architectural plans.
- Demonstrate the usefulness of, and ability to interpret, the different scales used for various types of drawings.
- Differentiate different scales and types of scales in their differing applications.

TABLE OF CONTENTS

INTRODUCTION TO SCALING AND DIMENSIONS

Scaling and dimensioning are critical to drawing blueprints that ensure the successful construction of a building. A designer could not draw a building's foundation or other features on a sheet of paper with full-size dimensions; size restrictions are why one-to-one drawings rarely appear on construction plans.

Architects solve the size problem by using decreasing scales to draw the building. Scales such as ⅛ inch = 1 foot or ¼ inch = 1 foot are examples of these reduced scales. Engineers use the 1:1 scale for drawings of small objects that require detail, such as nuts and bolts. When drawing small items with a very tight tolerance (not commonly seen in construction, but more prevalent in manufacturing), the scale is increased. With an increasing scale, the drawing of the object is larger than the actual item. **See Figure 2-1.**

Scales are used with the metric and imperial measurement standards. The imperial scale, usually used by architects in the United States, has a format of inches, or parts of an inch, equal to one foot. An example of an imperial scale is ½ inch = 1 foot. This scale means that every ½ inch of an object's length on a drawing represents one foot. For example, an item that is one inch long on the drawing is two feet long when it is constructed. Imperial scales are commonly referred to in a shorthand manner as ¼", which is short for ¼ inch = 1 foot.

The metric scale is used in most of the world's countries, other than the United States. It is formatted as a ratio with the first number representing the drawn size and the second number representing the object's actual size. For instance, a standard metric scale is 1:50; this scale means that for every centimeter that an object is in length on a drawing, the item it represents is 50 centimeters in real life. If an object

For additional information, visit qr.njatcdb.org Item #6710

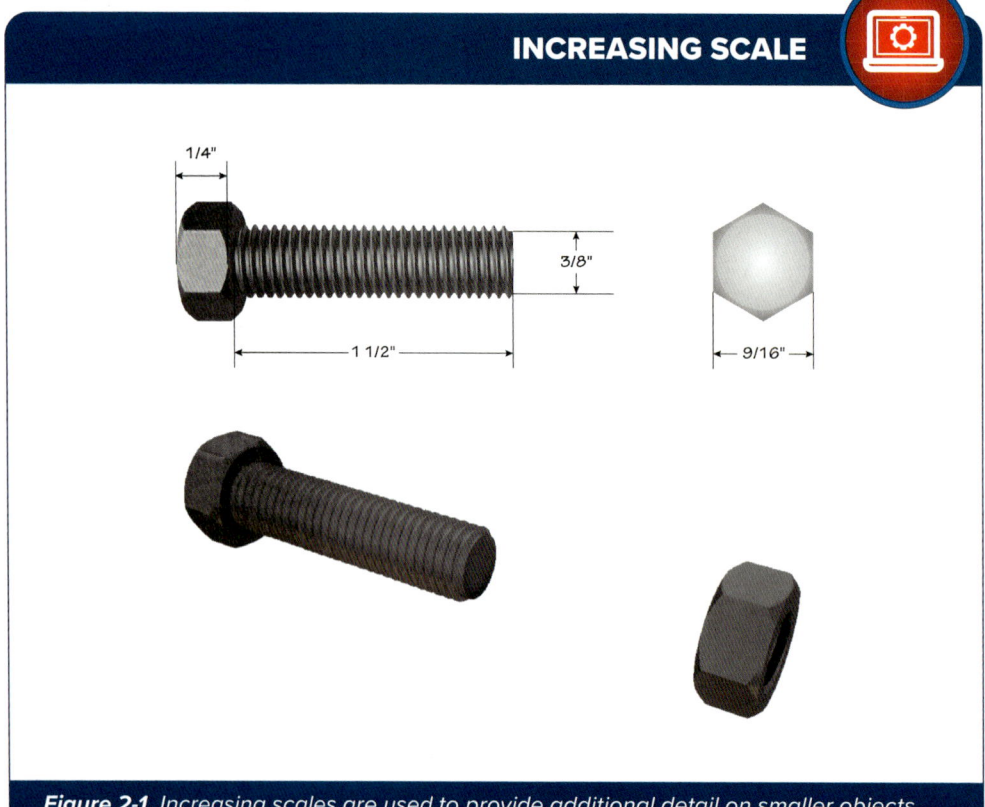

INCREASING SCALE

Figure 2-1. Increasing scales are used to provide additional detail on smaller objects.

is drawn as two centimeters long, it will be 100 centimeters long when constructed. **See Figure 2-2.**

Clarity

An architect's use of accurate varying scales is one of the most critical aspects of creating blueprints. Proper scales improve readability by making a drawing large enough to provide the needed dimensioning information clearly. Scaling is a process that creates a scale model of a building no different than scale models of cars or the solar system. It is not easy to fully understand the relative sizes and relationships of objects if there is nothing for comparison.

METRIC SCALES

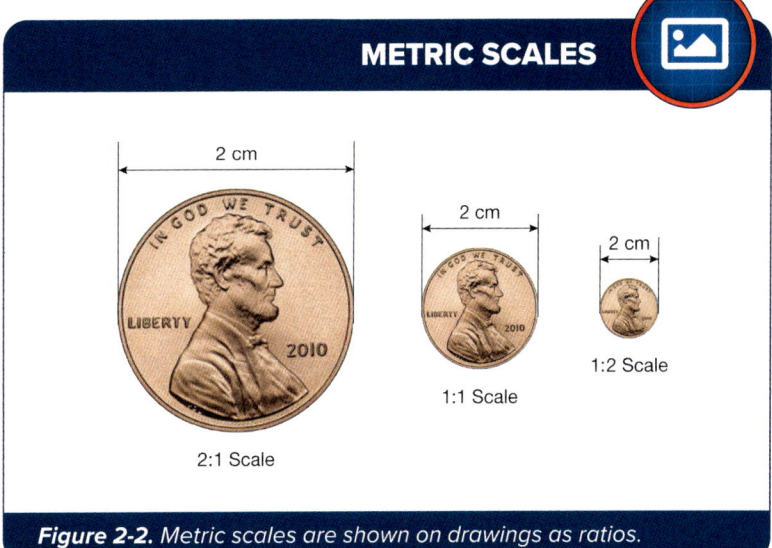

Figure 2-2. *Metric scales are shown on drawings as ratios.*

Scale of the Solar System

We cannot fathom the solar system's size unless we have things to compare it to. To begin to understand the size of the solar system, we can compare the Earth's size to that of the moon. We can also gain a better sense of the distance between the Earth and the moon by showing the distance using a scale. **See Figure 2-3.** This scale and dimensions help to give us an idea of the size of the elements of the solar system. Similarly, we use standard units of measurement to understand the building drawn on a set of blueprints.

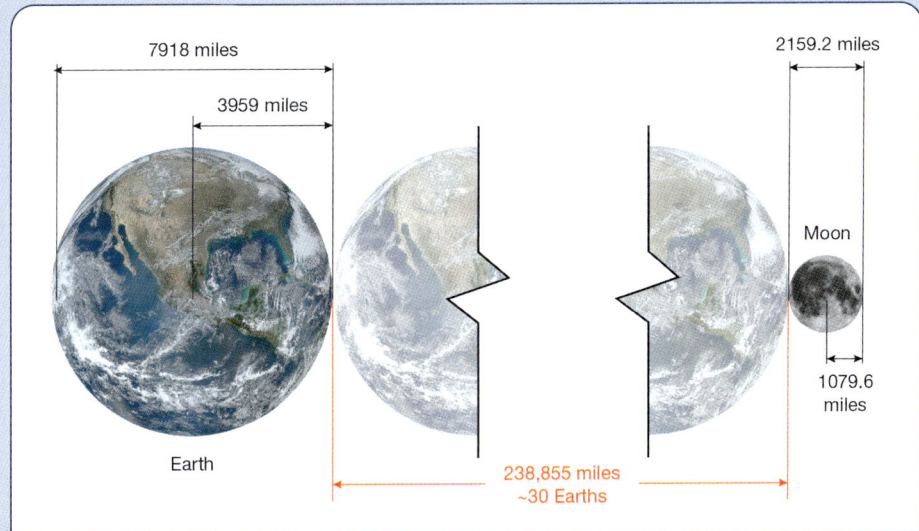

Figure 2-3. *The use of scale helps with the understanding of both size relative to other objects and the distance between objects.*

For additional information, visit qr.njatcdb.org Item #6711

Size and Location

Three significant items determine drawing scales: the size of the blueprint paper used, the size of the object being drawn, and the level of detail required. The paper size used for a print sheet helps define the drawing's scale and allows designers to show the entire object on the page. In most cases, designers use architectural paper that conforms to one of the standard sizes defined by the American National Standards Institute (ANSI). ANSI lists five standard sheet sizes for blueprints:

- ANSI A: 8.5" × 11"
- ANSI B: 11" × 17"
- ANSI C: 17" × 22"
- ANSI D: 22" × 34"
- ANSI E: 34" × 44"

Because architectural floor, ceiling, and exterior elevation plans have a large area to represent, they are typically drawn at ⅛-inch scale, while some residential drawings use a ¼-inch scale. In larger buildings, designers draw the floor and ceiling plans in sections with each section drawn on a separate sheet. **See Figure 2-4.** Each of these drawings provides essential details about the dimensions needed for construction.

When greater detail levels are needed, other scales, including ¼ inch or ½ inch, are used for architectural building sections based on the amount of necessary clarity. In some cases, scales ranging from ¾ inch to 3 inches are used where intricate complexity levels are required, such as wall sections or interior elevation drawings.

Although the relationship between the types of drawings and the scale used is commonly similar, the architectural team may vary the scales used to present the information and necessary level of detail with clarity. The size of the area or object that the designer intends to show on the sheet helps define the drawing's scale. For instance, even when imperial units are used for the rest of the sheets in the construction drawings, the site plan often uses a decimal scale of 1:60.

Additionally, architects may draw details, sections, and interior elevations on dedicated sheets or sheets with other drawings. Some sheets may have

For additional information, visit qr.njatcdb.org Item #6712

SCOPE OF CONTENT ON SHEETS

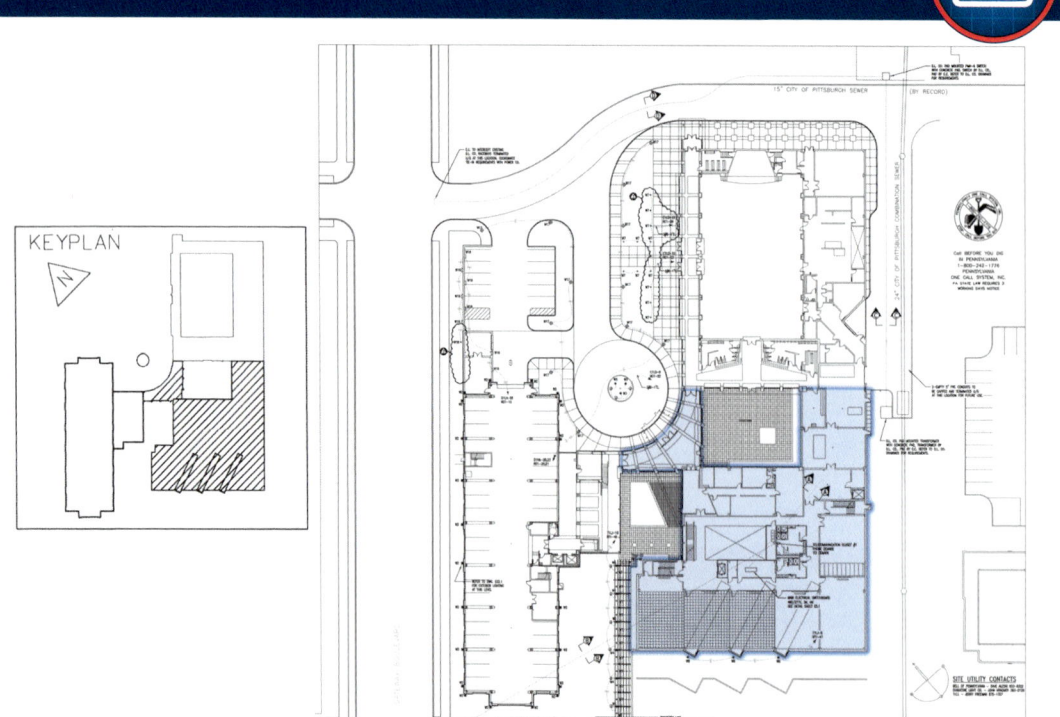

Figure 2-4. *When a large building will not fit on a single sheet, it is commonly split onto multiple sheets within the construction drawing set.*

drawings with different scales, which means close attention must be given to locating the scale used for each drawing. **See Figure 2-5.**

Information Manageability

Managing data on a drawing is tricky; if the architect placed every dimension on a drawing, it would become cluttered to the point that the print may become illegible. To eliminate clutter, designers limit the number of dimensions used to those that are essential. For example, a floor plan usually provides the outside dimensions of the building and, in most cases, centerline measurements to windows, doors, and other openings. Floor plans also include the dimensions for the interior partitions and openings in them. These are key to the building's construction, but they limit the amount of information on the drawing to maintain clarity.

More detailed dimensioning is often found on wall sections, interior elevations, and detail drawings. Construction workers can also determine dimensions using an architectural scale. Workers often install trade-specific features with measurements obtained by scaling the drawing. For instance, electrical devices are not usually dimensioned unless they must be installed at an exact location, such as near or in cabinetry. Managing data on blueprints provides clarity and leads to a successful job.

For additional information, visit qr.njatcdb.org Item #6713

CONTEXTUAL SCALE

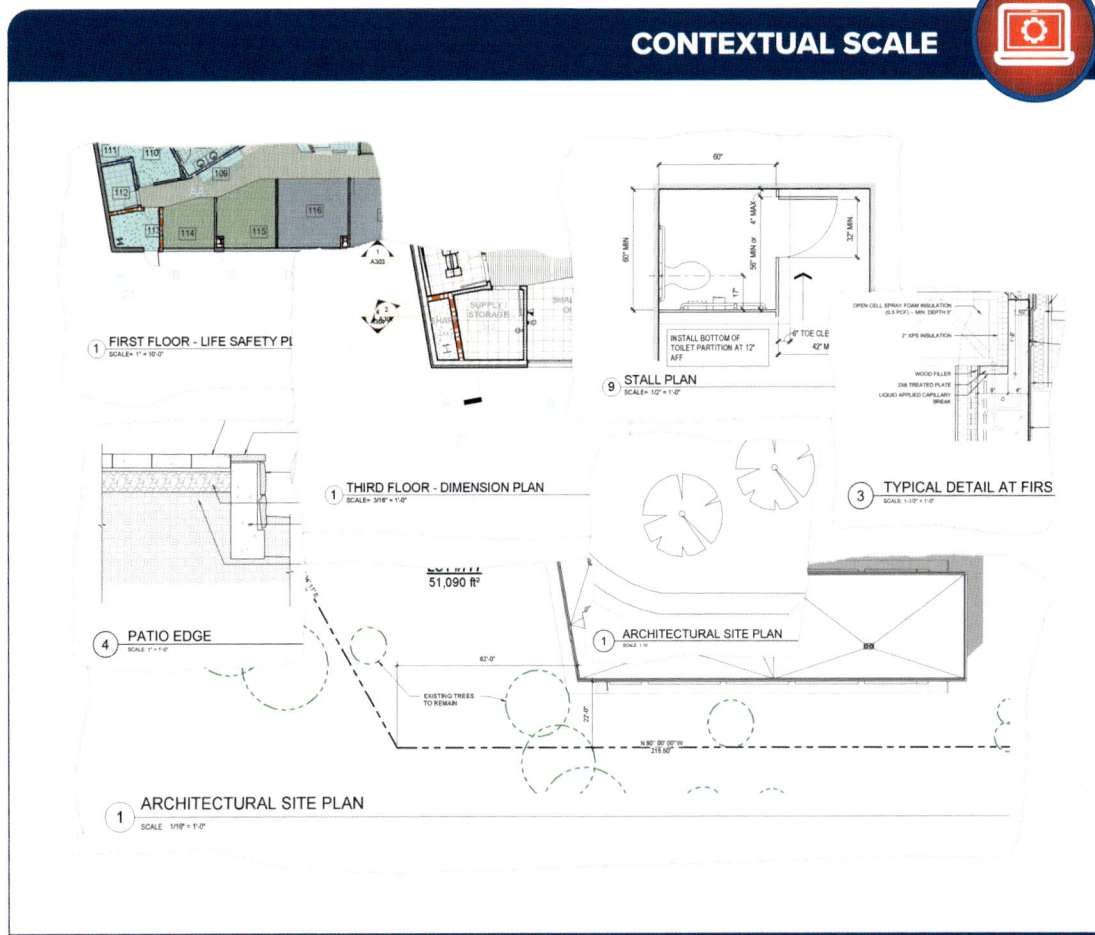

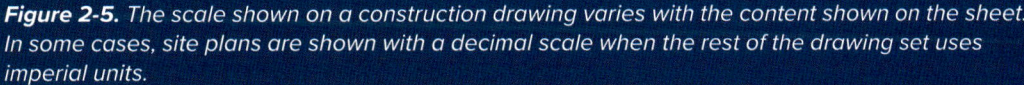

Figure 2-5. *The scale shown on a construction drawing varies with the content shown on the sheet. In some cases, site plans are shown with a decimal scale when the rest of the drawing set uses imperial units.*

TECHNICAL DRAWING STANDARDS

ISO Standards for Technical Drawings		
ISO 128-1:2020	General Principles of Representation Part 1: Introduction and Fundamental Requirements	General drafting rules relating to two- and three-dimensional drawings
ISO 128-2:2020	General Principles of Representation Part 2: Basic Conventions for Lines	General rules for lines (types, designations, and general rules for drafting) used for diagrams, plans, and maps
ISO 128-3:2020	General Principles of Representation Part 3: Views, Sections and Cuts	General rules for presenting views, sections, and cuts following orthographic projection

Figure 2-6. *The International Organization for Standardization (ISO) creates many industry standards including those used in architecture, engineering, construction, and shipbuilding.*

Standards

Many standards regulate the scope of the work in the construction industry. Federal, state, or local building codes mandate requirements applicable to almost all aspects of the building's construction. Many jurisdictions enact architectural standards that apply within a set of geographical boundaries.

Scaling and dimensioning practices also follow industry standards based on the object the designer is drawing. For example, a machining or engineering drawing requires greater detail and closer tolerances than architectural drawings for a construction project. The machined part may be an assembly that connects to another component requiring additional precision levels. Measurements must be within very close tolerances.

Architectural industry standards and guidelines promote standardization and clarity in construction blueprints. Standards and guidelines address drawings' appearance by categorizing line thickness and darkness and managing arrowheads and text size. These standards and guidelines aim to provide consistency in how the information is presented and result in a drawing that is easy to read. **See Figure 2-6.**

SCALING

As it applies to drawings and print reading, the term *scale* has three common usages in construction: one as a noun, one as a verb, and one used to describe the relationship between an object and its drawing.

When used as a noun, a scale is a specialized ruler with evenly spaced graduations to measure a building component on a print. The scale has incremental dimensions with a ratio corresponding to the actual dimensions of the object. The most common scales

SCALE RULER

Figure 2-7. *Scale rulers are created for every common type of imperial and metric scaling.* © Klein Tools, Inc. All rights reserved.

are standard-inch rulers and metric rulers that are used around the house and school to measure objects and distances. Workers use folding rulers and tape measures on every construction job. The inch and metric scales measure the actual size and imply no ratio of increase or decrease. **See Figure 2-7.**

As a verb, scale refers to the task of using a ruler (or scale) to find the actual dimensions of a component on a print. Architectural and mechanical engineering scales are not full-scale rulers (like folding rules or tape measures).

Finally, the term scale as an adjective describes the relationship between an object and its rendering on a drawing. In reality, almost all construction drawings are represented by some ratio (mathematical relationship or conversation

factor) between the drawing and the actual structure. The ratio between an object's drawing and its real size can increase or reduce the drawing's size depending on the need. Architects draw blueprints to scale for feasibility and to provide exact dimensions that represent actual proportions. **See Figure 2-8.**

In this manner, scaling is best used to solve the problem of fitting a 50-foot by 100-foot building on a sheet of ANSI E paper, sized 34" by 44". The sheet area is 1,496 square inches, while the building area is 720,000 square inches (5,000 square feet). Without scaling, the architect would need to break the floor plan into more than 482 full sheets, allowing room for sheet borders and title blocks. Reading these plans would be a nightmare, and the building's construction

RELATIONSHIP BETWEEN LIFE SIZE AND CONSTRUCTION SHEET SIZE

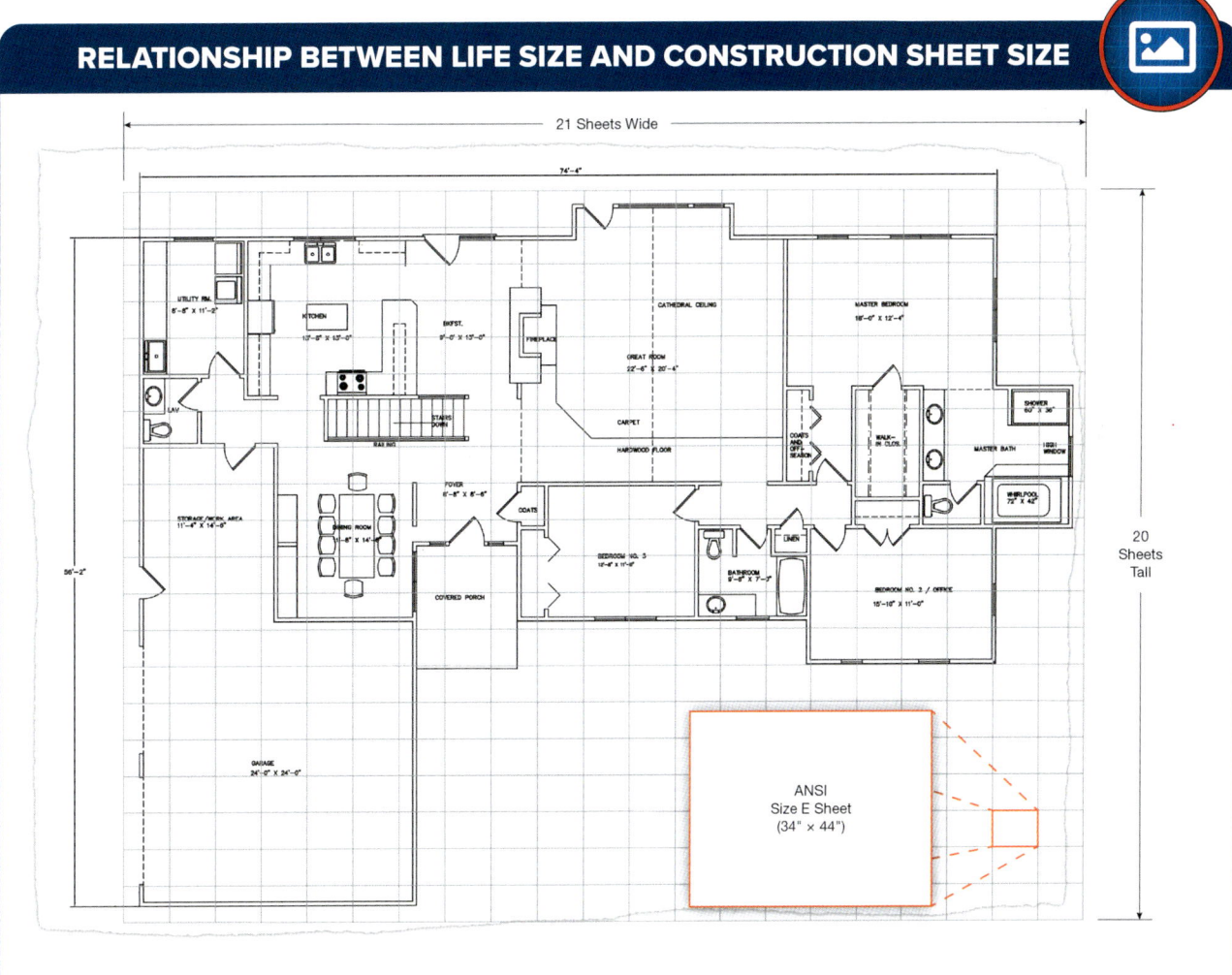

Figure 2-8. Reducing the size of an object allows very large objects to be shown in a more manageable manner.

would be impossible; the final set of blueprints would have several thousand sheets. An example such as this makes the benefits of scaling clear in the world of construction.

SCALING CONSIDERATIONS

Creating a set of plans for the construction of a building is a structured process. The architect will include site plans, floor plans, exterior elevations, interior elevations, and details. These drawings are common to most projects, but they are just the beginning. Each of these drawings will be drawn to a scale. The primary purpose of using a scale is to provide all the needed information for the construction team to build the structure as designed. There are several considerations the architect must consider before the drawing starts.

For additional information, visit qr.njatcdb.org Item #6714

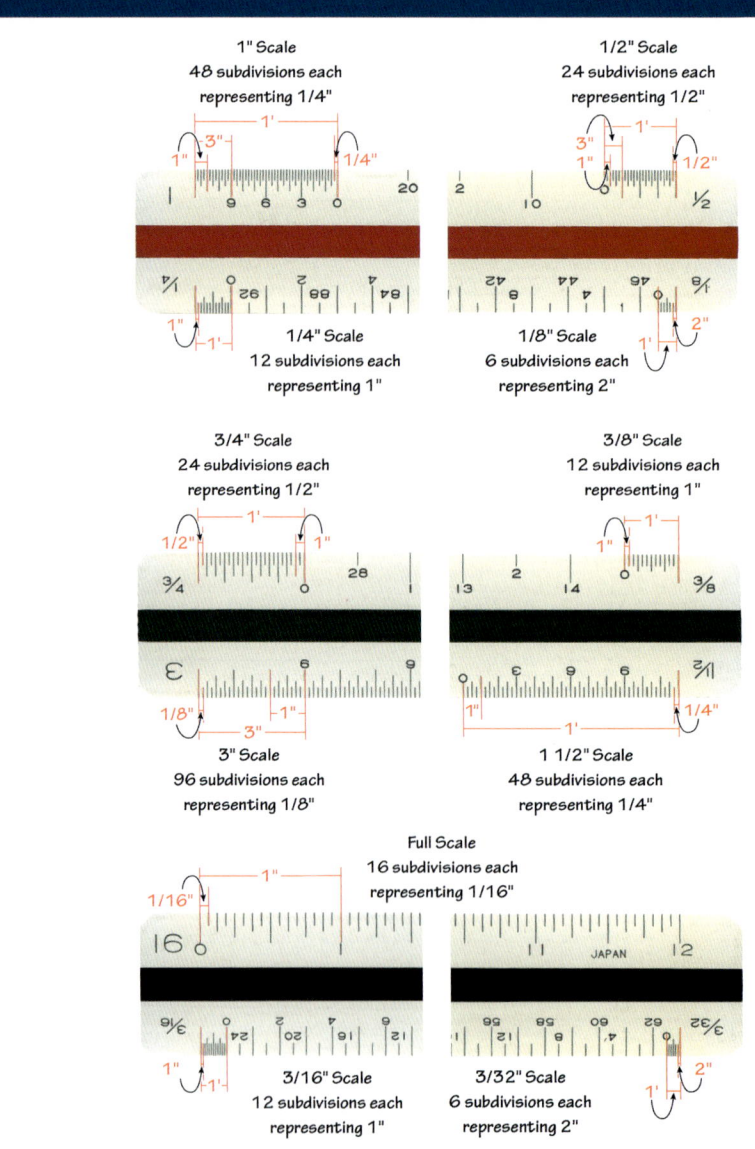

SCALES REPRESENTED ON AN ARCHITECTURAL SCALE

Figure 2-9. *An architectural scale is a specialized ruler used to ascertain detailed measurements from a construction drawing and usually contains many different scales on one ruler.*

Application

How large is the building to be built? The size affects the scale that must be used for the site plan, foundation plan, and the floor plan. The foundation and floor plans must provide critical dimensions. Foundation and floor plans usually are drawn to a scale of ⅛ inch equals 1 foot, or ¼ inch equals 1 foot. Smaller buildings may use the ¼-inch scale, and larger buildings may require the floor plan to be divided into sections and drawn on separate sheets.

Other considerations involve the amount of detail that will be needed to construct the building. Buildings with an intricate design will require more information than simple building construction. This information will result in more details that will have scales chosen to accurately show the construction details. Selecting the correct scale for a drawing is one of the most important tasks an architect has.

Common Scales

Architectural scales are available in two shapes: flat and triangular. Both flat and triangular scales are used to interpret blueprints for buildings. The flat scale looks like an ordinary ruler except for the marks on the edges, representing various scales. Most flat scale rulers have six imperial scales: ⅛ inch, ¼ inch, ½ inch, 1 inch, 1 ½ inches, and 3 inches.

The triangular scale has scales on all three edges—each edge has scales on both sides, resulting in six faces printed with increments. Most faces, except the one with the full-scale increments, have pairs of scales on their faces. Scale rulers with pairs of scales, such as ⅛ inch and ¼ inch on the same line, are dual-reading scales. In these cases, one scale is read from left to right and the other one from right to left.

Triangular scale rulers have 11 scales with varying subdivisions in the representative one foot at the beginning of their scales. The subdivisions represent differing values depending on the scale. **See Figure 2-9.**

The small areas at the end of the scale (between the 0 and the 1) are divided into subdivisions delineating fractions of one foot, which has 12 inches. For example, there are 8 or 16 small divisions for the ⅛-inch and ¼-inch scales, respectively.

There are times when a standard ruler is used to scale a drawing, but close attention must be given to the conversion that is necessary to get the measurement as it was intended by the designer. Because the measurement will be in "full inches" the measurement must be multiplied by the proper amount to derive the accurate intended length. For instance, if a 1" measurement is observed with a standard ruler on a drawing whose scale is ½" equals a foot, the 1" measurement must be multiplied by 2 (since there are two ½" lengths in one inch) to get the scaled measurement of 2 feet. **See Figure 2-10.**

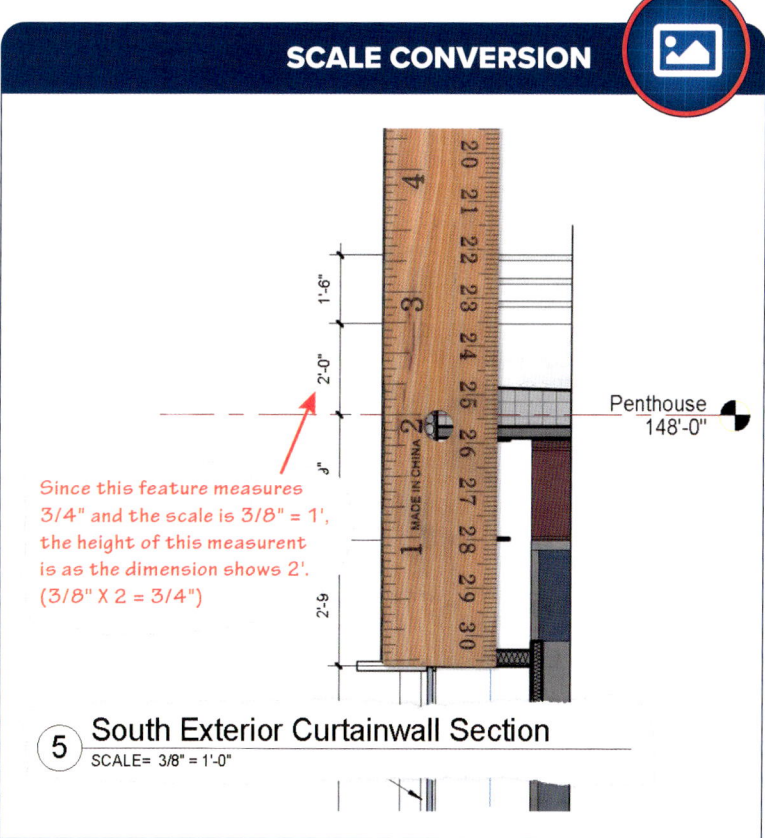

SCALE CONVERSION

Since this feature measures 3/4" and the scale is 3/8" = 1', the height of this measurent is as the dimension shows 2'. (3/8" X 2 = 3/4")

Penthouse 148'-0"

⑤ South Exterior Curtainwall Section
SCALE= 3/8" = 1'-0"

Figure 2-10. *When using a standard ruler on a scaled drawing, the actual measurement must be converted to obtain the measurement intended for the finished product.*

Scaling with a Tape Measure

Construction workers may have to determine a needed measurement on a plan but may not have the necessary ruler. This is not a problem, as the plan can be scaled using a tape measure. **See Figure 2-11.**

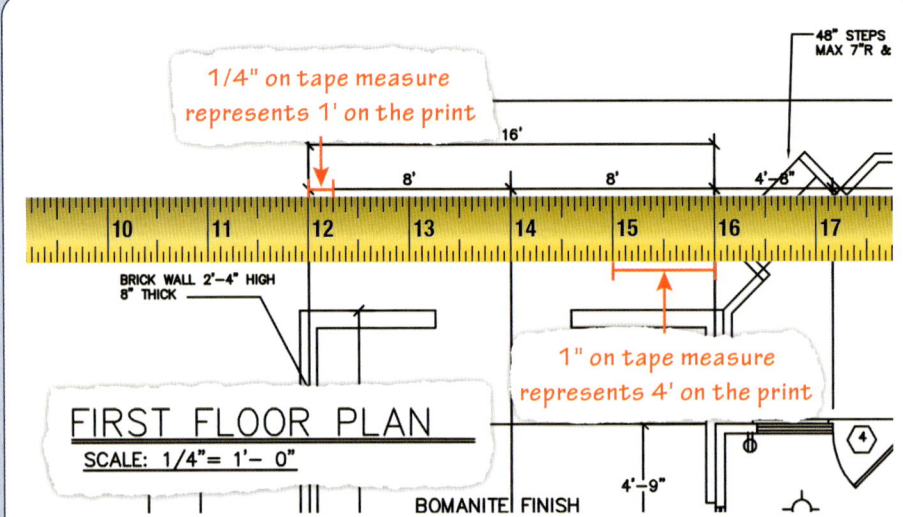

Figure 2-11. *Tape measures can be used to obtain scaled measurements, but they are most accurate on the larger scales.*

There are a larger number of subdivisions in each scale, starting with the $\frac{1}{2}$-inch scale. These scales are used for drawings of smaller portions of the building, such as interior elevations, wall sections, and detail drawings. When the size of a subdivision decreases, the accuracy of the measurement increases. For example, a detail drawn with a three-inch scale is accurate to the nearest $\frac{1}{16}$ inch, while a floor plan at a $\frac{1}{4}$-inch scale is accurate to the nearest inch.

An error of $\frac{3}{4}$ inch on a floor plan does not create a significant flaw. If the floor plan has a feature that must be installed within a $\frac{1}{4}$-inch tolerance, the architect can include it in an interior elevation with a $\frac{1}{2}$-inch scale or with a detail that includes the required dimensions.

A 10-foot measurement for an object drawn to a $\frac{1}{8}$-inch scale can be made with a tape measure. Each $\frac{1}{8}$ inch is equal to 1 foot and each inch is 8 feet. Ten feet, full-size, would equal 1 $\frac{1}{4}$ inches (10 one-eighth inches) using a scale of $\frac{1}{8}$ inch equals 1 foot. Measurements using a tape measure should start at the one-inch mark to eliminate inaccuracy that may occur due to tape hook play. Do not scale when the needed measurements are on the plans, especially with a tape measurer. Written measurements prevail over measurements that are scaled where there has been an installation error. Mistakes cost time and money.

Architects draw almost all of their drawings to scale in order to provide the information in a manner that can be easily read and understood. Construction drawings rarely include drawings of components small enough to draw at full scale and not clutter a sheet. These items would be included as shop drawings usually supplied on standard sheets of paper sized 8.5" by 11".

The civil engineering scale is mainly based on ratios with scales of 10, 20, 30, 40, 50, and 60 feet per inch (1:10, etc.). **See Figure 2-12.** For example, every inch on the "10" line on the scale is equal to 10 feet, 1 inch would equal 20 feet on the "20" line, and so on. Civil engineers are involved with site plans, including grading, drainage, and landscaping, which require scales ranging from 1:200 to 1:2,500. They also design foundations, footings, and other structural items for buildings in addition to roads, bridges, dams, location maps, and other infrastructural installations.

Location maps often use scales with a ratio of 1:100,000 (1" = 100,000').

THE SCALING PROCESS

A drawing scale is essential to accurately convey the information needed to construct a building that meets the designer's intent. To ensure accuracy, designers draw plans with an appropriate architectural or engineering scale (ratio), which installers use to determine the actual size. Remember, the drawing provides dimensions in two manners by including the numerical dimension and

CIVIL ENGINEERING SCALES

1:10 Scale
1 inch represents
10 feet

1:20 Scale
1 inch represents
20 feet

1:30 Scale
1 inch represents
30 feet

1:40 Scale
1 inch represents
40 feet

1:50 Scale
1 inch represents
50 feet

1:60 Scale
1 inch represents
60 feet

Red text indicates the intended size of the component being shown.

Blue text indicates the length of the item on the blueprint page.

For additional information, visit qr.njatcdb.org
Item #6715

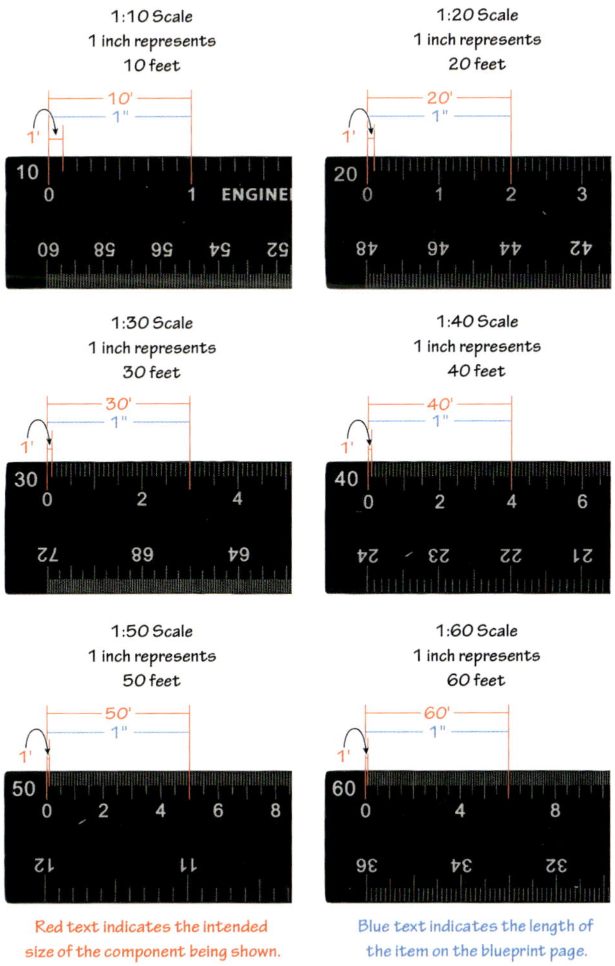

Figure 2-12. *Civil engineering scales are used on larger areas, like building sites, or roads, and represent a number of feet per inch.*

DRAWING SCALE

Figure 2-13. *Attention must be given to the scale of each drawing with a set of construction drawings to accurately interpret the information.*

drawing the object's shape using the appropriate scale to be accurately discerned. The scale for a sheet is usually found in the title block—or where details, sections, or elevations are on the same page—in the drawing description of the item. **See Figure 2-13.**

Reproduction Errors

Care must be taken to ensure that any paper drawing has been reproduced at 100%. Many photocopying machines allow for a copy to be created at larger or smaller than 100%. Obviously, if the print has not been reproduced at 100% any dimension that is obtained by scaling will be inaccurate. To prevent this error from impacting the final object any reproduced (photocopied) drawing should be checked against a printed dimension in both the horizontal and vertical orientation.

The intent is to either shrink or enlarge an object to a manageable size. Scaled drawings are accurate when the architectural team draws them carefully and when exact printing procedures are followed that do not skew or change the objects' size on the page. Before using the plans to obtain a dimension, ensure the scale being used matches the scale shown on the sheet.

Obtaining a Measurement Using a Scale (Ruler)

A standard procedure is used to determine a measurement when a dimension is not printed on a construction drawing:

1. Start the measurement from the zero point on the appropriate scale (as shown on either the title block or drawing title), not the end of the scale or the first notch (the small series of notches before the 0 on the scale divide the scale into smaller divisions).

2. Place the zero at the start of the feature being measured.

3. Look at the number at the other end of the feature being measured. If this number is not a whole number, slide the scale to the previous whole number.

4. This measurement is stated by the main scale number and the number of inches (for example, 8 feet, 6 inches). **See Figure 2-14.**

DIMENSIONING

Dimensioning begins when the designer applies the necessary dimensions to the plans and ends when construction personnel read them and use them to estimate and construct the building or structure. The best way to ensure accuracy is to provide a printed dimension on the print; if it is not on a plan, it is time to use a scale.

Types

Two types of dimensions are used on construction prints: size and location. Size dimensions define the length, width, and height of a feature. They are often used for individual objects and

For additional information, visit qr.njatcdb.org Item #6717

THE SCALING PROCESS

Step 1
Use this point on the scale to begin the measurement.

Step 2
Begin with the scale positioned with the zero line on one side of the object

Step 3
Slide the scale to the left so that the left hand side of the object is aligned with the next "whole-foot" graduation on the ruler.

Step 4
The resulting measurement is 1'5"

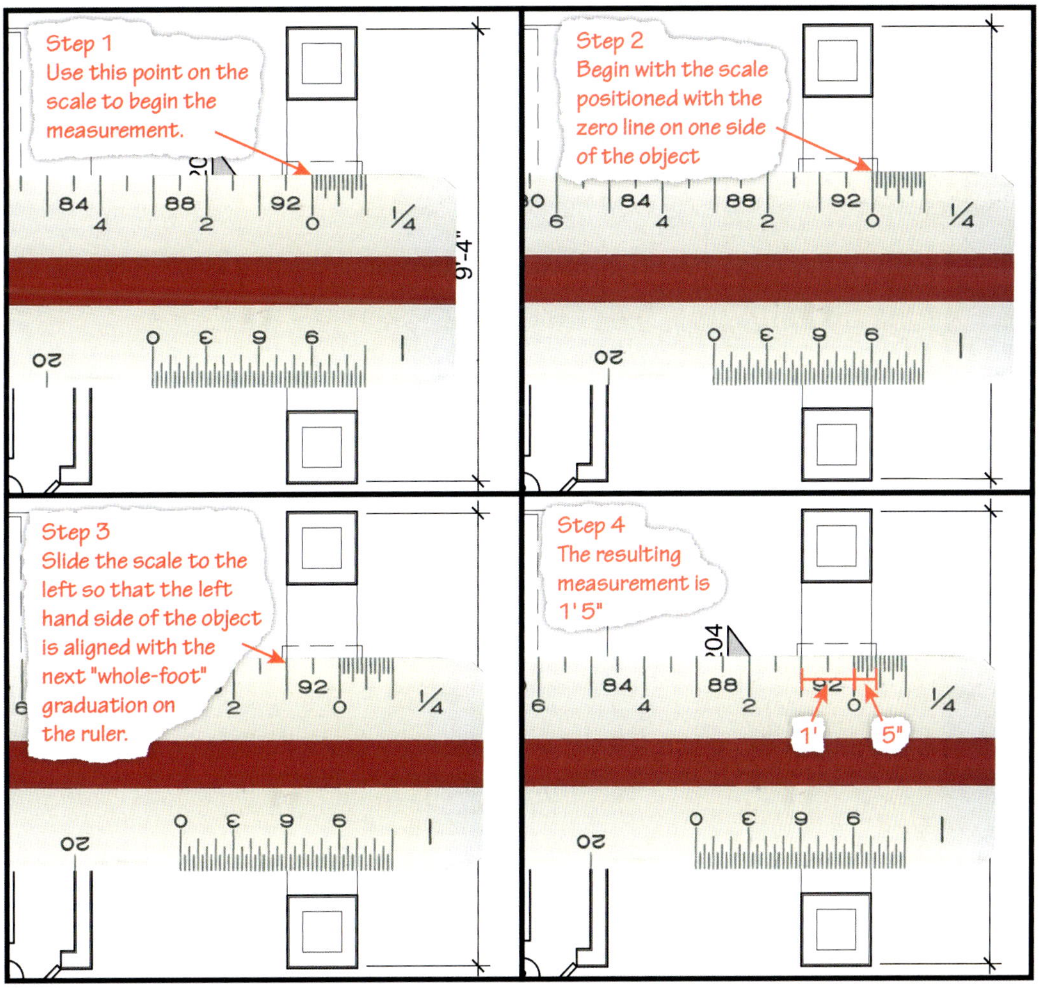

Figure 2-14. *A specific process must be utilized to obtain accurate scaled measurements from a construction drawing.*

EXTENSION LINES

For additional information, visit qr.njatcdb.org Item #6718

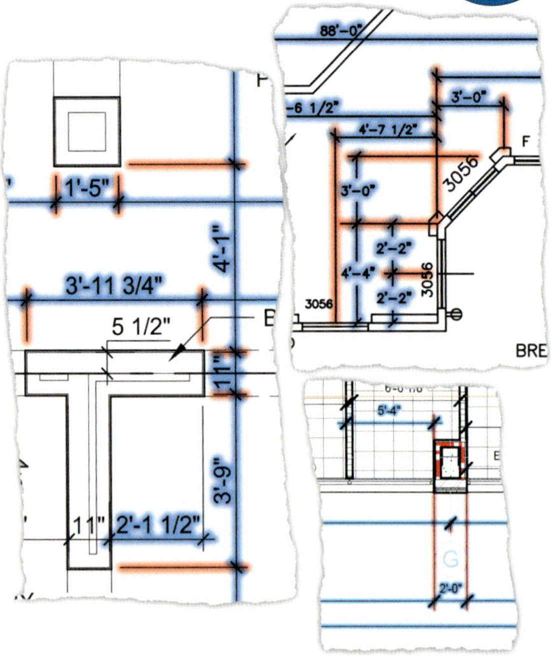

Figure 2-15. *Extension lines are tools used to place the dimension on a part of the drawing page that is less crowded.*

DIGITAL PLAN MEASURING DEVICES

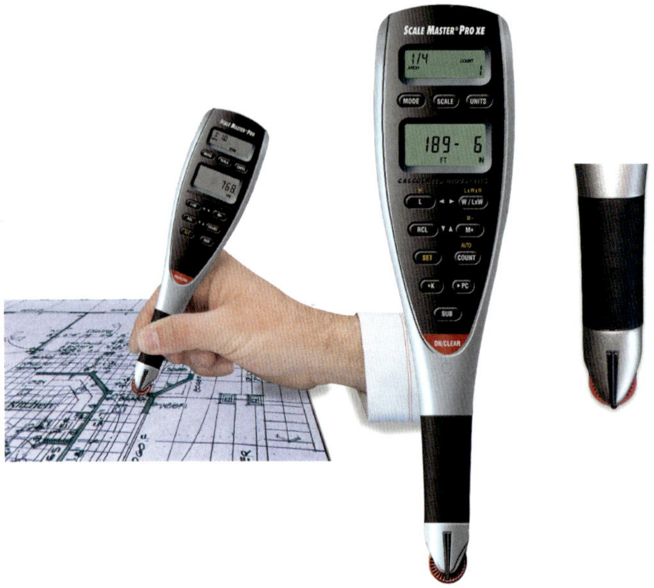

Figure 2-16. *Digital tools help to ease the scaling of construction documents.*

Dimension Inconsistency

If there is a discrepancy between printed dimension and one obtained by scaling a drawing, the printed dimension will always be assumed to be the correct dimension. If a dimension seems wrong, the architect or engineer who drew the prints will decide how to proceed.

building components. Location dimensions define the distance a feature is located from a known reference point, which is essential for proper object placement within a building.

Dimension Documentation

For dimensions to be functional on a construction drawing they require three critical pieces of information:

1. Extension lines
2. Dimension lines
3. Dimension types

Extension lines are short perpendicular lines with a small space between the beginning of the line and the measured object. The lines and spacing create a clean print, which is easier to read. Designers use extension lines for more than one dimension. **See Figure 2-15.**

Dimension lines indicate the starting and stopping points of the measurement. The measurement may be from one extension line to another or between points on the drawing. The ends of the dimension line usually have arrowheads, slashes, or dots.

Where there is insufficient room to print a dimension, leaders are used. At one end of the leader, there is an arrow pointing to the dimensioned object's location, and at the other end is a dimension. The actual dimensions are typically placed over the dimension line or in a break in the dimension line.

ELECTRONIC SCALING TOOLS

In addition to physical rulers used to determine needed dimensions on a set of construction drawings, electronic devices are available that accomplish the same task. Each electronic device has a specific function and use, but all of them improve the workflow and reduce the effort required to obtain measurements from a set of construction drawings.

Digital Plan Measuring Devices

Digital plan measuring devices are available for construction bidding and estimating. While many manufacturers offer these devices, they all perform the same primary task—each device uses a wheel to measure distances on a plan. Some models can calculate the area or volume of objects after measuring the lines creating their shapes. **See Figure 2-16.**

Most devices have multiple scales, both imperial and metric. They usually have storage memory and have a line starting at the measuring wheel axis that moves upward. Users align the line with the starting point and the endpoint of the measurement. The electronics have an accuracy of approximately 99%. However, the measurement accuracy is generally within 2% to 4% due to user inaccuracy in starting and stopping the measurement.

Installers should never use dimensions read by one of these devices for construction. A 2% error in the measurement of a 20-foot wall could result in the measurement of a 20-foot wall being as short as 19.6 feet or as long as 20.4 feet. This is as much as 10 inches of variation, which is unacceptable. These tools are best used for estimating and bidding where errors like these do not create a problem.

Computer Models

The use of computers in the design and construction process is growing each year. In many cases, the software manages the creation of the documentation relating to the construction drawings.

Unlike digital plan measuring devices, the software can handle all aspects of a construction project, including planning, designing, building, and building management. Very accurate measurements are available via software. **See Figure 2-17.**

COMPUTER-AIDED TOOLS

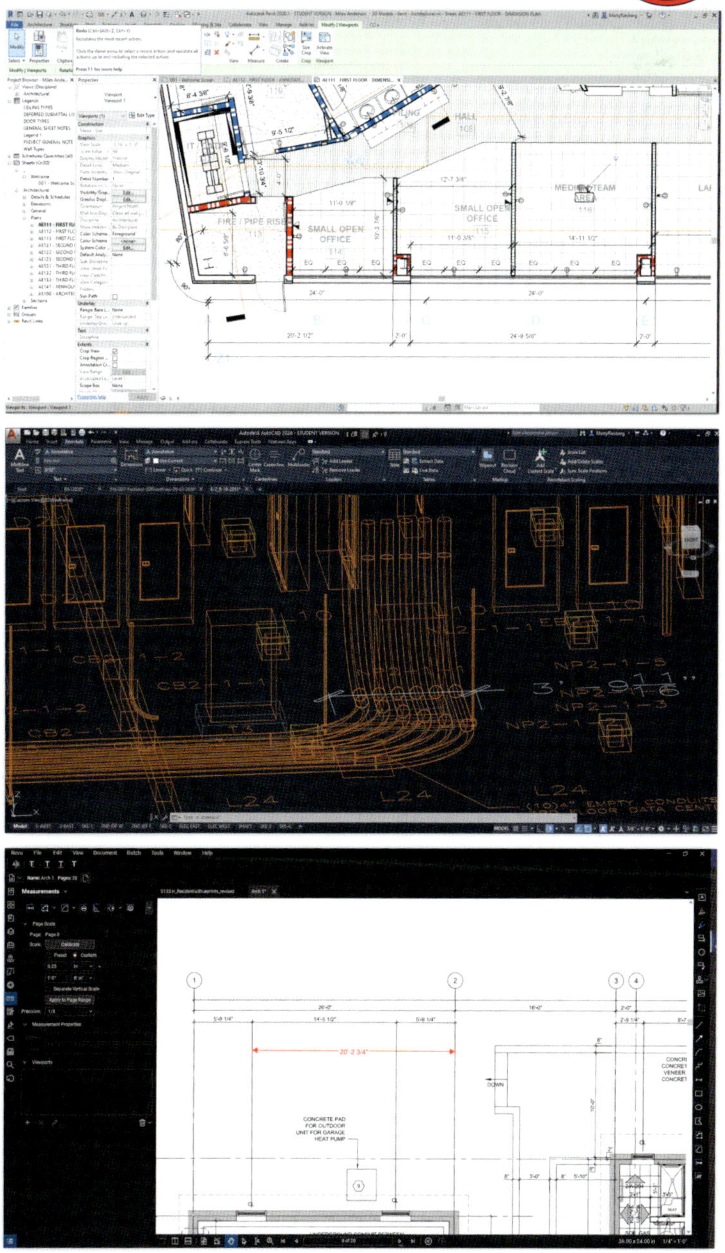

Figure 2-17. Many software tools allow for the ability to obtain needed measurements on construction drawings.

Applications

Electrical print reading often requires the use of a scale to find dimensions, although residential plans may not need a scale for the placement of receptacle outlets. The *National Electrical Code®* (*NEC®*) regulates the placement of receptacle outlets in Article 210. One requirement states that no location along a wall line can be further than six feet, zero inches from a general-purpose receptacle. An electrician may receive a "not approved" tag from an inspector if the measurement is six feet, one inch. Other areas of a residence, such as a kitchen, have other spacing requirements. Special outlets, lighting outlets, and receptacle outlets in cabinets often require exact dimensions.

Commercial and industrial construction requires many exact measurements that may require the use of the scale. Equipment often requires the electrician to provide power in a specific area. Appliances such as drinking fountains and commercial cooking equipment have very specific power rough-in dimensions, and have tight tolerances for the location of the receptacle outlet. **See Figure 2-18.**

For additional information, visit qr.njatcdb.org Item #6719

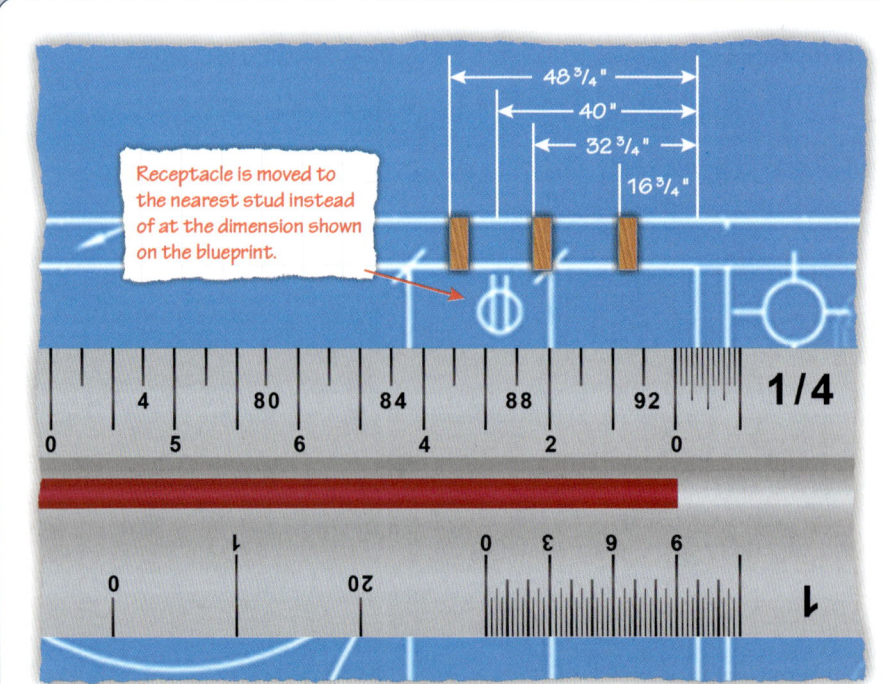

Figure 2-18. Electrical receptacles are not always placed precisely as drawn on electrical power plans but are most often placed on the nearest wall stud, while still maintaining the maximum spacing requirements of the NEC.

SUMMARY

An understanding of dimensioning and scaling is critical to ensure a construction project is built as designed. The accurate communication of details pertaining to an object's size results in the ability to construct a building as it was intended. The use of standard units of measure in conjunction with standard scales (conversion factors) enables this form of communication.

Scales are another piece in the puzzle that will provide a complete picture of how the construction of a building is to be completed. Without proficiency with interpreting scales, it is likely that workers will make errors in scaling a drawing resulting in the use of the wrong dimensions. After the communication of size information these scales are applied to most all construction drawings including plans, elevations, details, and many others. Just like with a puzzle, every piece is necessary to complete the project.

For additional information, visit qr.njatcdb.org Item #6641

REVIEW QUESTIONS

1. The __?__ scale, usually used by architects in the United States, has a format of inches, or parts of an inch, equal to one foot.

   a. British
   b. imperial
   c. metric
   d. none of the above

2. Because architectural floor, ceiling, and exterior elevation plans have a large area to represent, they are typically drawn at __?__ scale.

   a. $\frac{1}{16}$"
   b. $\frac{1}{8}$"
   c. $\frac{3}{8}$"
   d. $\frac{1}{2}$"

3. Designers include all of the necessary dimensions on a set of construction drawings.

   a. True   b. False

4. __?__ lines are short perpendicular lines with a small space between the beginning of the line and the measured object.

   a. Center
   b. Extension
   c. Hidden
   d. Object

5. Triangular scale rulers have __?__ scales with varying subdivisions in the representative one foot at the beginning of their scales.

   a. 9
   b. 10
   c. 11
   d. 12

6. As it applies to drawings and print reading, the term *scale* has __?__ common usages in construction.

   a. 2
   b. 3
   c. 4
   d. 5

CHAPTER 3
PLAN VIEWS

Elevation drawings, of the outside of the structure, are usually drawn first to aid in the initial design process; plan views follow closely. Plan views, showing the building from an overhead view, establish interior features such as walls, doors, windows, footers, and foundations. They are the most widely used method of showing the interior layout of a structure.

The architectural plan views are the "plan" for the construction of a building. The primary purpose of other drawing types is to provide the aesthetic appearance of the building and are needed to present the design intent, but they cannot be used to construct the building without additional specific and detailed information. Plan views provide additional information by showing the interior layout of the building and incorporating structural features to ensure the building's safety.

There are various types of plan views that provide information about specific applications and disciplines of the construction process. Plan views are also supplemented by symbols, abbreviations, and notations to ensure a complete, unambiguous explanation of the desired final structure.

OBJECTIVES

- Identify the aspects of plan views and the information they provide.
- Identify the types of plan views and the details provided in each view.
- Recognize the specific information provided in "trade-specific" drawings.

TABLE OF CONTENTS

INTRODUCTION TO PLAN VIEWS

A plan view is a two-dimensional view of a structure that looks straight down from overhead and sees the result from directly over the object or structure. The word "plan" indicates a top down view.

Floor plans are the most common type of plan views but there are many other types as well, including plot plans, foundation plans, trade specific plans (like mechanical or electrical), reflected ceiling plans, and others. **See Figure 3-1.**

PLAN VIEWS

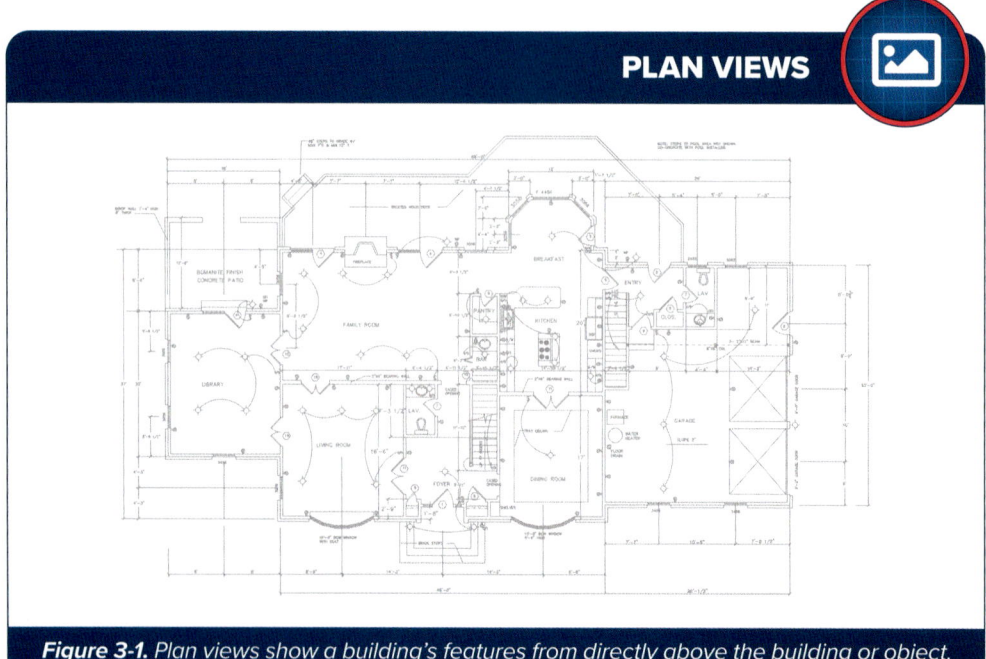

Figure 3-1. Plan views show a building's features from directly above the building or object.

PLANE TO CREATE PLAN VIEWS

For additional information, visit qr.njatcdb.org Item #6539

Figure 3-2. By removing the portion of the building above the cut line, a building's features can be seen on a plan view.

Description

A floor plan is a top-down scaled view of a building. This drawing is produced by visually removing everything above an imaginary plane and looking down upon the floor of the building. **See Figure 3-2.** The plane that is used to remove the upper portion of a building is called a cutting-plane.

Although different architects may use different heights, the cutting plane is typically at a height of about four feet and runs through the doors and windows. Any object or wall that is cut by, or below, the cutting-plane line is shown with an object line. **See Figure 3-3.** For example, partition walls, base cabinet units, doors, and windows will be represented with an object line. Any item

VISIBLE FEATURES ON PLAN VIEWS

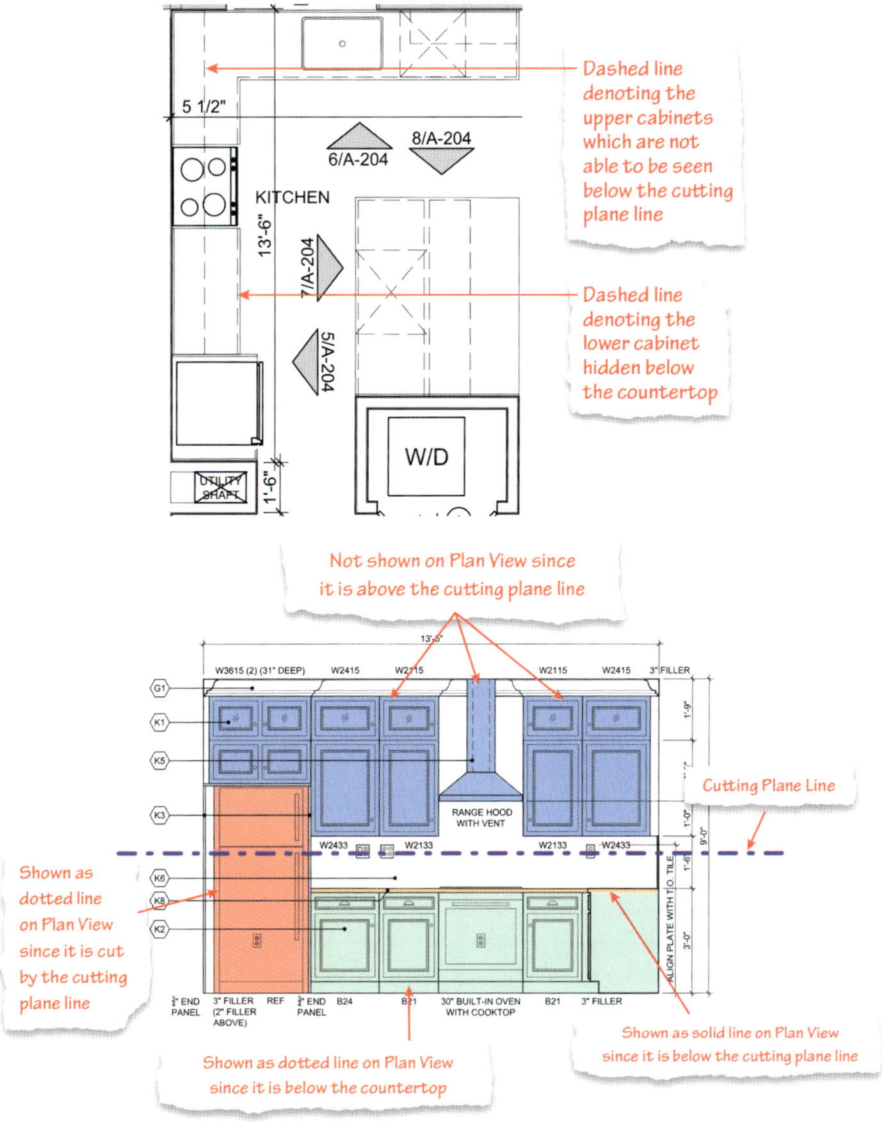

For additional information, visit qr.njatcdb.org Item #6540

Dashed line denoting the upper cabinets which are not able to be seen below the cutting plane line

Dashed line denoting the lower cabinet hidden below the countertop

5 1/2"

8/A-204
6/A-204

KITCHEN

13'-6"

7/A-204

5/A-204

1'-6"

UTILITY SHAFT

W/D

Not shown on Plan View since it is above the cutting plane line

13'-6"

W3615 (2) (31" DEEP)   W2415   W2115   W2115   W2415   3" FILLER

G1
K1
K5
K3

RANGE HOOD WITH VENT

W2433   W2133   W2133   W2433

Cutting Plane Line

Shown as dotted line on Plan View since it is cut by the cutting plane line

K6
K8
K2

ALIGN PLATE WITH T.O. TILE

1'-9"   1'-0"   9'-0"   1'-6"   3'-0"

3" END PANEL   3" FILLER (2" FILLER ABOVE)   REF   3" END PANEL   B24   B21   30" BUILT-IN OVEN WITH COOKTOP   B21   3" FILLER

Shown as solid line on Plan View since it is below the cutting plane line

Shown as dotted line on Plan View since it is below the countertop

Figure 3-3. Objects are shown as either solid or dotted lines based on if they are above or below the cutting plane.

MULTIPLE FLOOR PLANS

For additional information, visit qr.njatcdb.org Item #6541

Figure 3-4. *Each floor of a building has its own floor plan. Often the same exterior walls are shown on multiple floor plans.*

above the cutting-plane line is shown with a hidden line to indicate that it cannot be seen in this view. For example, upper cabinets in a kitchen, cased openings, roof lines, and vaulted ceilings will be represented with a hidden line.

The floor plan shows the layout and relationships of rooms and walls.

Floor plans are created for each floor, or level, of a building, since including information or components from multiple levels of a building would result in a confusing and crowded drawing. For instance, the floor plans for the first and second floors of a building will show much of the same building outline but will have information specific to items on that floor. **See Figure 3-4.**

FEATURE RELATIONSHIPS ON FLOOR PLANS

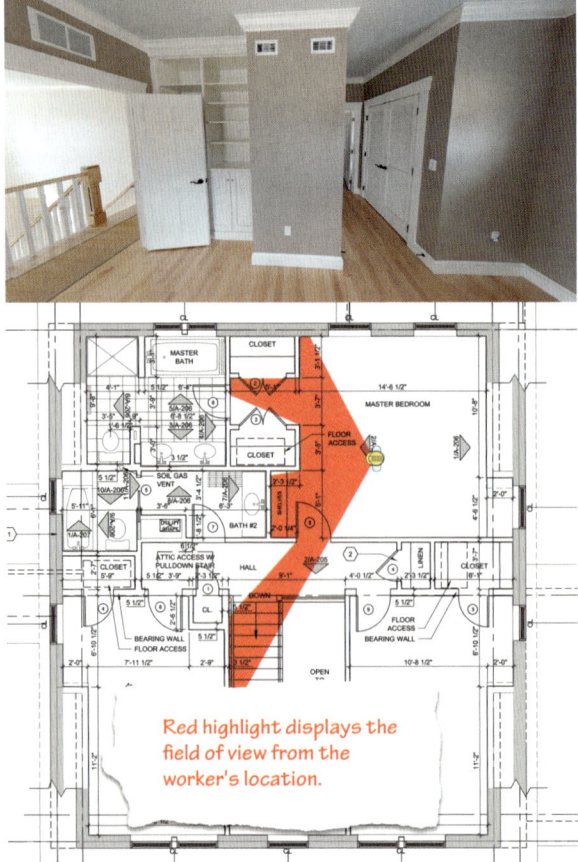

For additional information, visit qr.njatcdb.org Item #6542

Red highlight displays the field of view from the worker's location.

Figure 3-5. *Interpreting a floor plan helps understand the final room layout.*

The floor plan shows the entire footprint of each level of the building in a two-dimensional drawing.

By looking at a floor plan, a tradesperson should be able to visualize the layout of the building and imagine what the finished project will look like. Floor plans give the relationships of doors, windows, walls, and any other permanently installed feature. The floor plan will also give detailed information about the sizes and placement of these features within a building. **See Figure 3-5.**

Information Conveyed

A floor plan shows a variety of information including the location of stairs, windows, and doors, the room layout, and things as simple as the room names. This information is helpful in visualizing what the finished building layout will be when completed. **See Figure 3-6.** Since plan views, including floor plans, include a great deal of information, often symbols, abbreviations, and notations are used to keep the drawing clean while still presenting all the necessary information.

Dimensions

Most of the dimensioning is done on the floor plans, indicating both size and location. Not every plan will contain every dimension; only the necessary dimensions for that discipline or type of drawing will be included on that print. Having only the most needed dimensions on each type of plan will prevent the print from becoming too cluttered. **See Figure 3-7.**

Although most electrical devices do not have location dimensions, a device may occasionally require installation in a very specific location. If a device does require a specific location, it may have horizontal and vertical dimensions. Horizontal dimensions to electrical devices are typically to center. Dimensions on a drawing are usually given to either the edge or the center of the component. These dimensions are commonly referred to as either "to the edge" (top, bottom, left or right) or "to center." Most vertical dimensions to

INFORMATION ON FLOOR PLANS

For additional information, visit qr.njatcdb.org Item #6543

Figure 3-6. *Symbols, abbreviations, and notations are used to show multiple types of material on a floor plan without crowding the plan.*

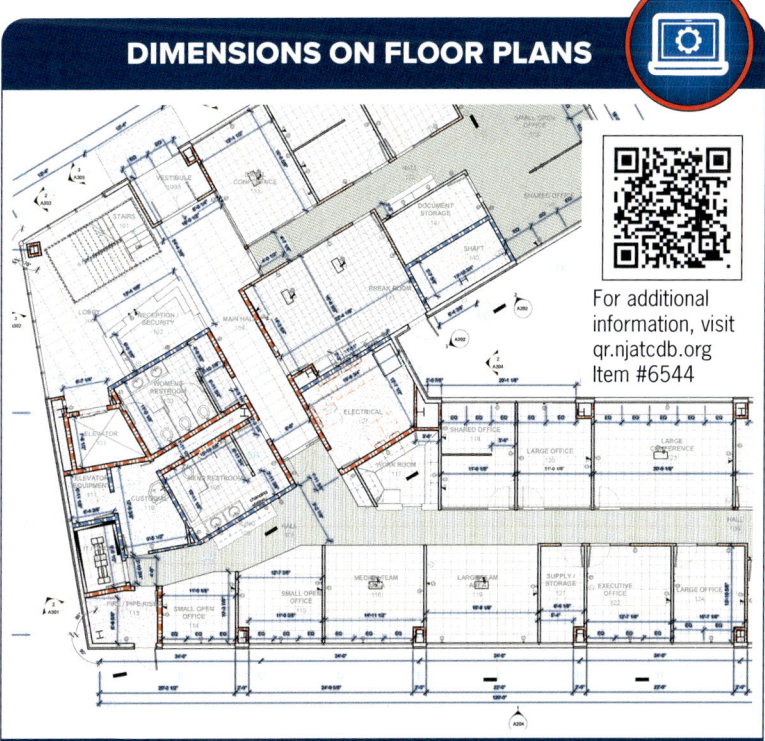

DIMENSIONS ON FLOOR PLANS

For additional information, visit qr.njatcdb.org Item #6544

Figure 3-7. *Dimensions that indicate key sizes and locations aid in maintaining concise drawings.*

devices are to the edge. Often the vertical dimension for receptacles and switches will be identified by a note on the drawing that gives the height for a typical receptacle or switch. Any switch or receptacle height that deviates from the typical dimension will have a specific note giving the height of that specific device.

If a person wants to be able to lay out and draw notes on a plan, it is convenient that he or she receive a print without any notes or dimensions. This is not necessarily helpful with determining locations, but it gives a person a clean print for jotting down notes and

information about a job. Computer-aided design (CAD) drawings simplify the process of selective printing.

Symbols

Most construction drawings have a legend to identify the symbols used on the sheets. **See Figure 3-8.** If a symbol on the sheet seems unfamiliar and is not identified in the legend, review other drawings in the set, reference materials (textbooks), or ask the designer of the drawings to define the symbol.

There are many symbols shown on the floor plan that give the appropriate information without cluttering the

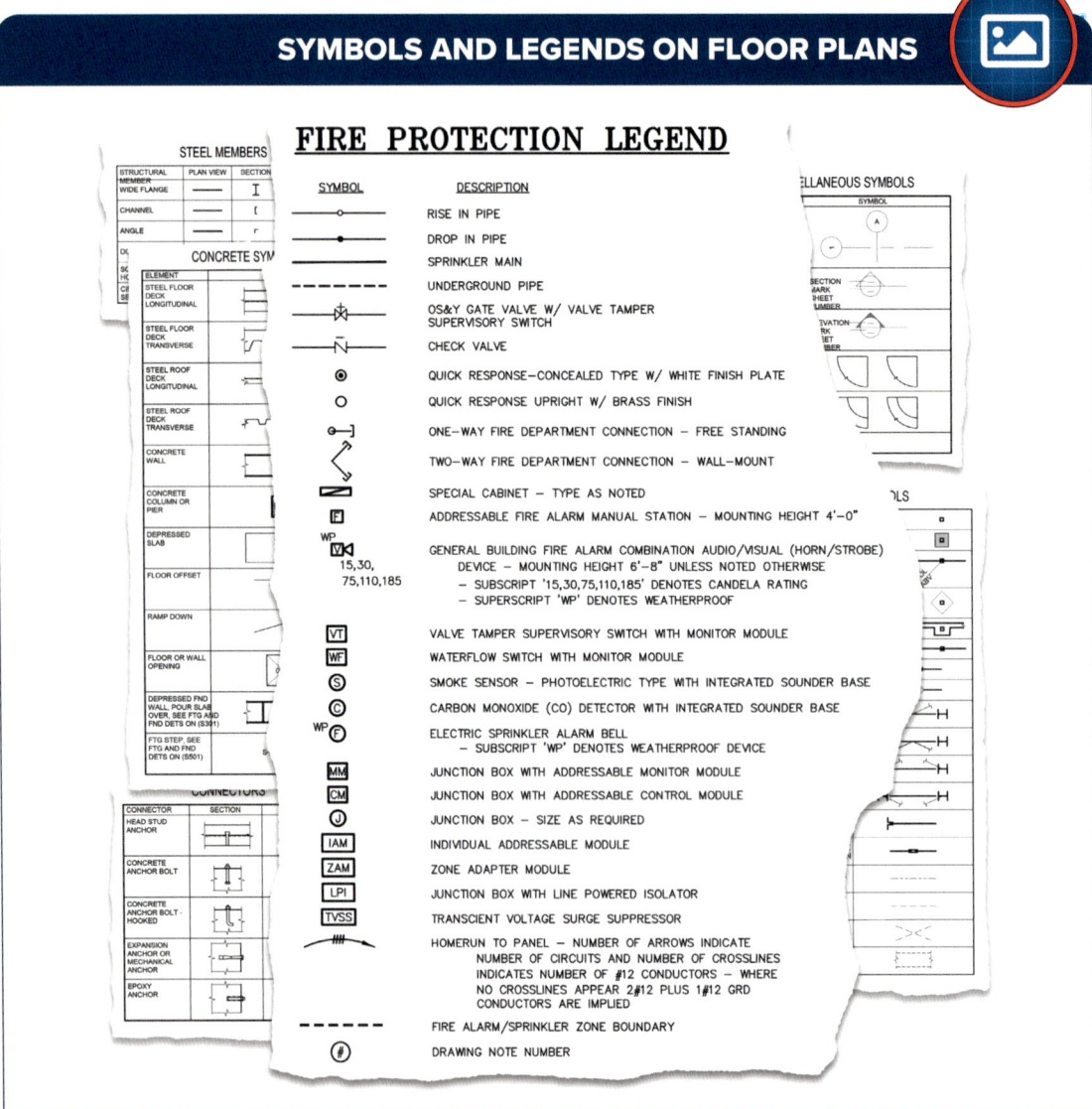

SYMBOLS AND LEGENDS ON FLOOR PLANS

Figure 3-8. The use of symbols makes the legend a helpful tool to accurately interpret floor plans.

print. Most designers use standardized symbols put forth by the American National Standards Institute (ANSI), although this is not required; designers may choose to use their own, or company-specific, symbols that do not align with the ANSI standards.

Some of the most common symbols on prints are door and window symbols. Door and window symbols are usually somewhat generic in nature with the specifics about each instance of a door or window symbol annotated with the addition of a type indicator; this is usually done with a number or letter next to the door symbol. Additional information about each door and window type is found on a door or window schedule. **See Figure 3-9.**

Symbols Library

For more information on symbols, visit the <u>online Symbols Library</u>.

For additional information, visit qr.njatcdb.org Item #6545

NECA/NEIS 100

For more information on symbols, open the <u>NECA/NEIS 100 standard</u>.

For additional information, visit qr.njatcdb.org Item #6553

COMMON SYMBOLS ON FLOOR PLANS

For additional information, visit qr.njatcdb.org Item #6546

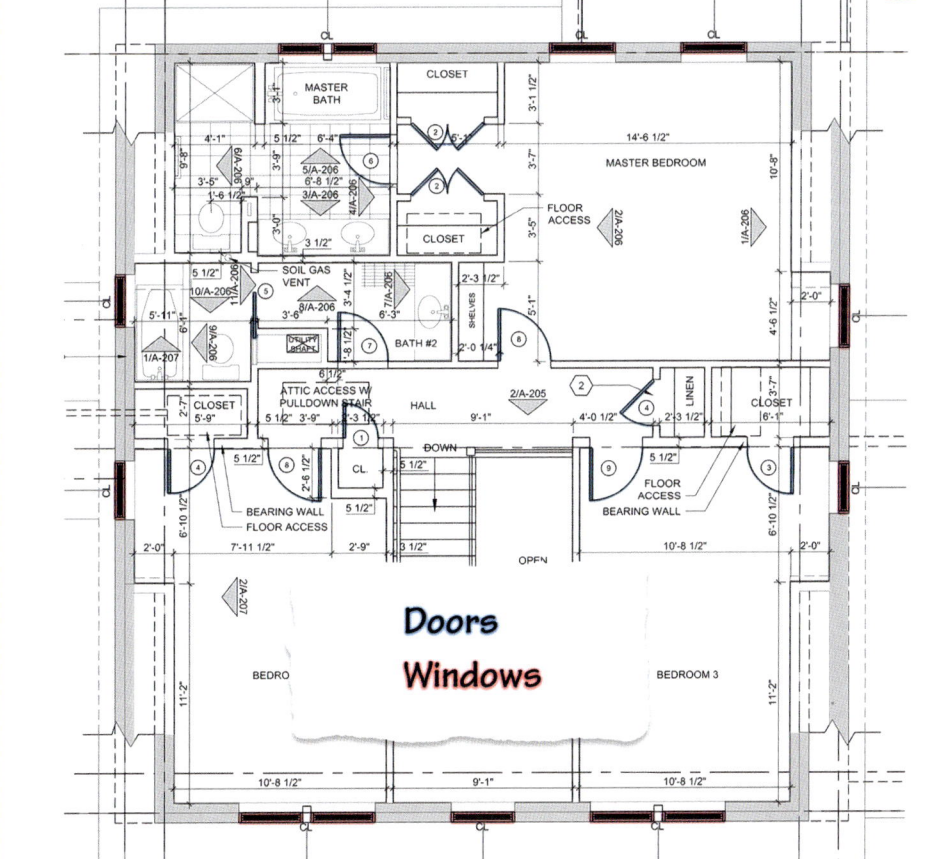

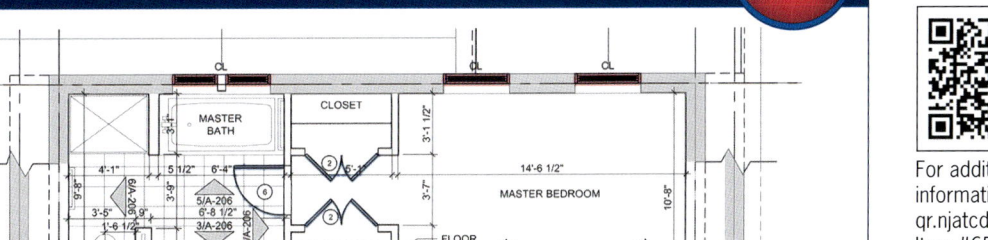

Figure 3-9. *Door and window symbols are among the most common on floor plans. Usually, additional information (from schedules and details) is needed to attain a full understanding of the component.*

Abbreviations

Like symbols, abbreviations also help to minimize clutter on a print by shortening important information. Most construction drawings have a designated location on one of the sheets that defines the abbreviations, similar to a legend. **See Figure 3-10.**

If an abbreviation is unfamiliar and not identified in the legend, one should check reference materials (textbooks) or ask the designer of the drawings to define the abbreviation.

> ## Appendix A
>
> For more information on abbreviations, see Appendix A.

Notations

Notations, or notes, are often found on floor plans. A notation can vary in length from only a few words to several sentences. The notes are used to convey additional information and can apply generally to the entire set of plans or specifically to one point on the drawing. A general notation could denote specific dimensioning requirements. **See Figure 3-11.** Specific notations will typically be written on the drawing where the note applies or will have a leader pointing to the location where the note applies.

TYPES OF PLANS

Although floor plans are the most common type of plan view, there are many

For additional information, visit qr.njatcdb.org Item #6547

ABBREVIATIONS ON FLOOR PLANS

ABBREVIATIONS

A.F.F.   ABOVE FINISHED FLOOR

Figure 3-10. *To keep floor plans concise, many designers use abbreviations for common items. Similar to legends for symbols, legends are normally defined for abbreviations.*

NOTATIONS ON FLOOR PLANS

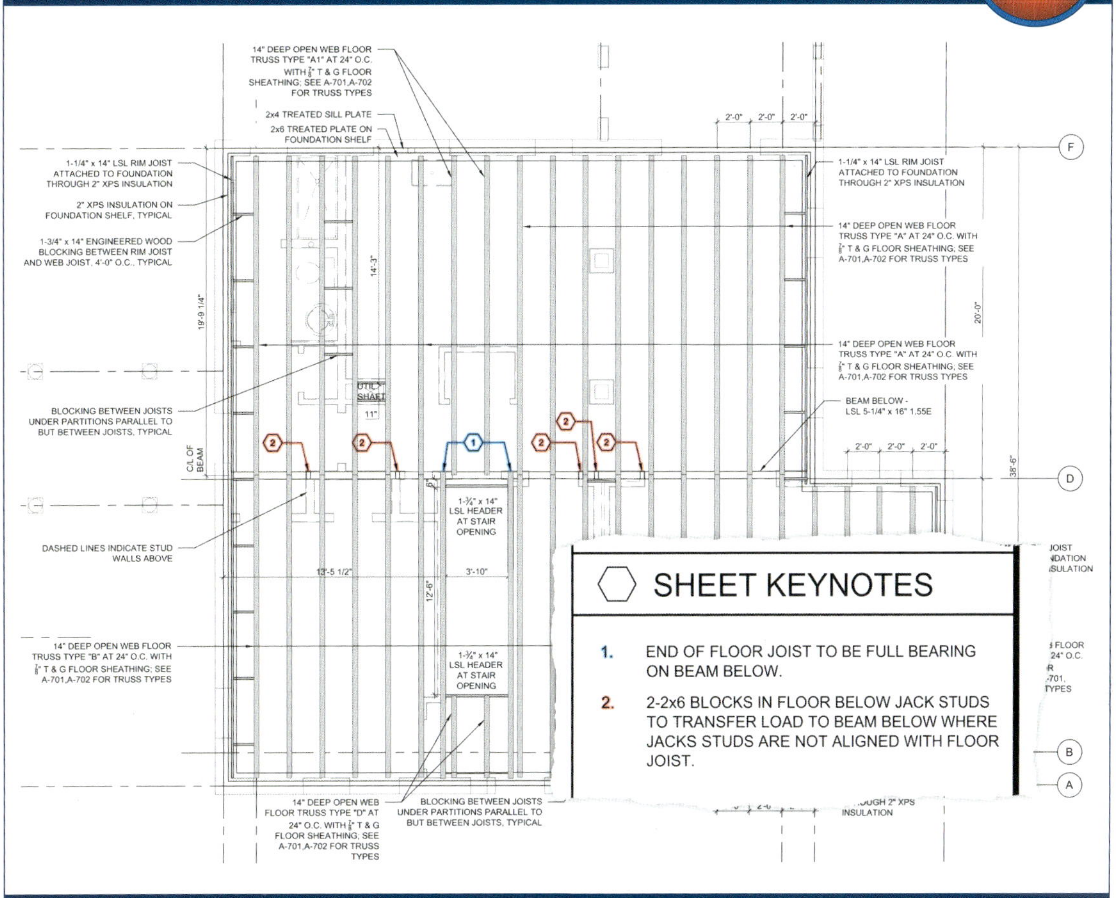

14" DEEP OPEN WEB FLOOR TRUSS TYPE "A1" AT 24" O.C. WITH ¾" T & G FLOOR SHEATHING. SEE A-701, A-702 FOR TRUSS TYPES

2x4 TREATED SILL PLATE

2x6 TREATED PLATE ON FOUNDATION SHELF

1-1/4" x 14" LSL RIM JOIST ATTACHED TO FOUNDATION THROUGH 2" XPS INSULATION

2" XPS INSULATION ON FOUNDATION SHELF, TYPICAL

1-3/4" x 14" ENGINEERED WOOD BLOCKING BETWEEN RIM JOIST AND WEB JOIST, 4'-0" O.C., TYPICAL

BLOCKING BETWEEN JOISTS UNDER PARTITIONS PARALLEL TO BUT BETWEEN JOISTS, TYPICAL

DASHED LINES INDICATE STUD WALLS ABOVE

14" DEEP OPEN WEB FLOOR TRUSS TYPE "B" AT 24" O.C. WITH ¾" T & G FLOOR SHEATHING; SEE A-701, A-702 FOR TRUSS TYPES

1-1/4" x 14" LSL RIM JOIST ATTACHED TO FOUNDATION THROUGH 2" XPS INSULATION

14" DEEP OPEN WEB FLOOR TRUSS TYPE "A" AT 24" O.C. WITH ¾" T & G FLOOR SHEATHING, SEE A-701, A-702 FOR TRUSS TYPES

14" DEEP OPEN WEB FLOOR TRUSS TYPE "A" AT 24" O.C. WITH ¾" T & G FLOOR SHEATHING, SEE A-701, A-702 FOR TRUSS TYPES

BEAM BELOW - LSL 5-1/4" x 16" 1.55E

1-¾" x 14" LSL HEADER AT STAIR OPENING

1-¾" x 14" LSL HEADER AT STAIR OPENING

14" DEEP OPEN WEB FLOOR TRUSS TYPE "D" AT 24" O.C. WITH ¾" T & G FLOOR SHEATHING, SEE A-701, A-702 FOR TRUSS TYPES

BLOCKING BETWEEN JOISTS UNDER PARTITIONS PARALLEL TO BUT BETWEEN JOISTS, TYPICAL

SHEET KEYNOTES

1. END OF FLOOR JOIST TO BE FULL BEARING ON BEAM BELOW.

2. 2-2x6 BLOCKS IN FLOOR BELOW JACK STUDS TO TRANSFER LOAD TO BEAM BELOW WHERE JACKS STUDS ARE NOT ALIGNED WITH FLOOR JOIST.

Figure 3-11. *Clarifying statements about the designer's intent are often provided on floor plans. These notations can be general or specific in nature.*

For additional information, visit qr.njatcdb.org Item #6548

types of plan views. Any top-down view that shows the building's, or site's, features is a plan view. Other plan views include foundation, site, ceiling, and trade-specific plan views.

Floor

Each level in a building has at least one floor plan, but most commercial and industrial prints have several. The basic layout of walls, doors, and windows for each of the drawings will be the same, however, each drawing details different aspects of the job. For example, the first-floor framing plan will have the information necessary to construct and place the walls of the first floor; it will not have any information about the lighting, receptacles, or plumbing fixtures. That information would be found on the first-floor lighting plan, power plan, or plumbing plan.

Foundation

A foundation plan is similar to a floor plan in that it looks down on the building as if everything above the cutting plane line were removed. It does not, however, give the same information as a floor plan. The foundation plan is a view of the foundation walls, footings, and any load-bearing posts or columns. It does not show partition walls, plumbing fixtures, cabinetry, or similar features. This is the drawing that will be used by concrete workers to build the footings and foundation walls.

Any wall or post cut by the cutting-plane line will be an object line. The footings, which are underground or

FOUNDATION PLANS

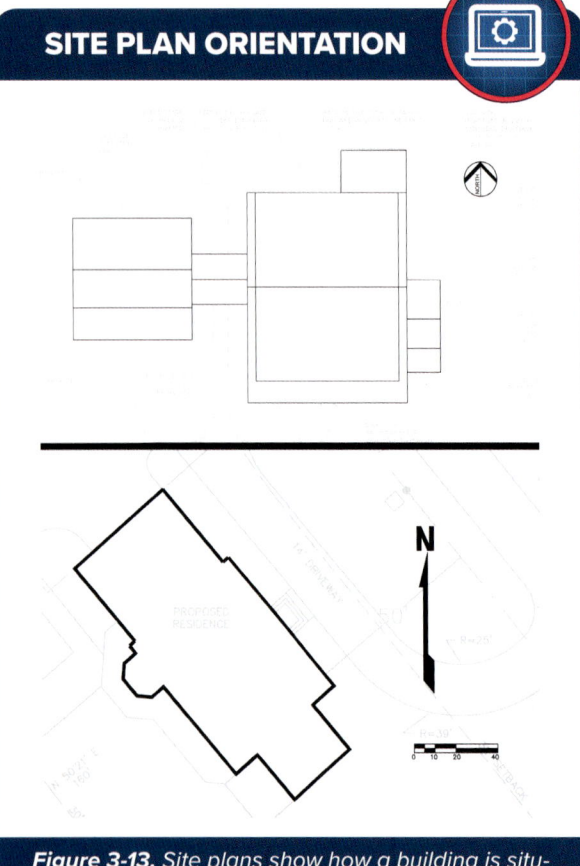

Figure 3-12. Foundation plans provide information about the structural foundation of the building. The information above the cut line is not shown to keep the view of the foundation clear and concise.

SITE PLAN ORIENTATION

Figure 3-13. Site plans show how a building is situated in relationship to North.

under the concrete, will be shown with a hidden line. **See Figure 3-12.** Residential drawings sometimes have a plan that serves as both the foundation plan and the basement floor plan. Commercial and industrial drawings will have a foundation plan separate from any lower-level or basement plans.

Site (Plot)

Site plans, often referred to as plot plans, are a plan view that provides information about the parcel of land on which the building is to be built. Site plans show how the building sits on the piece of land, as well as other specific information about the lot. Other types of information shown on a site plan include the contour of the land, the property lines, utility feeds to the building, and property easements.

Symbols and Abbreviations

As with all types of construction drawings, site plans have many line types, symbols, and abbreviations used to make the drawings easier to read. A very important symbol common to all site plans is the North arrow, which

GRADE ON SITE PLAN

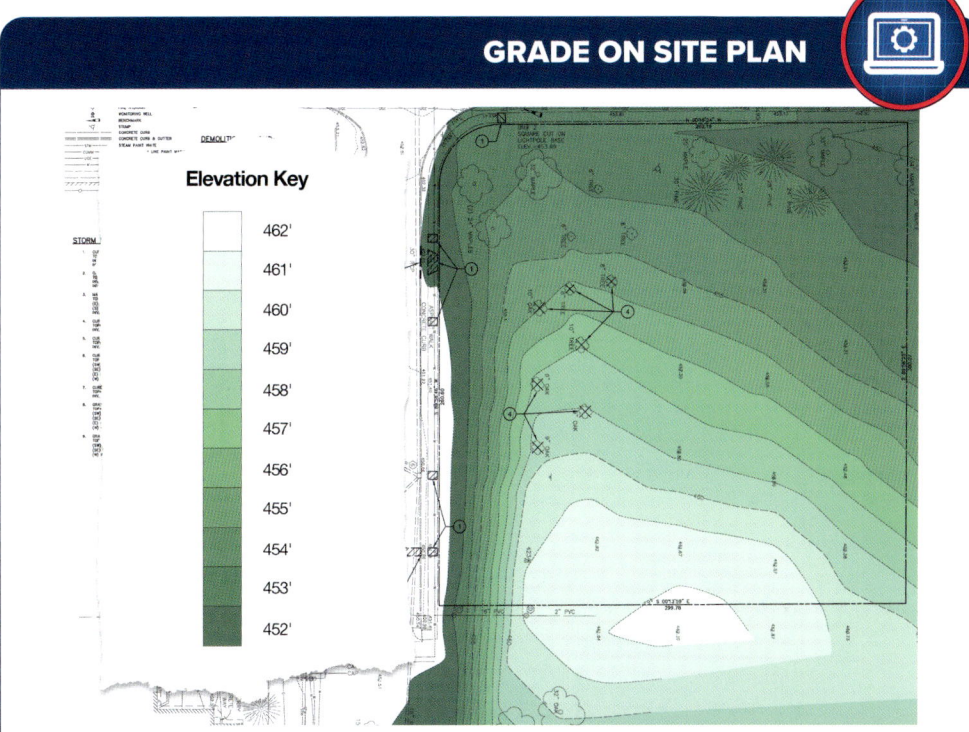

Elevation Key

	462'
	461'
	460'
	459'
	458'
	457'
	456'
	455'
	454'
	453'
	452'

For additional information, visit qr.njatcdb.org Item #6551

Figure 3-14. *Changes in grade are indicated on site plans with contour lines and an indication of the elevation that the grade changes along the contour line.*

indicates how the property and building sit with respect to the due or magnetic North direction. **See Figure 3-13.**

Elevation
Elevation is not only a type of construction drawing, but also a vertical dimension. A change in elevation, often referred to as grade, is shown on the site plan with contour lines. The elevation of the contour lines may be written on the high side of the contour line, in a break in the contour line, or to the side of the contour line. **See Figure 3-14.** Contour lines that are far apart represent a slight slope, whereas lines close together represent a steeper slope.

Natural grade is the elevation or slope of the earth before construction begins. Finished grade is the elevation or slope of the earth when the project is finished. The finished grade of a property is often not the same as the natural grade was. Contour lines representing natural grade are represented as dashed lines, while finished grade is represented with solid lines. **See Figure 3-15.** The elevation of contour lines

NATURAL AND FINISHED GRADE

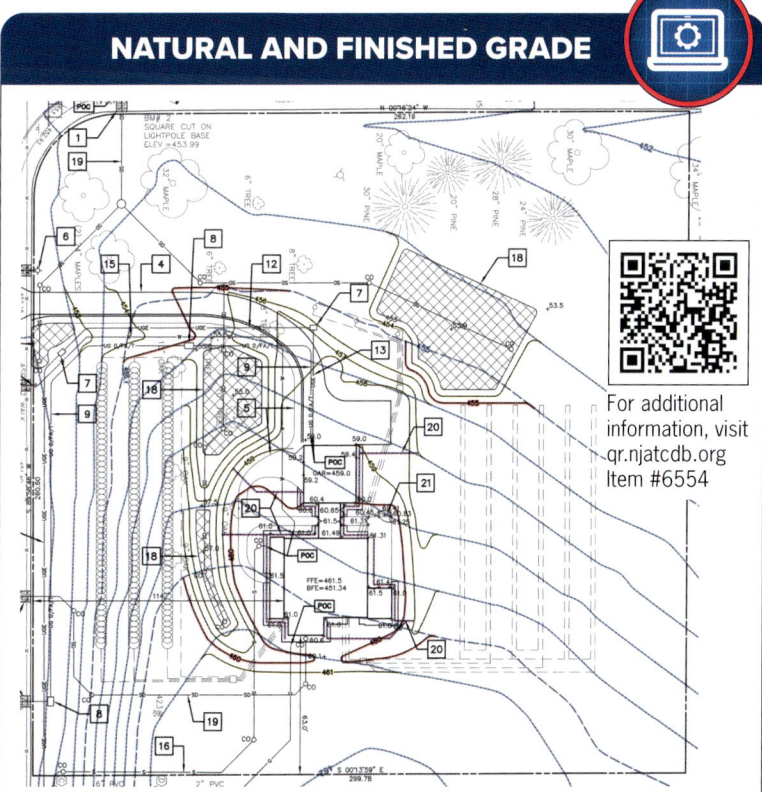

For additional information, visit qr.njatcdb.org Item #6554

Figure 3-15. *Site plans that show natural and finished grade help to provide an understanding regarding the amount of change there will be to the property.*

PROPERTY LINES ON SITE PLAN

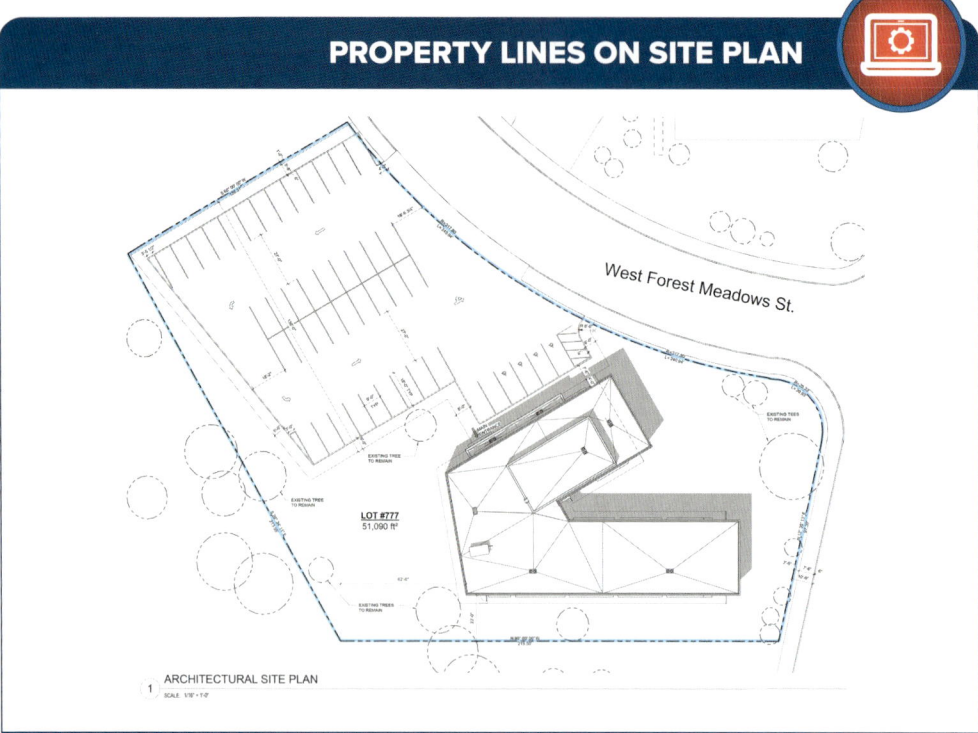

West Forest Meadows St.

LOT #777
51,090 ft²

ARCHITECTURAL SITE PLAN

Figure 3-16. Property lines indicate where a building sits in relationship to the entire building site (or property).

UNIQUE SCALES ON SITE PLAN

Figure 3-17. Because the size of the site is much larger than the size of the building, unique scales are used for site plans. Often, civil engineer's scales are used instead of the more common architect's scale. © Klein Tools, Inc. All rights reserved.

could be in reference to sea level, a reference point for the community, or the point of beginning on the drawing. The point of beginning, if shown on the drawing, is the starting point for all horizontal and vertical measurements; it is a benchmark of where the location and elevation are known. It may be a stake or pin buried in the ground, or a point on a street or curb.

Property Lines
Property lines, which represent the edges of a property, will typically be marked with the length of the line, as well as with the bearing angle—given in degrees, minutes, and seconds from North, South, East, or West. The location of the building and other features on the site plan will be indicated with dimensions from the property lines or the point of beginning. **See Figure 3-16.**

Scale
The scale used on a site plan is not only smaller than the other drawings in a set of prints but is a different type of scale. Site plans are typically drawn by a civil

engineer and will have a scale that uses tenths of a foot rather than inches. Remember that 10.5 feet is not the same as 10 feet, 5 inches. While this difference may not seem significant, there is still a difference.

Imagine making 25 measurements that were an inch off. When finished, the measurement would be more than two feet off from the intended location. Having a tape measure with tenths of a foot rather than inches will save having to convert all dimensions to inches. **See Figure 3-17.**

Easements and Utilities

Site plans will often include the locations of easements and utilities. An easement is a portion of land dedicated to public utilities (or access to utilities and the like), such as water, gas, sewer, and electricity. **See Figure 3-18.** It is

EASEMENTS AND UTILITIES ON SITE PLAN

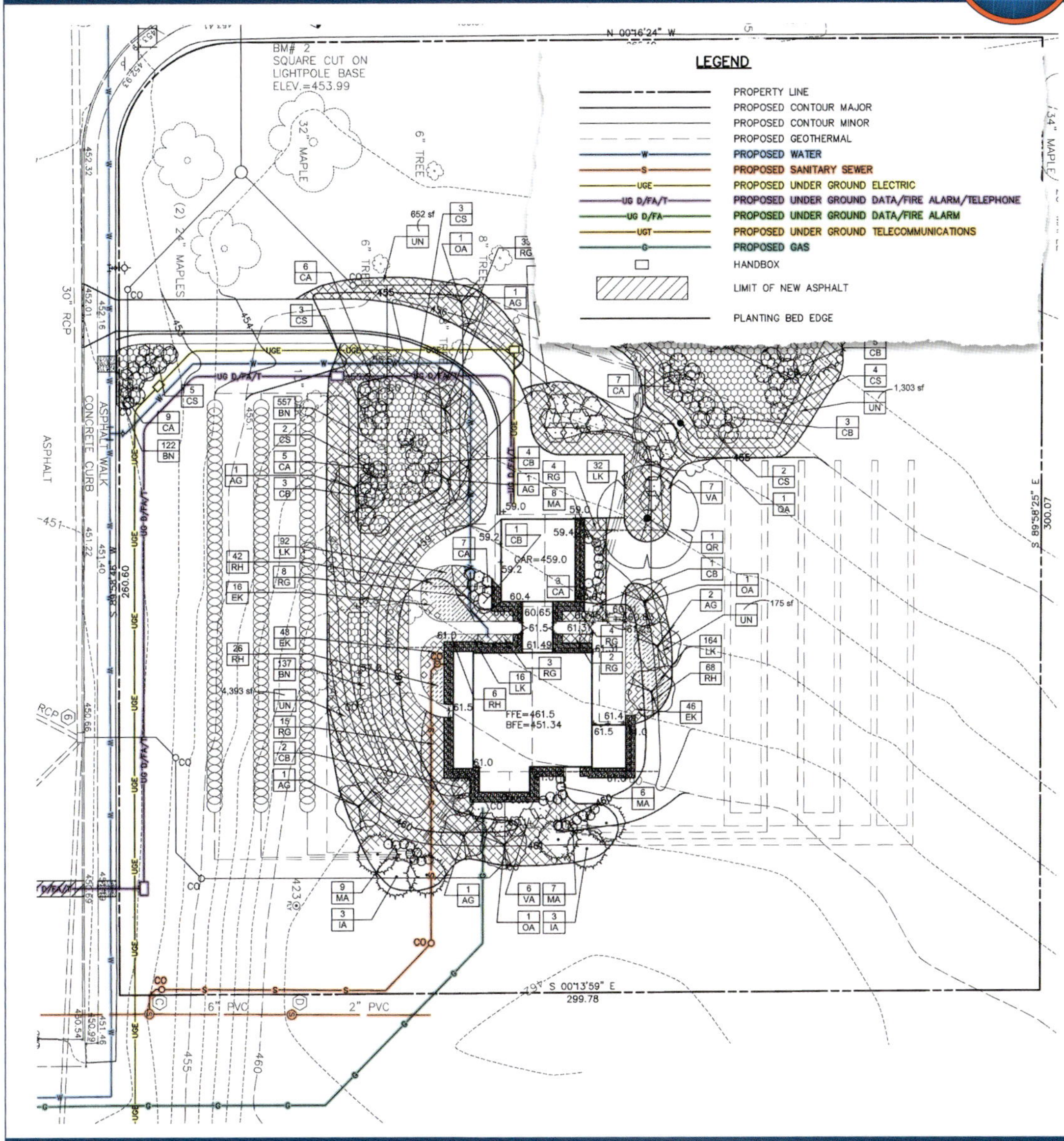

LEGEND

	PROPERTY LINE
	PROPOSED CONTOUR MAJOR
	PROPOSED CONTOUR MINOR
	PROPOSED GEOTHERMAL
W	PROPOSED WATER
S	PROPOSED SANITARY SEWER
UGE	PROPOSED UNDER GROUND ELECTRIC
UG D/FA/T	PROPOSED UNDER GROUND DATA/FIRE ALARM/TELEPHONE
UG D/FA	PROPOSED UNDER GROUND DATA/FIRE ALARM
UGT	PROPOSED UNDER GROUND TELECOMMUNICATIONS
G	PROPOSED GAS
	HANDBOX
	LIMIT OF NEW ASPHALT
	PLANTING BED EDGE

For additional information, visit qr.njatcdb.org Item #6556

Figure 3-18. *Information about the location and direction of utilities is shown on the site plan, to both aid in connecting the building and to ensure that utility lines are not cut when excavating.*

important to know where all buried cables and pipes are located so that trenching through them can be avoided. Before digging or trenching, the public utilities must be located and marked. Some areas of the country have a centralized agency that will locate all public utilities on the property. Keep in mind that only the cables and pipes owned by the public utilities will be marked.

Instead of a public water supply, some properties have private utilities, like a well and septic system, that can be more difficult to locate.

Electrical Information

The electrical information found on a site plan is typically anything electrical outside the structure or building. Some jobs, such as small houses, may not have any electrical information except for the location of the utility cables that will feed the house. Many commercial and industrial jobs will have one or more sheets dedicated to the electrical that exists outside the structure or building. **See Figure 3-19.**

The following are examples of electrical information found on site plans:

- Parking lot light and receptacle locations
- Circuitry used for exterior lighting and receptacles
- Sign location and circuitry
- Raceway locations (duct banks) to connect to utility power
- Raceway locations (duct banks) to connect communication circuits
- Utility transformer location
- Exterior well location and circuitry
- River pump location and circuitry
- Exterior security and cameras
- Underground sensors
- Landscape lighting

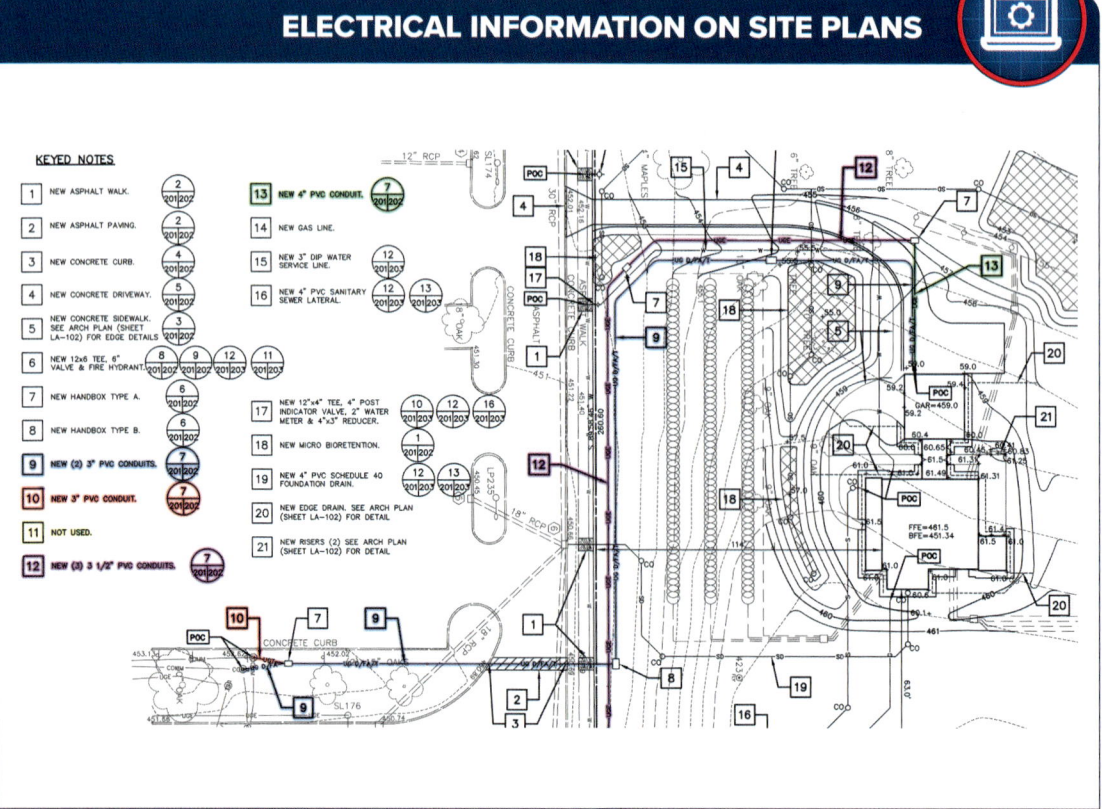

Figure 3-19. *Information about the electrical that extends beyond the building is commonly shown on the site plan.*

SYSTEM- OR TRADE-SPECIFIC PLANS

Figure 3-20. There are often multiple plans of the same area of a building, each showing information about a specific type of content that is installed by a specific construction trade.

For additional information, visit qr.njatcdb.org Item #6558

SYSTEM- OR TRADE-SPECIFIC PLANS

In many cases, there is enough information specific to a system or construction trade that the designers choose to have individual system information on a plan for each trade, or even each individual part of a system or trade. For instance, electrical plans are commonly split into power and lighting plans. System- or trade-specific plans are common for electrical, plumbing, heating, ventilation, and air conditioning, as well as other trades. **See Figure 3-20.**

> The complexity of the project determines how many trade-specific plans are in a set of construction drawings.

Electrical

Each of the disciplines will have drawings with the information pertaining to its aspect of the job. There may be several electrical drawings for the first floor alone, including a lighting plan, a power plan, or a systems plan. It is very important that a person completely understand the prints relating to their field and those of the other trades. If an electrician does not pay attention to the plumbing and mechanical plans, it is very likely that some of the electrical raceways and equipment will conflict with the plumbing and heating, ventilation, and air conditioning (HVAC) equipment and runs. By coordinating with other trades, not only will the job run more smoothly, but time and money will be saved.

Floor Plans Showing Electrical Information

Residential blueprints are not always drawn up by an architect or engineer. Sometimes, they are drawn by the contractor or by a draftsperson at a lumberyard. These prints are typically only a few pages long and will not be divided into disciplines in the way that commercial and industrial prints are.

The electrical contractor will usually be the one to draw in the symbols and lay out all the electrical on the drawing according to the *National Electrical Code (NEC)* and what the customer wants. Because the electrical contractor pencils in most of the symbols, there will typically not be a legend, the symbols will not be perfect, and the circuitry will usually not be laid out.

The set of drawings printed for an electrician on a residential job will typically have very few dimensions, and no information from the other disciplines. **See Figure 3-21.** Having a clean plan without most of the dimensions and other trade information makes it easier to draw in the electrical and make it legible. The downfall about not having information on the other trades is that the worker will not know where ductwork, plumbing, and the like will be. It is important for an electrician to get together with the other trades on the job to coordinate locations before the installation begins. This will save a lot of headaches, time, and money.

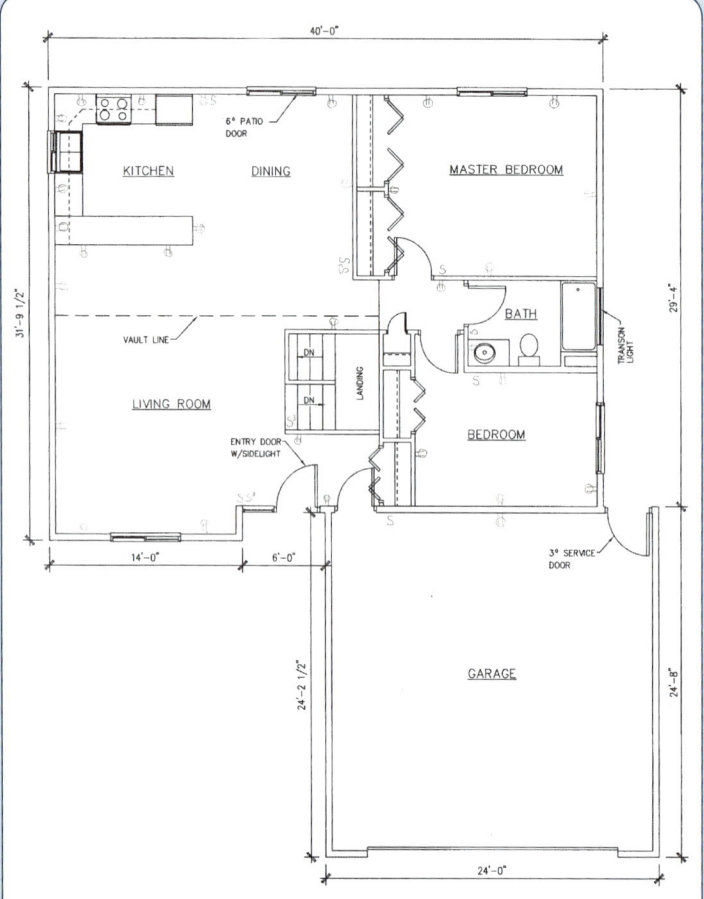

Figure 3-21. *Many times, information on residential buildings is not provided in as formal a manner as on larger construction projects. Consequently, Electrical Workers often utilize a copy of the floor plan to document the intent of their installation.*

Power Plan

The power plan is the drawing that will convey the information about where devices and equipment are to go. The power plan will also indicate how the circuitry is divided and how the raceways are to be run.

The electrical panels will be identified with a panelboard symbol and a series of letters, which are the panelboard identifiers. Panelboard identifiers are used in buildings with multiple panels to distinguish between panels. The panelboard identifier will typically indicate the voltage of the panel where there are multiple voltages on the premises. For example, a panel may have *LK* written next to it; the *L* in this case represents lower voltage (typically 120/208 volts), and the *K* indicates Panel K. **See Figure 3-22.** Another panel might have *HA* written next to it. The *H* in this case represents higher voltage (typically 277/480 volts), and the *A* indicates Panel A.

Panelboards will be typically separated by voltage and will be lettered starting

ELECTRICAL POWER PLAN

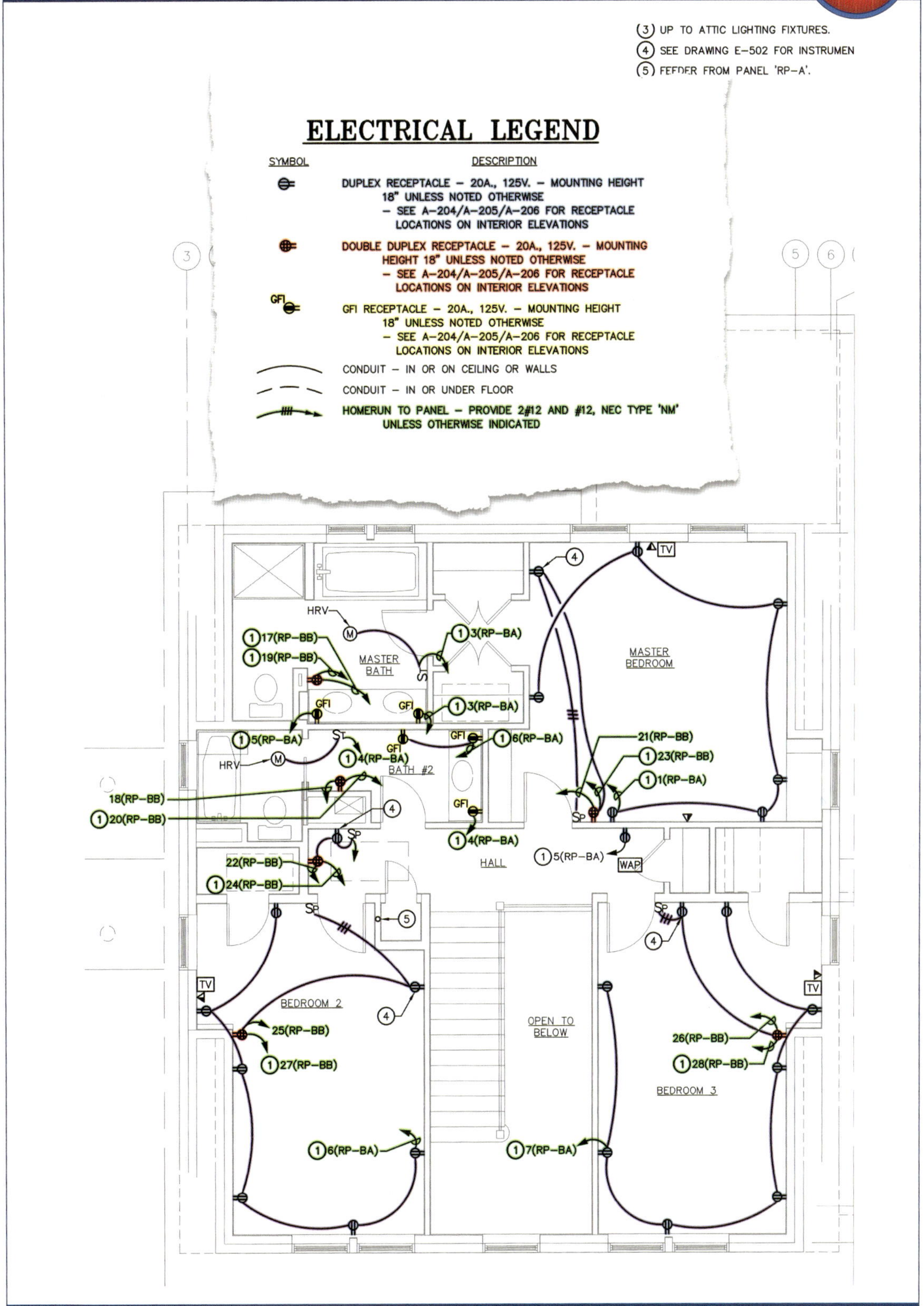
(3) UP TO ATTIC LIGHTING FIXTURES.
(4) SEE DRAWING E-502 FOR INSTRUMEN
(5) FEEDER FROM PANEL 'RP-A'.
ELECTRICAL LEGEND
SYMBOL
DESCRIPTION
DUPLEX RECEPTACLE – 20A., 125V. – MOUNTING HEIGHT 18" UNLESS NOTED OTHERWISE – SEE A-204/A-205/A-206 FOR RECEPTACLE LOCATIONS ON INTERIOR ELEVATIONS
DOUBLE DUPLEX RECEPTACLE – 20A., 125V. – MOUNTING HEIGHT 18" UNLESS NOTED OTHERWISE – SEE A-204/A-205/A-206 FOR RECEPTACLE LOCATIONS ON INTERIOR ELEVATIONS
GFI
GFI RECEPTACLE – 20A., 125V. – MOUNTING HEIGHT 18" UNLESS NOTED OTHERWISE – SEE A-204/A-205/A-206 FOR RECEPTACLE LOCATIONS ON INTERIOR ELEVATIONS
CONDUIT – IN OR ON CEILING OR WALLS
CONDUIT – IN OR UNDER FLOOR
HOMERUN TO PANEL – PROVIDE 2#12 AND #12, NEC TYPE 'NM' UNLESS OTHERWISE INDICATED
MASTER BATH
MASTER BEDROOM
BATH #2
HALL
BEDROOM 2
BEDROOM 3
OPEN TO BELOW
HRV
TV
WAP
17(RP-BB)
19(RP-BB)
3(RP-BA)
5(RP-BA)
4(RP-BA)
6(RP-BA)
21(RP-BB)
23(RP-BB)
1(RP-BA)
18(RP-BB)
20(RP-BB)
22(RP-BB)
24(RP-BB)
25(RP-BB)
27(RP-BB)
26(RP-BB)
28(RP-BB)
7(RP-BA)

Figure 3-22. *The electrical power plan provides information about the loads to be connected to the electrical system, as well as an indication of the panel that is intended to serve them.*

For additional information, visit qr.njatcdb.org Item #6559

ELECTRICAL CIRCUITING

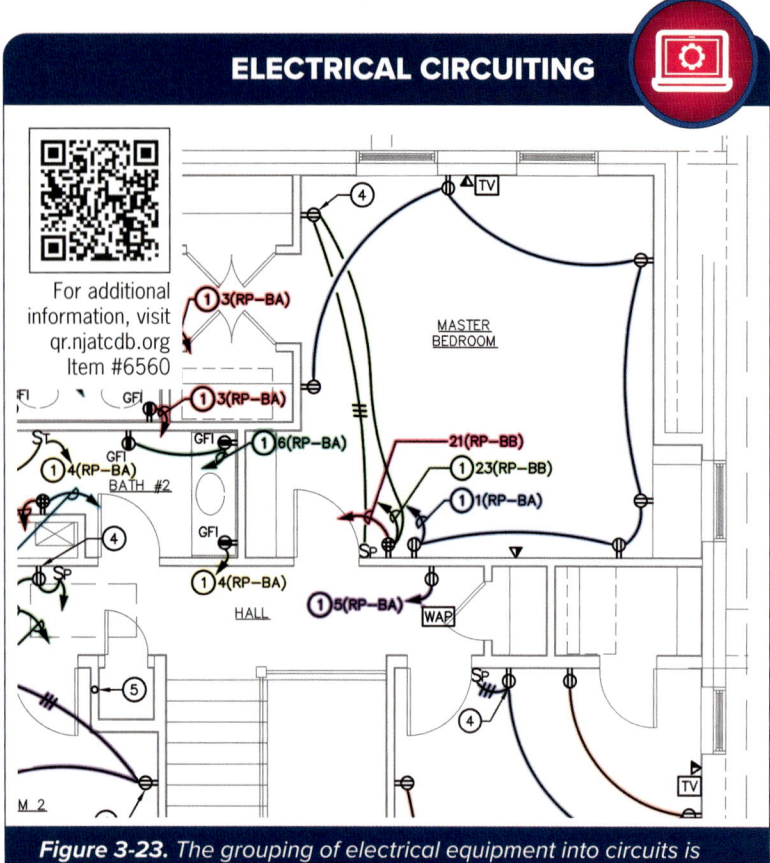

For additional information, visit qr.njatcdb.org Item #6560

Figure 3-23. *The grouping of electrical equipment into circuits is shown on the electrical power plan.*

with A. If there are four lower-voltage (120/208-volt) panels, they will be identified by the letters LA through LD. The *L* and *H* represent a comparison of the voltages available at the premises; the *L* represents the lower voltage available, and the *H* represents the higher voltage available. Larger buildings many times have additional distinguishing letters, numbers, and abbreviations to identify their panelboards by floor, area of the building, or purpose.

The power plan will show where the receptacles and equipment are to be located. The location of receptacles is typically approximate, meaning that the electrician can place the box on the nearest stud. Occasionally, a receptacle will have a very specific location, and dimensions or a note will give its exact details.

A home run symbol with a panel identifier will identify which panel the home run goes to and which circuit in that panel it connects to. To help distinguish them from a building's structure, curved lines are used to represent which equipment and devices are tied together by conduit

ELECTRICAL LIGHTING PLAN

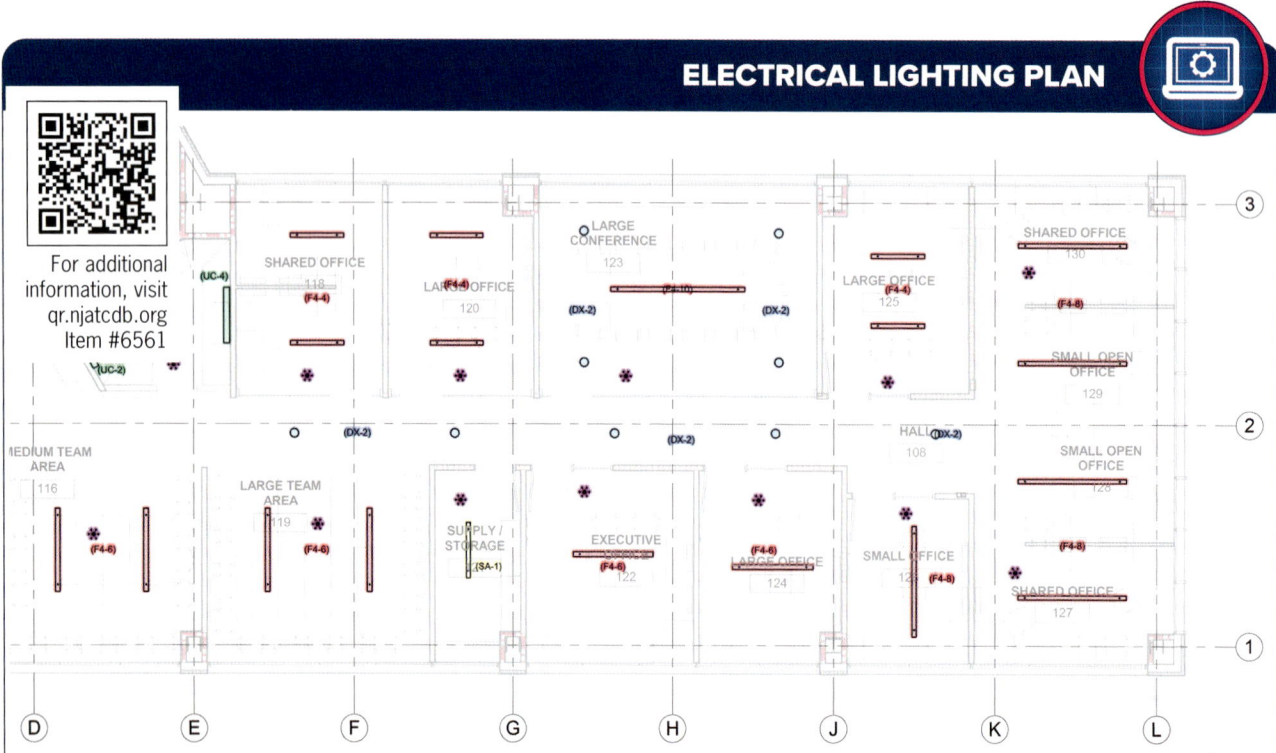

For additional information, visit qr.njatcdb.org Item #6561

Figure 3-24. *Information about the electrical luminaire types and locations, as well as how they are switched, is commonly shown on lighting plans.*

runs, by circuitry, or by both. The home run symbol and the curved lines connecting devices will sometimes have hash marks. The hash marks represent how many circuit conductors are installed in the raceway. Multiple arrows at the end of the home run depiction are also used to identify the number of circuits. **See Figure 3-23.**

Lighting

The lighting plan will have the information necessary to install the lights. The plan will have a lighting symbol with a capital letter, a number, or a combination of the two near it to identify which lighting fixture is to be installed. **See Figure 3-24.** The letter will correspond to a letter on the lighting schedule, which will give specific information about the light.

The lighting symbols drawn on the plan will sometimes have a lowercase letter written next to them. **See Figure 3-25.** This letter indicates which switch is controlling the lights. If there are two lowercase letters next to a lighting symbol, it would mean that part of the light is controlled by one switch and the other part by another switch. This is common with fluorescent lighting fixtures.

A curved line will often tie together lighting fixtures fed from the same switch or on the same circuit. A home run symbol with the panel identifier written next to it will indicate which panel the lights are fed from and which circuit the lights connect to.

The lighting plan will also indicate how the lighting is switched. It will indicate which lights are being controlled and where the switch is to be located. The switches will often have a lowercase letter by them to indicate which lights they switch. The height of the switches will typically be a standard indicated by a note or in the specifications. If the height of a switch varies from the standard height, it will be indicated on the plan near that switch.

The reflected ceiling plan is also used for the placement of lighting fixtures. The plan is the same as a floor plan,

FIXTURE SCHEDULE

LIGHT FIXTURE SCHEDULE

TYPE	MANUFACTURER	CATALOG NUMBER	LAMPS	MOUNTING	REMARKS
A	LITHONIA	WA440A277	4-40W	CEILING	WRAPAROUND ACRYLIC LENS
			FLUOR.	SURFACE	
B	KEYSTONE	2A440EXA277GPWS	4-40W	CEILING	2X4 GRID TROFFER
			FLUORESCENT	SURFACE	ACRYLIC LENS. AIR RETURN
C	KEYSTONE	2A440PWSGPW277S	4-40W	CEILING	2X4 GRID TROFFER
			FLUORESCENT	SURFACE	1/2"X1/2"X1/2" SILVER
					PARABOLIC LOUVER
					AIR RETURN
D	PHOENIX	DL-300D60-3	1-300W	WALL	DUAL ARM DOCK
			R40	7'-0" AFF	LIGHT, 62" LENGTH W/ VERT
					ADJUSTMENT, WIREGUARD, &
					BUILT-IN SWITCH
E	METALUX	DIM-296277	2-75W	PENDANT	INDUSTRIAL REFLECTOR
			FLUORESCENT	16'-0" AFF	8'-0" LENGTH
F	KEYSTONE	2SG440WFEXA277V	4-40W	RECESSED	2X4 GRID TROFFER
		GOLD LAMPS	GOLD FLUOR.		ACRYLIC LENS
			LAMPS		
G	LITHONIA	DD296277	2-75W	CEILING	MOLDED IMPACT-RESISTANT
			FLUORESCENT	SURFACE	WHITE PLASTIC HOUSING
					AND CLIPS. 8'-0" LENGTH
H	METALUX	DIM-296277	2-75W	CEILING	INDUSTRIAL REFLECTOR
			FLUORESCENT	SURFACE	8'-0" LENGTH
I	LITHONIA	DD296A277	2-75W	CEILING	MOLDED IMPACT-RESISTANT
			GOLD FLUOR.	SURFACE	WHITE PLASTIC HOUSING
			LAMPS		AND CLIPS. 8'-0" LENGTH
J	NOT USED				
	AS LIGHT FIXTURE				
K	HI-TEK	TWH200S277DMB	1-200W	WALL, AFG AS	WALL PACK

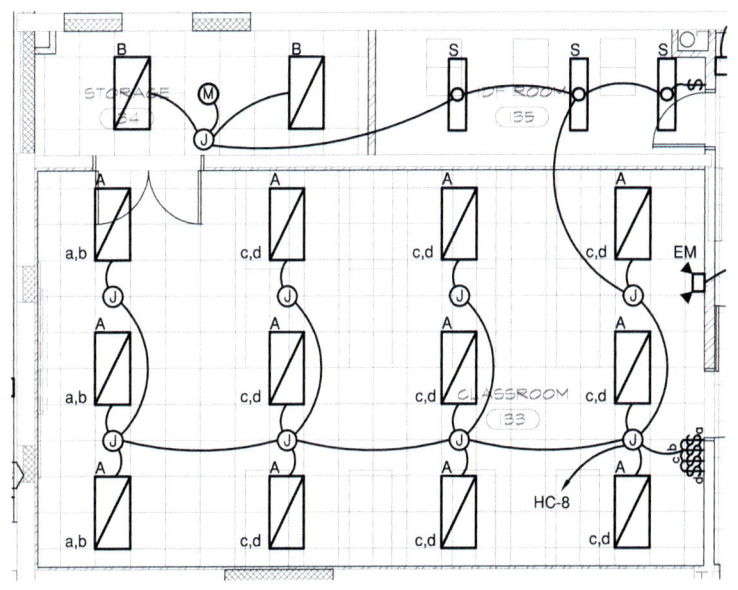

Figure 3-25. The fixture schedule gives more detailed information on each type of fixture than the electrical lighting plan.

REFLECTED CEILING PLAN

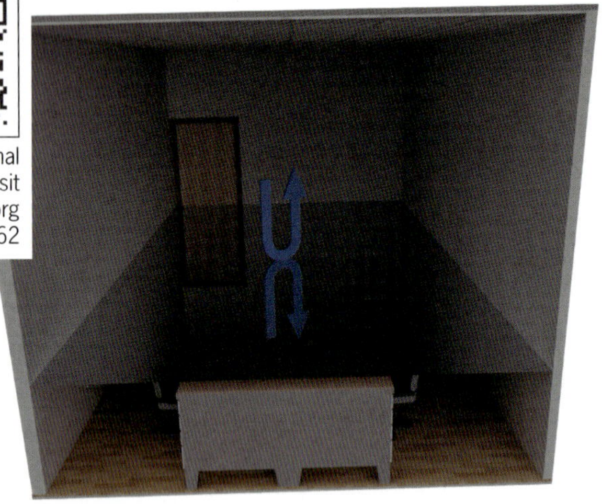

Figure 3-26. The reflected ceiling plan allows the viewer to view the face of the ceiling because the plane acts like a mirror.

PLUMBING PLAN

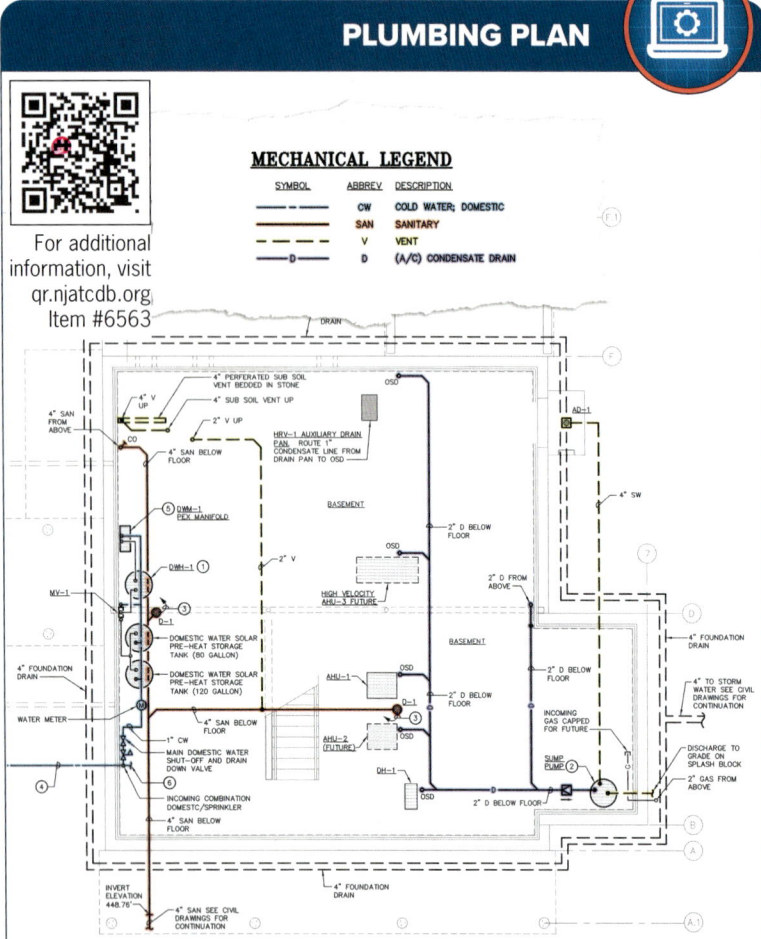

Figure 3-27. The plumbing plan shows plumbing equipment, like water and drain and gas lines, that are installed in the building.

but the "cut" or plane used to create the view can be thought of as a mirror which allows the viewer to see what is reflected upward, and thus view the ceiling. **See Figure 3-26.** The reflected ceiling plan is utilized by all trades who install components on, or in, the ceiling. Equipment shown on the reflected ceiling plan includes, lights, HVAC registers, sprinklers, and other equipment.

Plumbing

Much like electrical plans, the plumbing plans show the equipment and piping related to the plumbing system. Items typically included on a plumbing plan include sinks, toilets, water heaters, and other equipment relating to the supply of water to the structure. In addition to water supply, the plumbing plans typically include the drain, waste, and vent (DWV) system. **See Figure 3-27.** Many plumbing plans also show the gas supply to the various equipment using gas in a building.

HVAC

The HVAC plans show not only the HVAC equipment, but also the ducts and associated piping relating to the system. The location of things like ducts is very important to the construction of a structure because these are normally relatively large and meant to be hidden from exposure after the structure is complete. For this reason, there is a great deal of coordination between the installation of the HVAC system and all other systems and structure within a building. **See Figure 3-28.**

Demolition Plan

On a renovation or remodel, existing features of a building will often have to be removed. A demolition plan will indicate which items are to be demolished or moved. Each discipline may have a demolition plan indicating the demolition that pertains to that particular discipline.

Most renovations will have an electrical demolition plan, as the project will involve electrical that must be removed. The items to be removed or demolished typically have hash marks through them. **See Figure 3-29.** Be sure to

HVAC PLAN

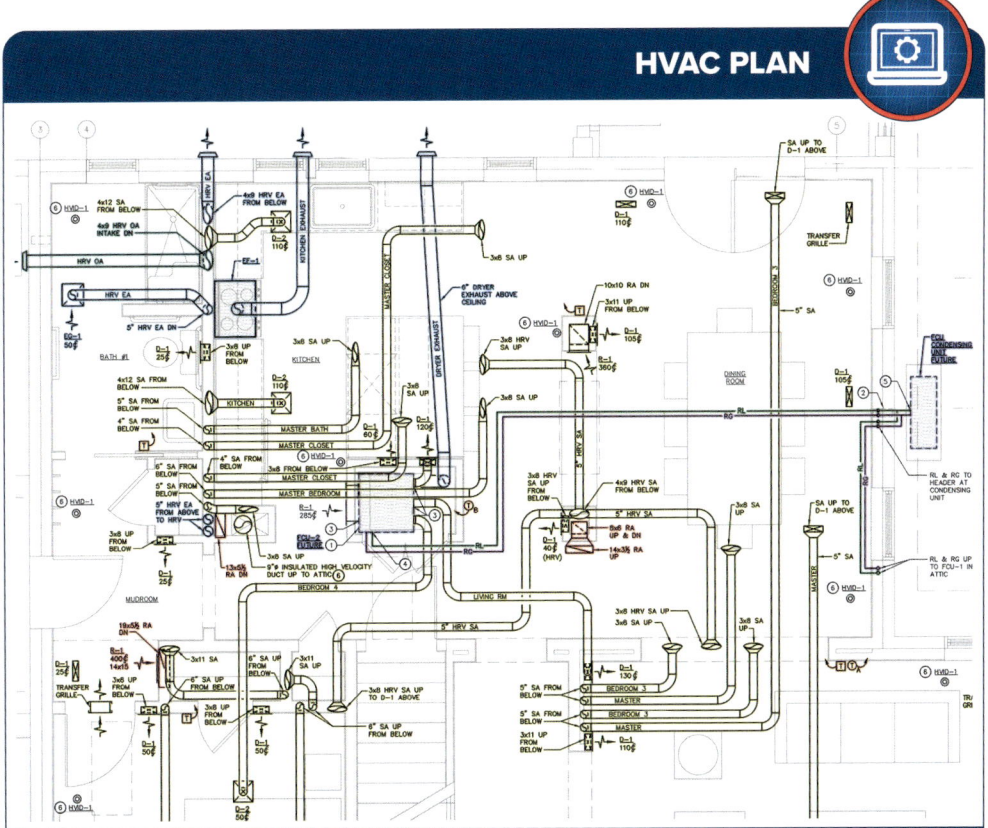

Figure 3-28. *The HVAC plan shows the location of the HVAC equipment and the ducts that connect them.*

For additional information, visit qr.njatcdb.org Item #6564

DEMOLITION PLAN

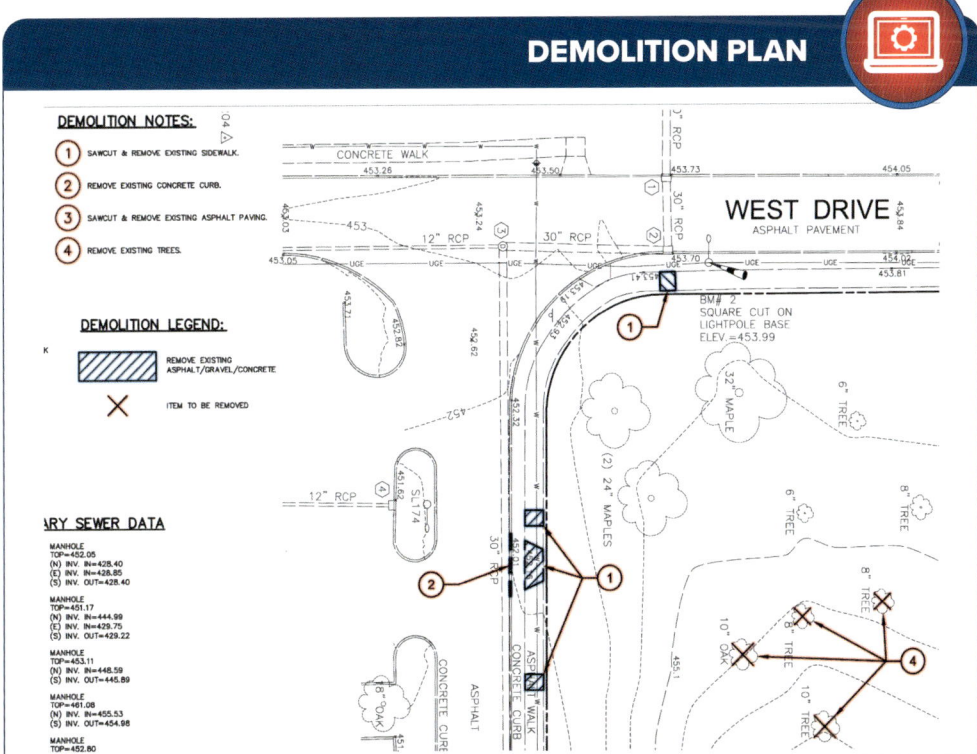

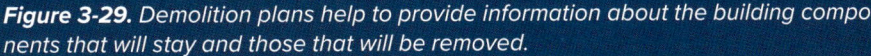

Figure 3-29. *Demolition plans help to provide information about the building components that will stay and those that will be removed.*

For additional information, visit qr.njatcdb.org Item #6565

check the legend on the prints to verify which symbols the designer used for demolition; removing something that was not meant to be removed can be a costly error.

Systems Plan

There may be several types of systems that will be on a systems plan. There may also be a separate plan for each system. Examples of items found on a systems plan are fire alarms, security, speakers, microphones, televisions, computers, and telephones.

The systems plan will also show where a raceway will be required for pulling in cables. An example would be raceways that need to be installed in the concrete for a data jack in the floor. Another example would be boxes installed in the wall with a pipe that extends out above the ceiling. Often a note will indicate that a ¾-inch pipe must be run up from each communication box and terminated (often referred to as stubbed out) above the ceiling tile or in another accessible location. That pipe will then be used to pull the computer or telephone cable down to the box in the wall.

Cable trays are often used to support the various communications cable used on a project. The path of the cable tray throughout a project will be indicated on the systems plan. **See Figure 3-30.** The symbols used to represent the various systems are not consistent from one designer to another. It is very important to check the legend to know what each of the symbols represents.

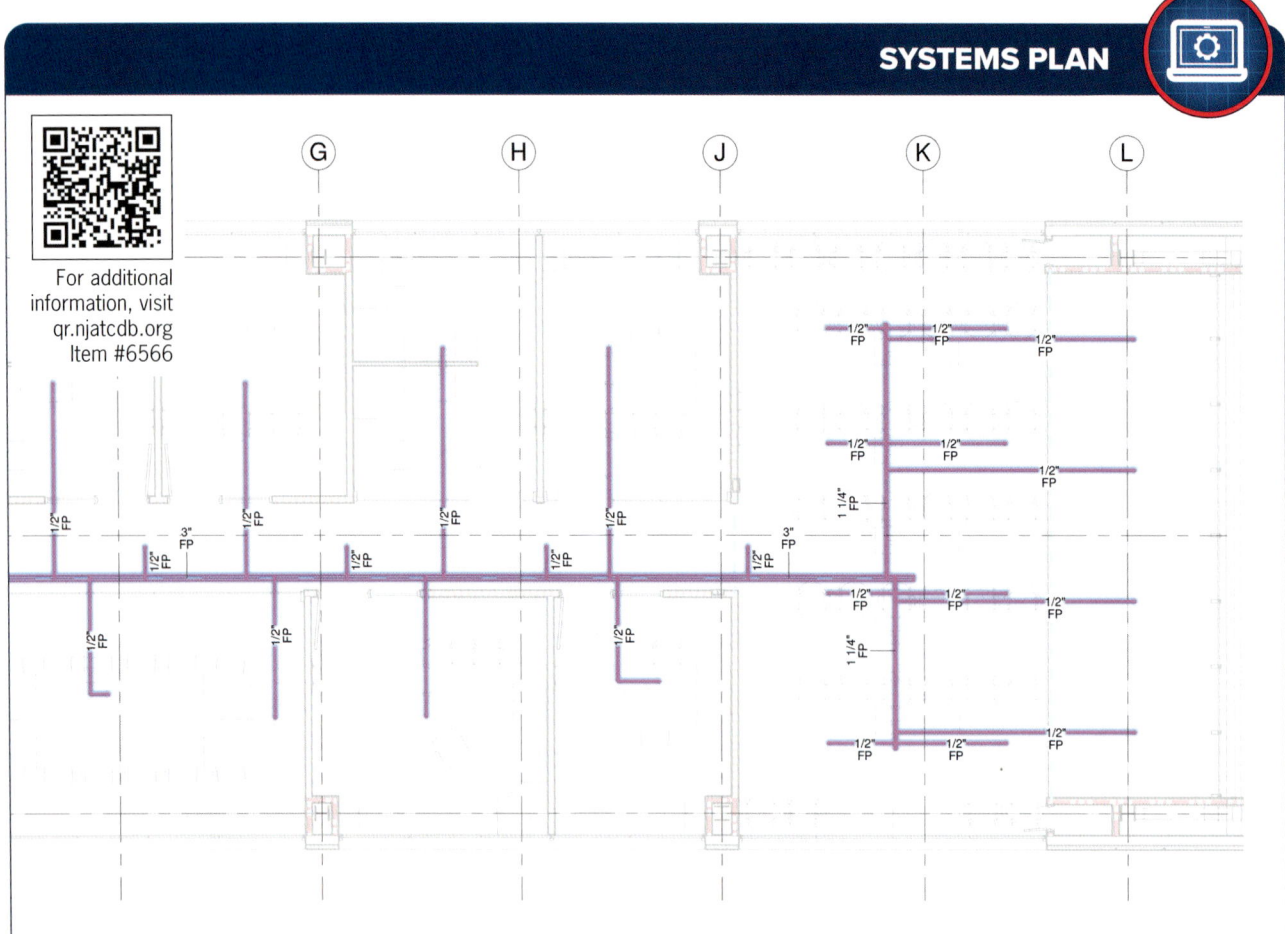

SYSTEMS PLAN

For additional information, visit qr.njatcdb.org Item #6566

Figure 3-30. *Because the fire alarm, security, audio visual, and other systems have information that may clutter an electrical plan, they are often combined onto a systems plan showing these and other building system components.*

SUMMARY

Plan views are the most referenced drawings in a construction set since they are used in such a wide variety of applications. From the beginning of a project to the end, plan views have information needed to construct the building. These details were thought up by the owner and architect at the point when the project began to come into reality. Every phase of construction and every trade discipline references the plan views for a variety of information including the building's layout, size, scale, and component locations, in addition to how the building sits upon a piece of land.

For additional information, visit qr.njatcdb.org Item #6567

REVIEW QUESTIONS

1. __?__ are the most common type of plan views.

    a. Floor plans
    b. Landscaping plans
    c. Reflected ceiling plans
    d. Site plans

2. Plan views are views created by removing the __?__ of the building.

    a. back
    b. bottom
    c. front
    d. top

3. If an electrical device requires a specific location, it may have __?__ dimensions.

    a. horizontal
    b. vertical
    c. both a. and b.
    d. none of these

4. __?__ are used to identify the meaning of symbols.

    a. Keys
    b. Legends
    c. Tables
    d. Tools

5. Most often, electrical devices like receptacles and switches have exact __?__ dimensions on a plan view.

    a. horizontal
    b. vertical
    c. both a. and b.
    d. neither a. nor b.

6. Contour lines representing natural grade are represented as __?__ lines.

    a. dashed
    b. dotted
    c. solid
    d. zig-zag

7. Footings, which are underground or under the concrete, will be shown with a(n) __?__ line on a foundation plan.

    a. center
    b. hidden
    c. object
    d. solid

8. Although different architects may use different heights, the cutting plane is typically at a height of about __?__ and runs through the doors and windows.

    a. 2'
    b. 3'
    c. 4'
    d. 5'

CHAPTER 4
ELEVATIONS

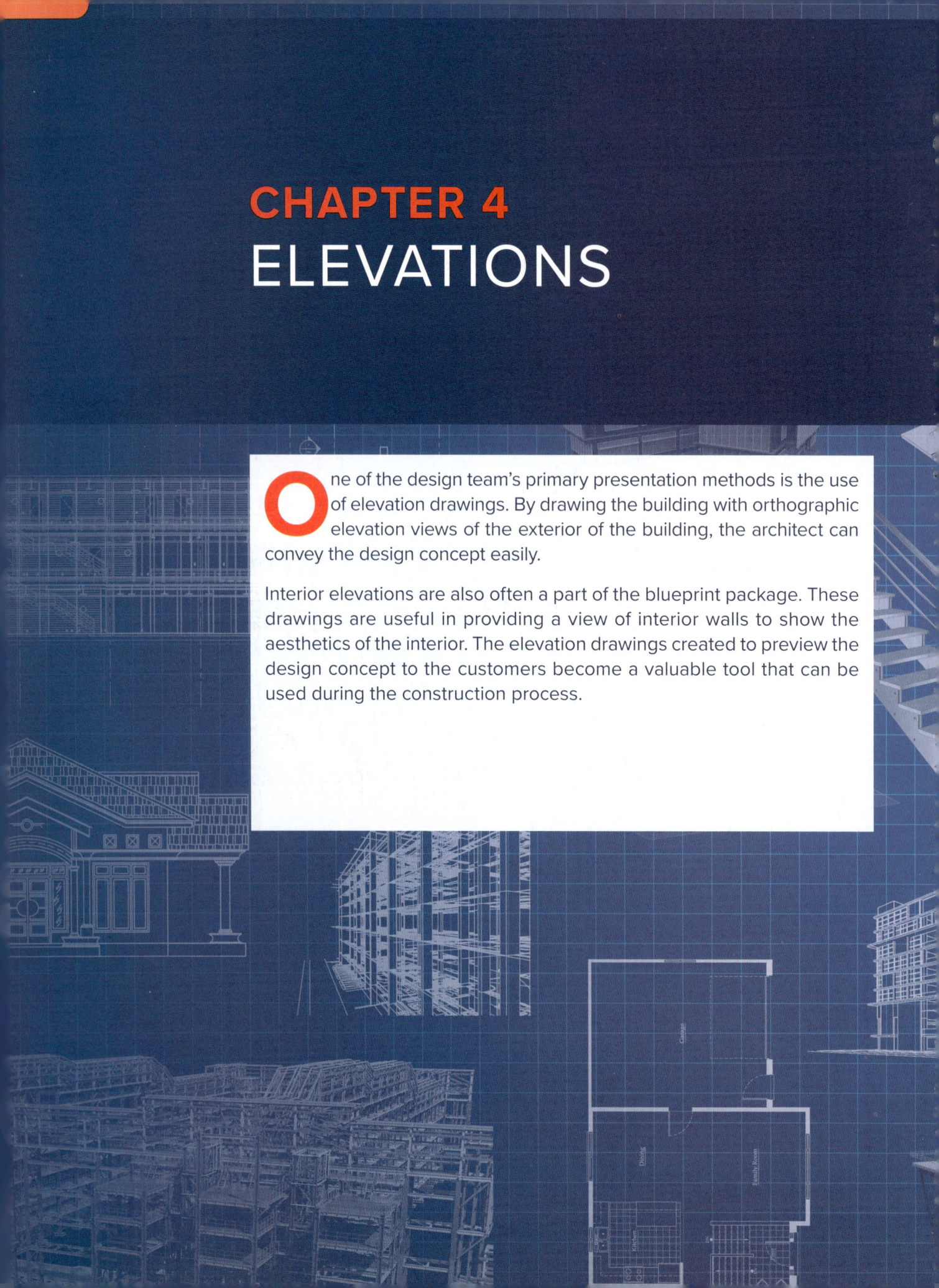

One of the design team's primary presentation methods is the use of elevation drawings. By drawing the building with orthographic elevation views of the exterior of the building, the architect can convey the design concept easily.

Interior elevations are also often a part of the blueprint package. These drawings are useful in providing a view of interior walls to show the aesthetics of the interior. The elevation drawings created to preview the design concept to the customers become a valuable tool that can be used during the construction process.

OBJECTIVES

- Recognize how elevation views are created and list the information they provide.
- Identify the types of elevation drawings.
- Recognize scales used on elevation drawings.
- Differentiate between elevation views and other drawing types.

TABLE OF CONTENTS

INTRODUCTION TO ELEVATIONS

An elevation is a view that looks at an object that is drawn on a vertical plane as opposed to a horizontal plane. In contrast to plan views that look down from above, elevation views represent a face-on view on what a person would see if standing on the floor looking directly at a wall (at a 90° angle). **See Figure 4-1.** Elevations show the exact vertical location of objects on walls and similar structures.

Description

The type of information contained on an elevation view is different than that of a plan view. The types of information shown can include finishes, doors, windows, and fixtures, as well as many other types of equipment.

Finished Appearance

Elevation views are able to give additional information about elements of the building that are not able to be discerned from plan views, including information about what the final item will look like and each object's vertical and horizontal proximity to other objects. **See Figure 4-2.**

Orthographic

Orthographic drawings are a series of two-dimensional (2D) drawings that represent a three-dimensional (3D) object. When 3D drawings are not available, orthographic drawings can provide much of the same information. An elevation drawing is one view in an orthographic drawing, generally a front view, a back view, or a side view. **See Figure 4-3.**

ELEVATION VIEWS

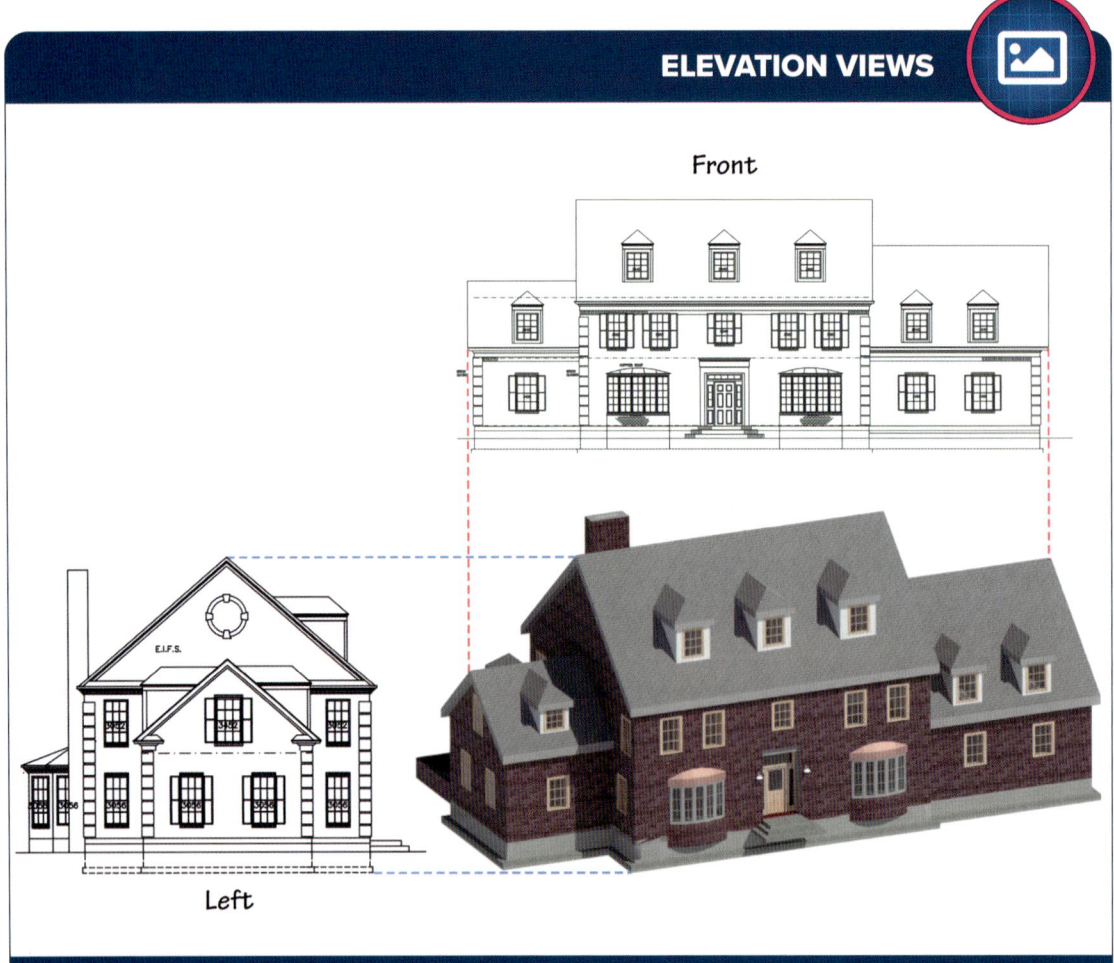

Figure 4-1. Elevation views are created to provide vertical details where plan views provide horizontal details about a structure.

FINISHED APPEARANCE

Figure 4-2. *Elevation views often provide more information to allow for a more complete understanding of the final look of a structure.*

ELEVATION VIEWS ARE ORTHOGRAPHIC VIEWS

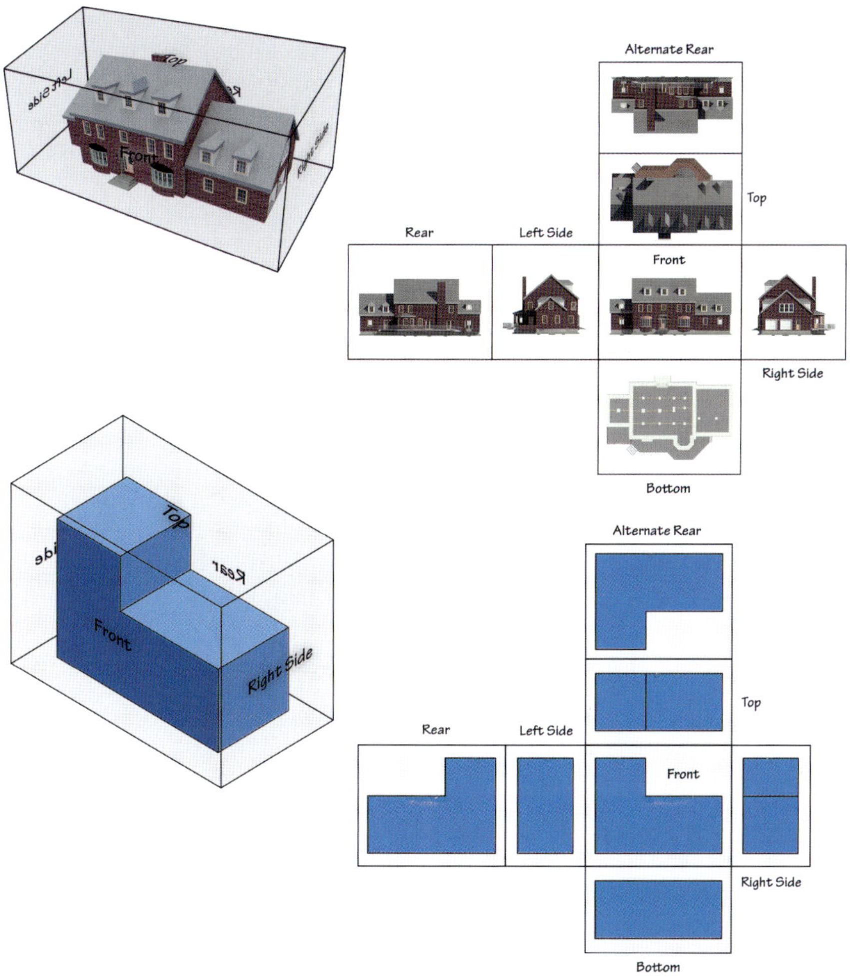

For additional information, visit qr.njatcdb.org Item #6695

Figure 4-3. *Elevation views show one side of an object as is the case with orthographic views.*

Information Conveyed

Although elevations can be drawn for any upright surface in a building, elevations are generally only used for items in the building that have unique construction factors requiring additional clarity.

Dimensions

Where multiple features are designed to be installed close to each other, elevation views are essential to ensure workers install them precisely as planned. Distances between components that are near to each other are much easier to see on an elevation view.

Applications of dimensions used on elevations views include:

- Grade line
- Finished floor height
- Ceiling heights
- Wall variations (offsets and corners)
- Windows
- Doors
- Roof features
- Porch
- Deck
- Patio

Most of the dimensions on elevations are for vertical dimensions since horizontal dimensions are usually shown on plan views. **See Figure 4-4.**

Scale

Like most other drawing types, elevation views are drawn to scale. Scales used on elevation views vary depending on the size of the objects being displayed. For example, an exterior side of a building will be at a much smaller scale than that of a kitchen wall with cabinets. Many times, elevations are drawn at a much larger scale (for instance 1 ½" = 1') to allow for a greater degree of detail on the drawing. As a result of the larger scale, the individual components on the drawing appear much larger and thus easier to view.

However, depending on component size, elevations may be drawn at a different scale than the plan views. For this reason, the scale used for the elevation is shown directly below the elevation view, as opposed to being shown on the title bar of the page, to alleviate any confusion about the scale of each individual elevation view. It is important that the scale of the elevation is determined prior to attempting to scale the drawing for additional dimensions. **See Figure 4-5.**

Use of Symbology

Elevation views typically have far fewer symbols than other view types because they are drawn to show the final view of the components and provide the most precise details of their construction and finishes.

For additional information, visit qr.njatcdb.org
Item #6696

ELEVATION DIMENSIONS

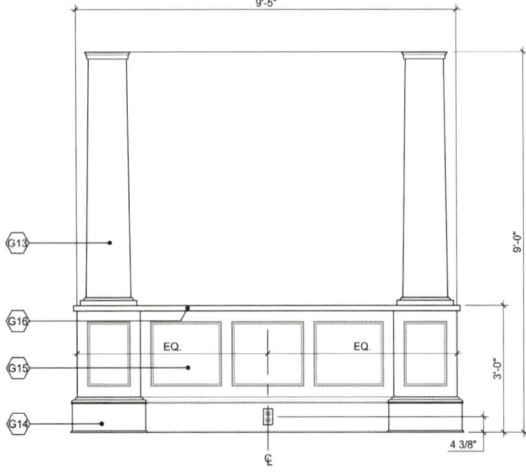

HALF WALL ELEVATION
SCALE: 1/2" = 1'-0"

Figure 4-4. *Dimensions on an elevation provide vertical elevations since these cannot be discerned from plan views. They also include horizontal elevations to provide more precise information about feature placement.*

Finishes

Designers often show the final finishes of components on elevation views, while they rarely do this on other views. These final views provide viewers with a better understanding of the components' intended design.

Abbreviations

Elevations contain abbreviations for materials, finishes, and other items to add clarity and manage the space needed due to the large amount of information shown on the view.

Notations

Notations are used for a variety of purposes on elevation drawing. Types of notations may include general sheet notes, penetration notes, sheet key notes, window key notes, and component notes. Notations may apply to several components on a sheet, to the entire sheet, or the entire set of plans.

ELEVATION SCALE

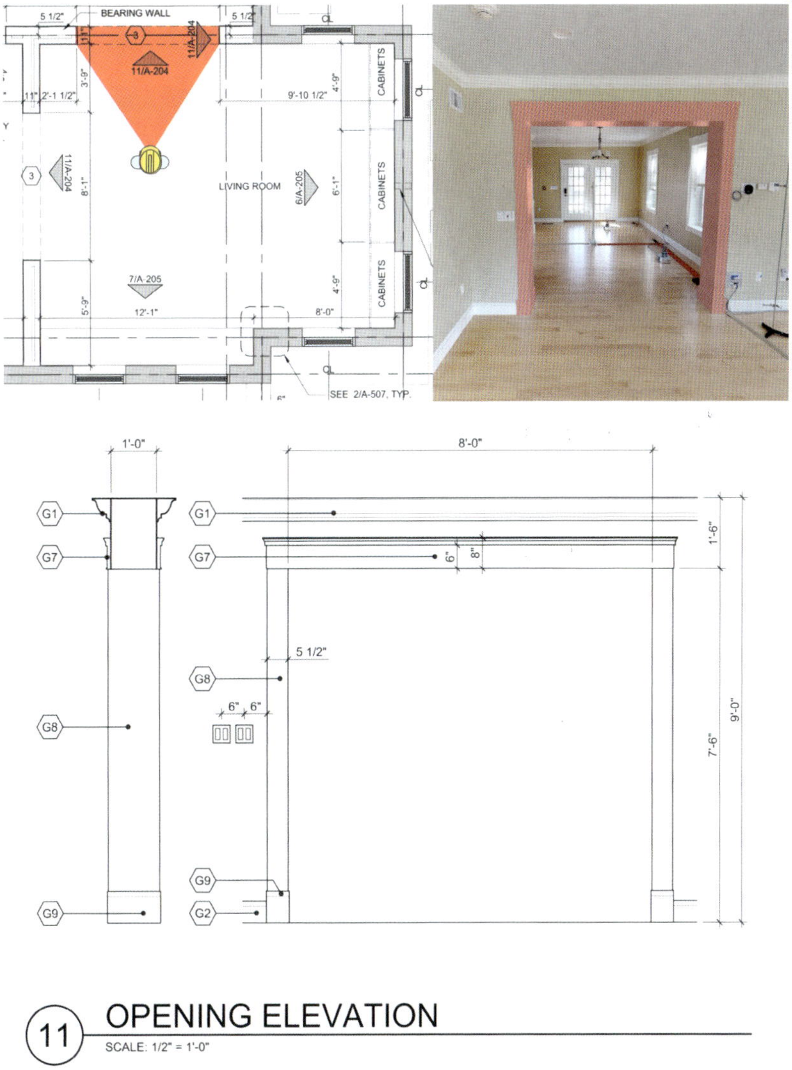

For additional information, visit qr.njatcdb.org Item #6697

OPENING ELEVATION
11 SCALE: 1/2" = 1'-0"

Figure 4-5. *Scales on an elevation are very often different than the scale on a plan view so special attention should be made to view the scale that is used by the elevation.*

ABBREVIATIONS AND NOTATIONS ON ELEVATIONS

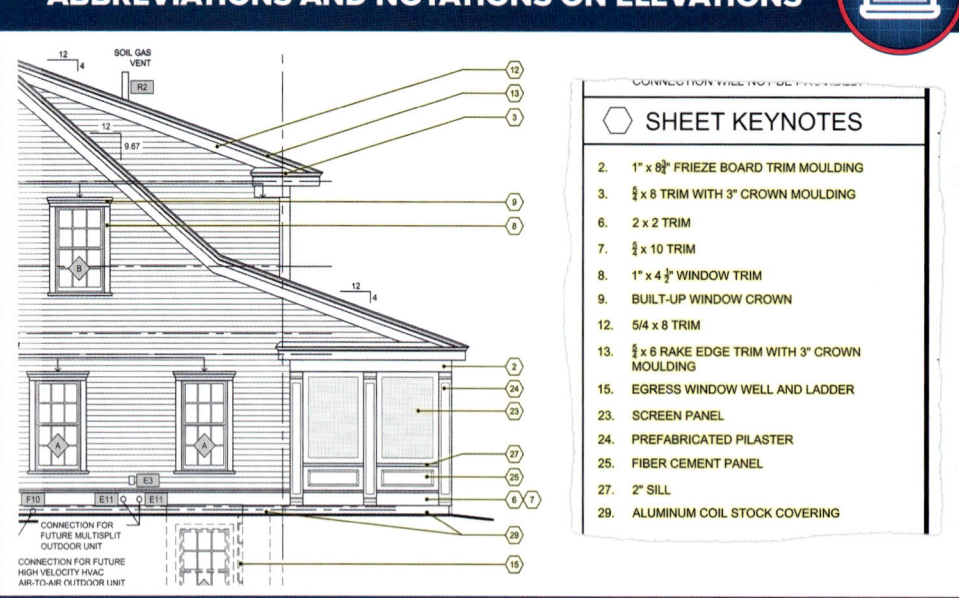

SHEET KEYNOTES

2.	1" x 8¼" FRIEZE BOARD TRIM MOULDING
3.	¾ x 8 TRIM WITH 3" CROWN MOULDING
6.	2 x 2 TRIM
7.	¾ x 10 TRIM
8.	1" x 4½" WINDOW TRIM
9.	BUILT-UP WINDOW CROWN
12.	5/4 x 8 TRIM
13.	¾ x 6 RAKE EDGE TRIM WITH 3" CROWN MOULDING
15.	EGRESS WINDOW WELL AND LADDER
23.	SCREEN PANEL
24.	PREFABRICATED PILASTER
25.	FIBER CEMENT PANEL
27.	2" SILL
29.	ALUMINUM COIL STOCK COVERING

Figure 4-6. *Notations on an elevation help to keep the drawing clear and concise.*

For additional information, visit qr.njatcdb.org Item #6698

For additional information, visit qr.njatcdb.org Item #6699

INTERIOR WALL ELEVATIONS

⑥ LIVING ROOM ELEVATION
SCALE: 1/2" = 1'-0"

Figure 4-7. *Interior wall elevations provide detail about walls that have a high density of features on the wall.*

Much like abbreviations, notations are used to provide clarity and manage space on drawings. **See Figure 4-6.**

TYPES OF ELEVATIONS

There are many types of elevations that are commonly grouped by the component or feature that is detailed in the drawing. Examples of this are interior elevations, exterior elevations, and trade-specific elevations and details.

Interior Elevations

Interior elevations are generally included whenever an interior feature is too complex to provide adequate detail on a plan view. They are typically drawn to a larger scale and provide important information about the construction of an interior feature. The drawing gives a pictorial view of the feature's design and how it looks when finished. Typical interior elevations include kitchen elevations, bathroom elevations, stairs, and elevations of other areas of the building.

Wall

A common interior elevation is a wall elevation, which may also include cabinetry on the drawing. Interior elevations with cabinetry typically include the height and width of each cabinet section. It will show the location of appliances, sinks, electrical switches, receptacles, and luminaires, and other features in the room. **See Figure 4-7.**

Electrical Information on Interior Elevations

The kitchen cabinet drawings are an example of interior elevation that is often referred to by electricians. **See Figure 4-8.** The following are a few examples of the types of detailed information that an Electrical Worker will use from a set of cabinet elevations:

- Height to the bottom of the upper cabinets. This is used when under-cabinet lights will be mounted below the upper cabinets. The electrician will need to know at what height the cable will need to be sticking out of the wall.

- Height to the top of the upper cabinets. This is used when outlets will be mounted above the upper cabinets for plugging in lights and the like.

- Location of the cabinet above the microwave. The outlet the microwave plugs into will be mounted in the cabinet above the microwave.

- Location of the oven or cooktop. The kitchen elevations will indicate at what height a cable should be left out to tie into the appliances.

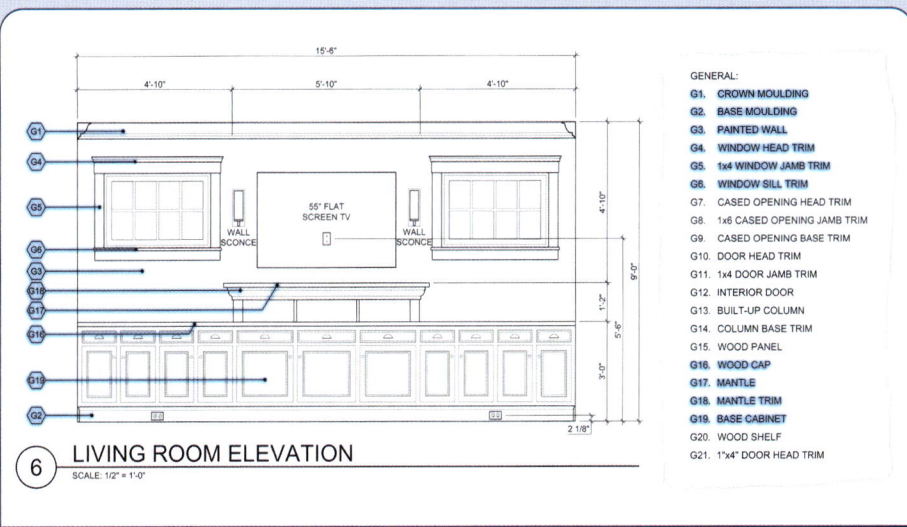

For additional information, visit qr.njatcdb.org Item #6700

Figure 4-8. *Cabinet elevations provide information about each of the individual cabinets and their mounting heights and relationships to each other.*

Exterior Elevations

Exterior elevations are used to give a view of what a building looks like from the exterior and are commonly shown for each side of the building. As is true for any elevation view, these sides of the building are shown from a directly straight ahead view, much like an orthographic projection.

Faces (North, South, East, West)

In some cases, elevation views of buildings are based on a directional orientation. In these cases, there are typically at least four main exterior elevations in a set of construction drawings: north, south, east, and west. The name used for a view title comes from the direction a side of the house faces. For

DIRECTIONAL EXTERIOR ELEVATIONS

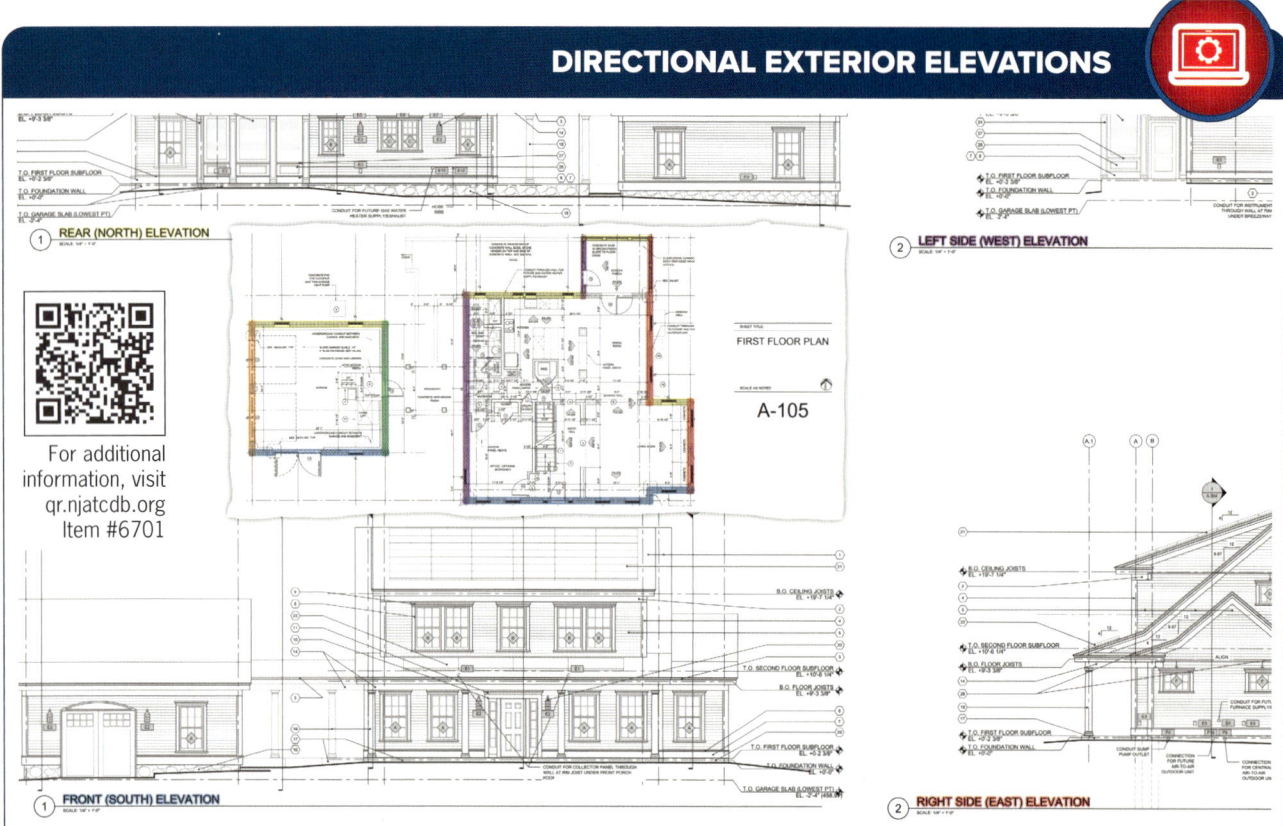

For additional
information, visit
qr.njatcdb.org
Item #6701

Figure 4-9. Exterior elevations are often referred to by the direction that the side of the house which is shown faces.

RELATIVE EXTERIOR ELEVATIONS

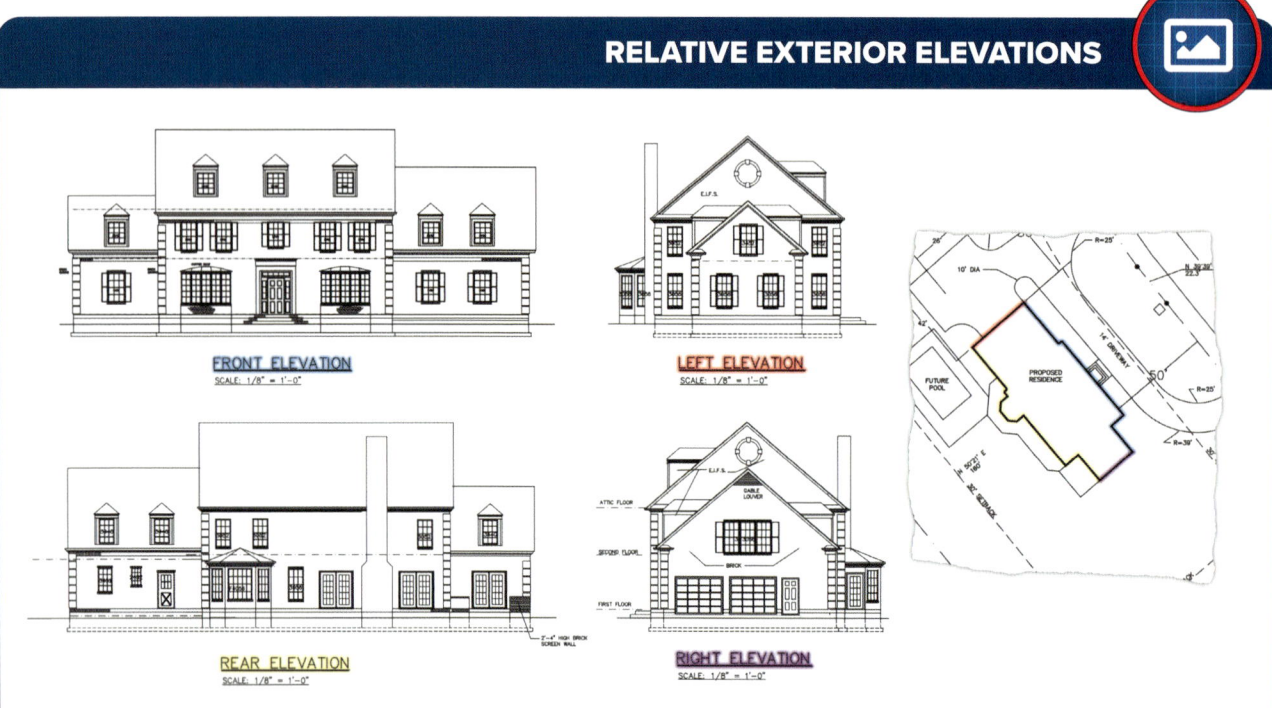

Figure 4-10. Because buildings very often do not sit true to magnetic directions, many times the elevations are referred to by the relative position on the building, such as front, back, left, and right.

example, the side of the house that faces south would be the south elevation. Most often north is shown toward the top of the page and south to the bottom of the page. **See Figure 4-9.**

The named dimension for an elevation may not be 100% accurate from a compass' point of view. Many times, these elevations are approximations of the direction so that a "general" discussion about the building can be held allowing everyone to understand which side of the building is being discussed. In some cases, plans are drawn without knowing where the building will be located, making it impossible to give the view a direction. In this case, they will be labeled as "front," "right side" (or "right"), "left side" (or "left"), and "rear" elevations based on the main entrance of the building. **See Figure 4-10.** The view of the building that faces the main entrance is the front elevation, the side of the building to the right while facing the main entrance is the right elevation, and so on.

The front view is typically drawn to the same scale as the floor plan. The other three views are sometimes drawn to a smaller scale than the floor plan and all placed on the same sheet. The scale will typically be printed below the drawing.

Exterior Wall Finish

Exterior elevations will indicate the wall finish to be used on the building. Notes often indicate the specific types of wall finish to be used and give other information that cannot be easily communicated by just looking at a drawing. This does not mean that the entire building will be drawn showing the finished wall material. Often only parts of the building will show the wall finish; either the wall finishes will fade off or there will be a break line where they end. When this is the case, there will be an outline of the building and openings only. **See Figure 4-11.** Not showing all details of the exterior finish minimizes clutter on the drawing.

Additional Information on Exterior Elevations

Vertical dimensions are sometimes given on exterior elevations. The dimensions will typically include the following information:

- The distance from grade to each of the finished floors in the building (first floor, second floor, third floor, etc.).
- The distance from grade to the top of windows and/or doors.

EXTERIOR FINISH ELEVATIONS

Figure 4-11. Exterior elevations often show more detail about the finish than many other drawings to allow for a greater ability to imagine the final look of the structure.

EXTERIOR ELEVATION INFORMATION

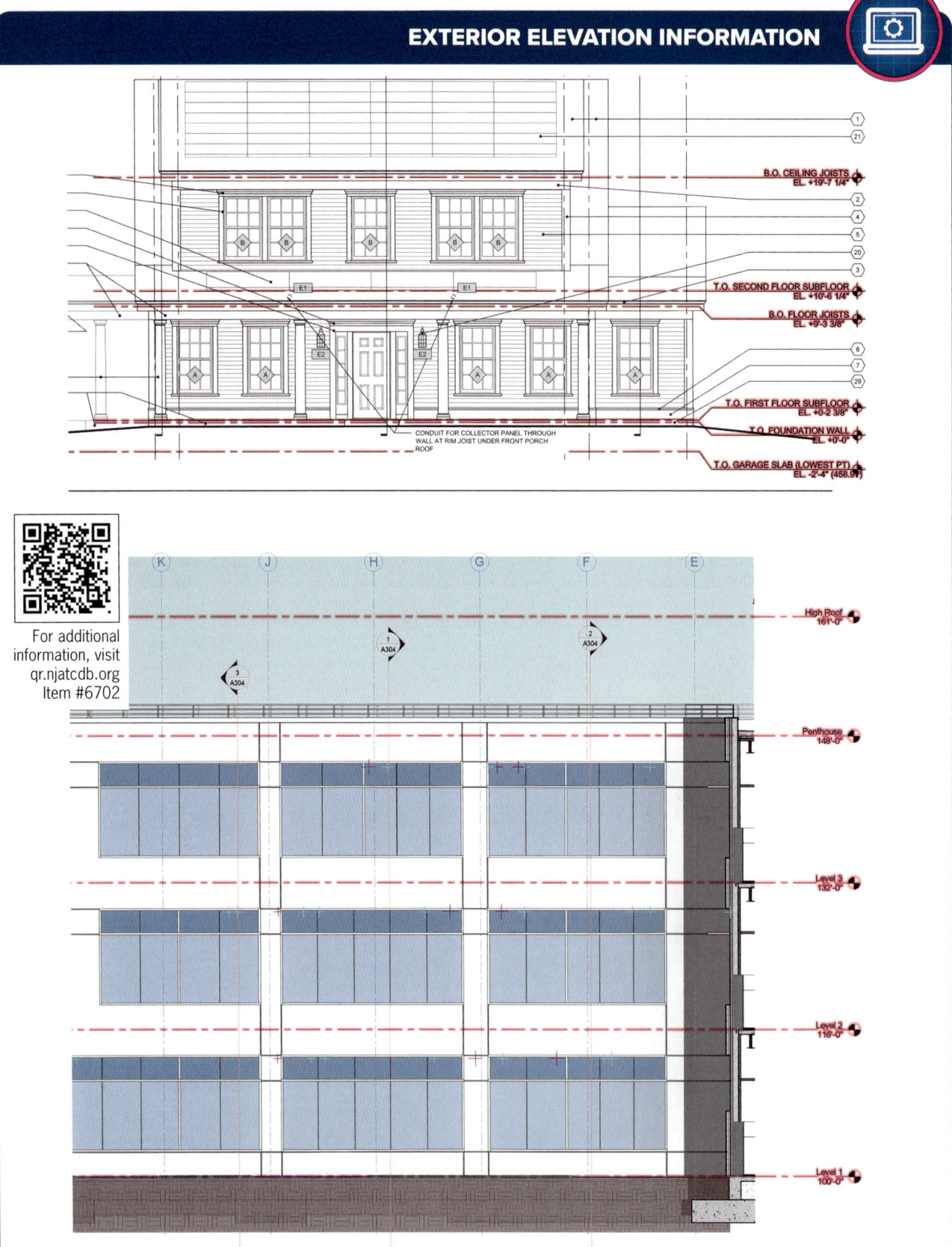

For additional information, visit qr.njatcdb.org Item #6702

Figure 4-12. *There are a variety of details provided on the exterior elevation to accurately describe the design intent.*

- The distance from grade to footings, as well as the thickness of the footings.
- The foundation walls and the footings of the building will be shown with a hidden line since they are "hidden" by the grade.
- The depths of the foundation and any elevation changes will also many times be indicated. **See Figure 4-12**.

First Floor Elevation

On most construction drawings the height of the finished first floor is represented by a designation of 100' 0". This is done so that anything lower than the first floor will not have a negative number for an elevation, as would be the case for the basement or footings of a building that had the first floor elevation represented by 0' 0". **See Figure 4-13**.

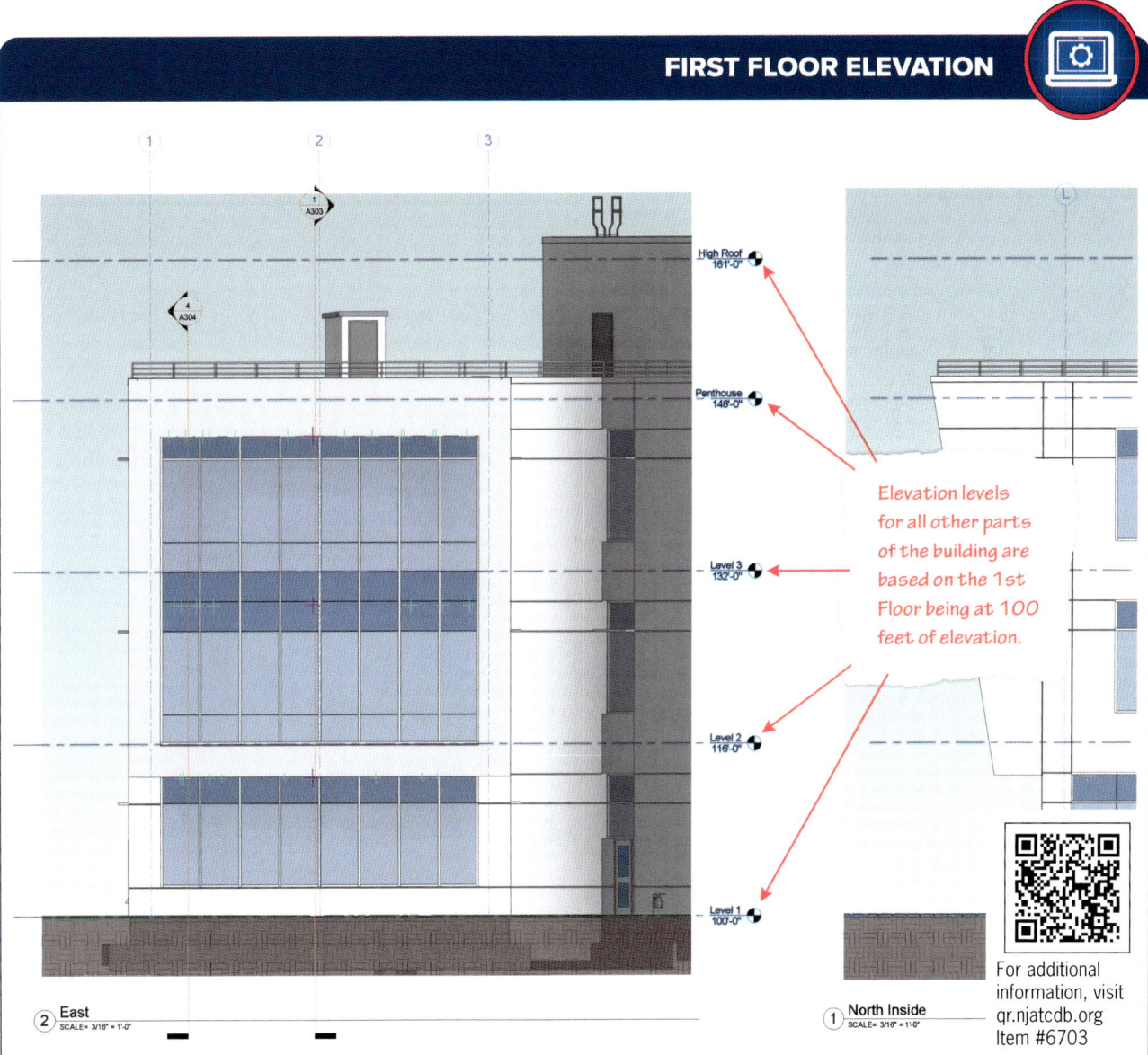

FIRST FLOOR ELEVATION

High Roof
161'-0"

Penthouse
148'-0"

Elevation levels for all other parts of the building are based on the 1st Floor being at 100 feet of elevation.

Level 3
132'-0"

Level 2
116'-0"

Level 1
100'-0"

For additional information, visit qr.njatcdb.org Item #6703

2 East
SCALE= 3/16" = 1'-0"

1 North Inside
SCALE= 3/16" = 1'-0"

Figure 4-13. Often the elevation of the first floor of a building is set at 100' 0" so that all dimensions can be made in reference to this vertical plane.

The roof pitch is often found on elevation drawings, shown as a right triangle drawn above the roof line. **See Figure 4-14.** Two numbers are typically shown beside the triangle: the number beside the vertical line of the triangle is the rise, and the number beside the horizontal line of the triangle is the run. These two measurements indicate the pitch, or the rise over the run, of the roof. If a roof has a rise of 4 and a run of 12, this means that the roof rises 4 inches for every 12 inches traveled horizontally. This is commonly referred to as a 4/12 pitch.

The layout and style of the roof are easily understood by looking at the elevations. Is the roof a gable, hip, or shed roof? Are there any dormers? All this information is clearly identified on the elevations. The type of material used on the roof will be identified by either a symbol or a note.

RELATIONSHIP TO OTHER DRAWING TYPES

Elevations do not stand alone; they are an extension of the other drawings within the set and are always referenced as a part of the larger whole as opposed to all-inclusive drawings. Elevations show many of the same spaces as the plan view, but they show a vertical view as opposed to a horizontal view. **See Figure 4-15.**

For additional information, visit qr.njatcdb.org Item #6704

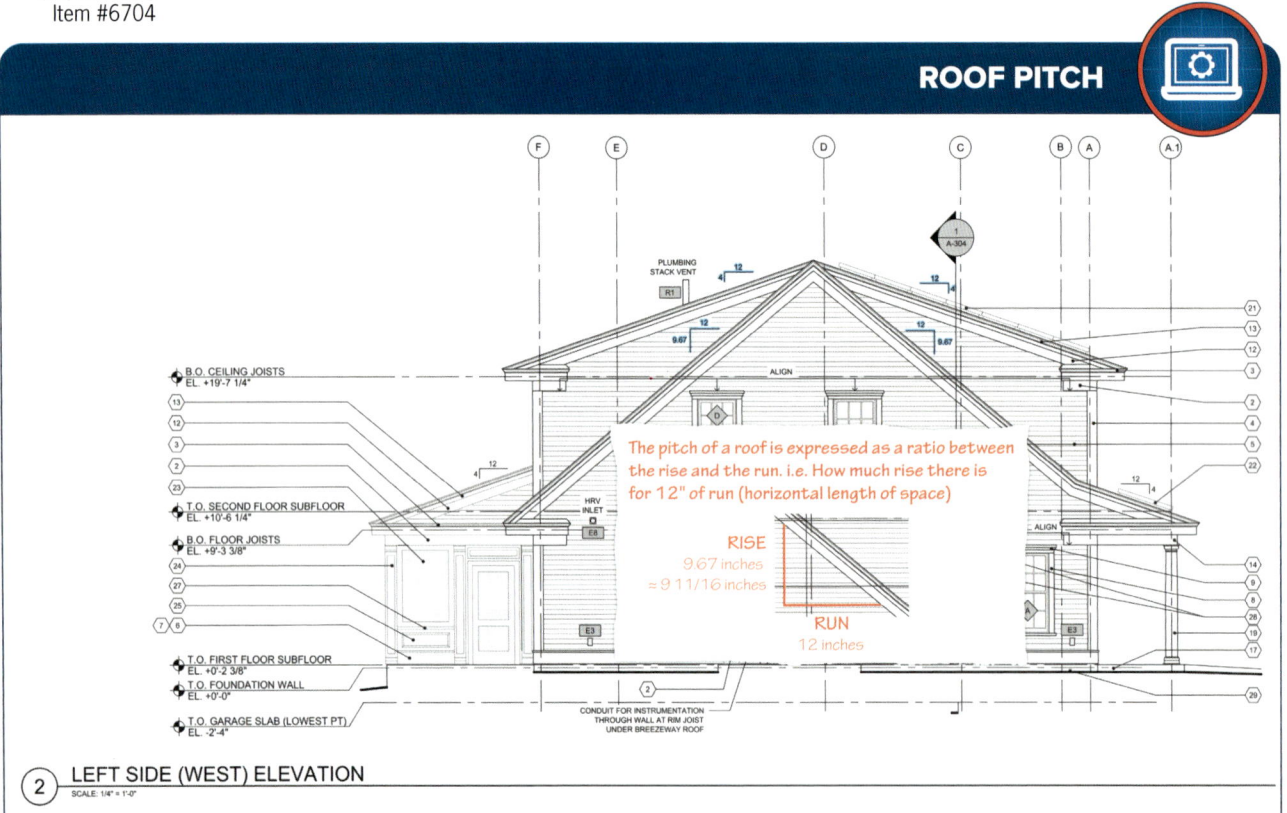

Figure 4-14. *The pitch of a roof is expressed as a ratio between the rise and the run. i.e. How much rise there is in 12 inches of run (horizontal length of space).*

ELEVATION RELATIONSHIP TO OTHER DRAWINGS

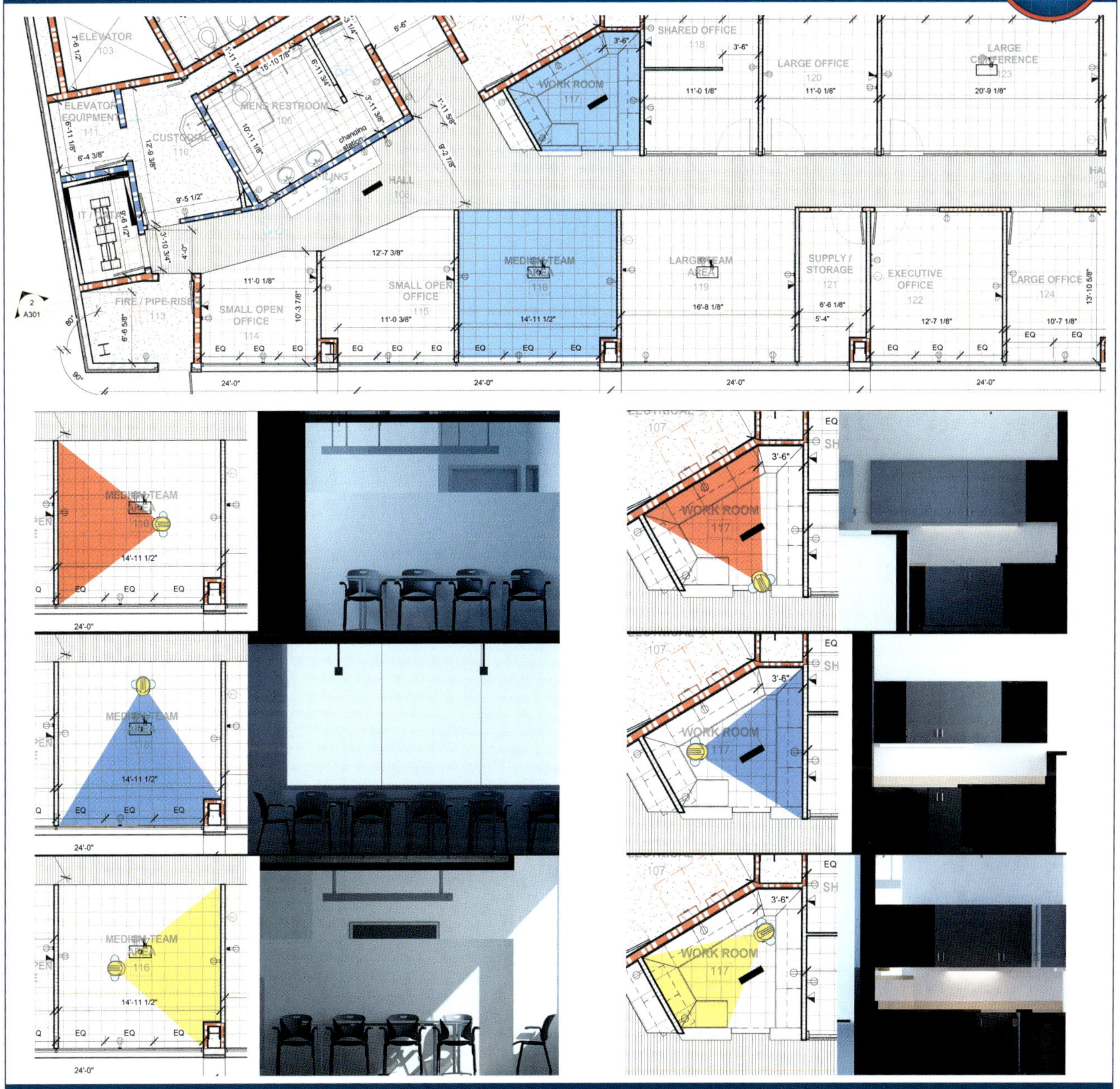

Figure 4-15. It is often necessary to view the elevation in reference to other drawing in the set of construction drawings to get a full understanding of the final structure.

The elevations also contain information about windows and doors that is not easily discerned from other drawings, such as plans. The types and sizes of windows used is usually identified by a dimension or a notation; for example, a

For additional information, visit qr.njatcdb.org Item #6705

letter corresponding to the window schedule. **See Figure 4-16.** If the window swings open, it will have an arrow with the point facing the hinge side of the window.

WINDOW AND DOOR INFORMATION ON ELEVATIONS

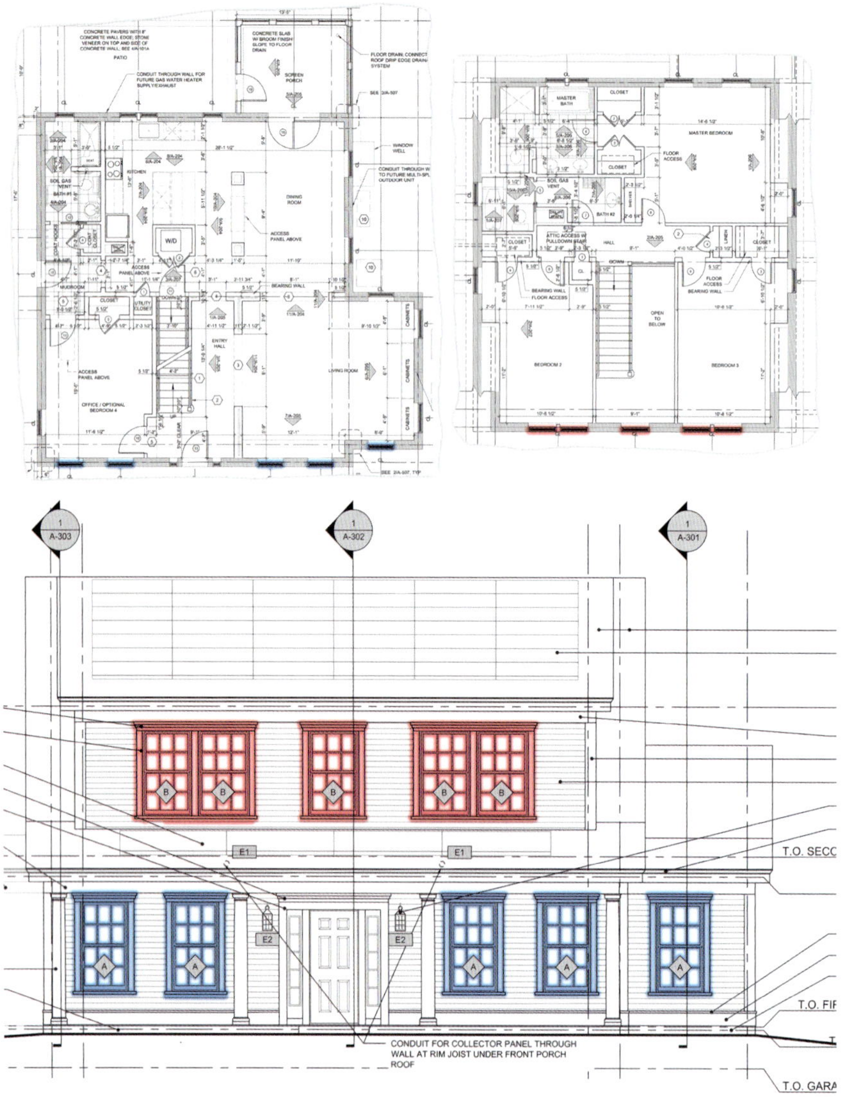

WINDOW SCHEDULE *							
TYPE	FRAME SIZE	TYPE	MATERIAL	GLAZING	MEETS EGRESS REQ.	QTY	NOTES
A	3'-0" x 5'-5"	DOUBLE HUNG	FIBERGLASS	SUPER-INSUL CLR LOW E	YES	13	1, 4, 5, 7, 8
B	3'-2 1/2" x 5'-2"	DOUBLE HUNG	FIBERGLASS	SUPER-INSUL CLR LOW E	YES	7	1, 3, 6, 7, 8
C	2'-1" x 3'-7"	DOUBLE HUNG	FIBERGLASS	SUPER-INSUL CLR LOW E	NO	2	1, 8
D	2'-8" x 2'-3"	AWNING	FIBERGLASS	SUPER-INSUL CLR LOW E	NO	2	1, 8
E	2'-3" x 4'-0"	DOUBLE HUNG	FIBERGLASS	SUPER-INSUL CLR LOW E	NO	4	1, 2, 8
F	3'-4" x 2'-3"	AWNING	FIBERGLASS	SUPER-INSUL CLR LOW E	NO	2	1, 8
G	3'-4" x 2'-7"	AWNING	FIBERGLASS	SUPER-INSUL CLR LOW E	NO	2	1, 8

Figure 4-16. Because there is so much detail associated with windows and doors it is necessary to reference them from drawings that supplement the elevation view.

SUMMARY

E levation drawings are an important part of the construction from the inception of a building design and throughout the construction process. They provide information that often cannot be found on other drawings. Examining elevation drawings reveals that they are used for many purposes and provide additional levels of clarity to everyone involved.

For additional information, visit qr.njatcdb.org Item #6642

REVIEW QUESTIONS

1. Distances between components that are near to each other (especially vertically) are much easier to see on a(n) __?__ view.

    a. detail
    b. elevation
    c. plan
    d. section

2. Elevation views typically have far fewer __?__ than other view types because they are drawn to show the final view of the components and provide the most precise details of their construction and finishes.

    a. abbreviations
    b. detail drawings
    c. notes
    d. symbols

3. An elevation drawing includes all views normally in an orthographic drawing; these are generally a front view, back view, and side view.

    a. True   b. False

4. The scale used for the elevation is shown __?__ to alleviate any confusion about the scale of each individual elevation view.

    a. as a sheet note
    b. at the top of the sheet
    c. directly below the elevation view
    d. on the title bar

5. Elevation drawings are used only for the exterior of buildings.

    a. True   b. False

6. Roof pitch is often found on elevation drawings, shown as a __?__.

    a. fraction drawn above the roof line
    b. general note on the sheet
    c. right triangle drawn above the roof line
    d. right triangle drawn below the roof line

7. A common designation for the first floor elevation in a building is __?__.

    a. 0'
    b. 25'
    c. 50'
    d. 100'

CHAPTER 5
DETAILS AND SECTIONS

Details and sections are drawings that provide the finest level of granularity in a set of construction drawings. Without them, the final building might not meet the original design intent. While other views are needed, they do not provide the small details that make the building safe or create the intended concept. Imagine an architect trying to show the attachment requirements for a wall where it connects to a floor using a $\frac{1}{8}$" or $\frac{1}{4}$" scale. The final drawing would not allow for enough clarity for the construction crew to see precisely how to make the attachment. Architects solve this problem by using a detail drawing with a larger scale that provides an accurate picture of the attachment method.

A section drawing is another view drawn to a larger scale but with a different purpose than the detail drawing. A section drawing provides a view of a portion of the building that is produced as though the building has been cut into two pieces. The cut that is made allows the viewer to see in one direction at the location of the cut. Plan views are very similar to section views; the primary difference is that plan views allow a horizontal plane to be visualized as opposed to a section view, which allows a vertical plane to be displayed at the point of the cut.

The importance of sections and details cannot be understated, as plan and elevation views are not able to show the same information. Detail and section views provide an added level of clarity that results in the final product matching the designer's and owner's intent as they conceptualized the final product.

OBJECTIVES

- Identify the different types of detail views, how they are used, and how they relate to other drawing types.
- Identify the different types of section views, how they are used, and how they relate to other drawing types.
- Identify the similarities and differences between detail and section views.

TABLE OF CONTENTS

INTRODUCTION TO DETAILS AND SECTIONS

Plan views and elevations do not contain all of the necessary information to construct a building. Additional information, such as architectural requirements, the structural intent of a wall (if it is load bearing), fire rating, wall cavity insulation requirements, and many other details are also necessary.

Elevation views show the outside appearance of the building or the appearance of interior walls, while plan views provide an overhead view of the layout of the interior. Section views and details provide additional information, such as information needed to construct walls as they are intended to be built when designed. Details and sections are included in a set of construction drawings when a building feature requires clarity and in-depth detail. **See Figure 5-1.**

There are two primary ways to depict a building: a vertical view or a horizontal view. The most common vertical view is an elevation and the most common horizontal view is a plan view. Sections and details are additional types of horizontal and vertical views of the building features. Each drawing type has a specific purpose and use case. **See Figure 5-2.**

DETAILS

The use of the word *detail* in a drawing title indicates its purpose: to provide more information about a portion of the building. In contrast to other drawings in a set of construction drawings, detail drawings concentrate on a very small part of the building. Since the area is so small, it can be drawn to a larger scale and provide specific information about the feature being depicted. Details are commonly drawn to show more information about a portion of a section view or a plan view. **See Figure 5-3.**

For additional information, visit qr.njatcdb.org Item #6497

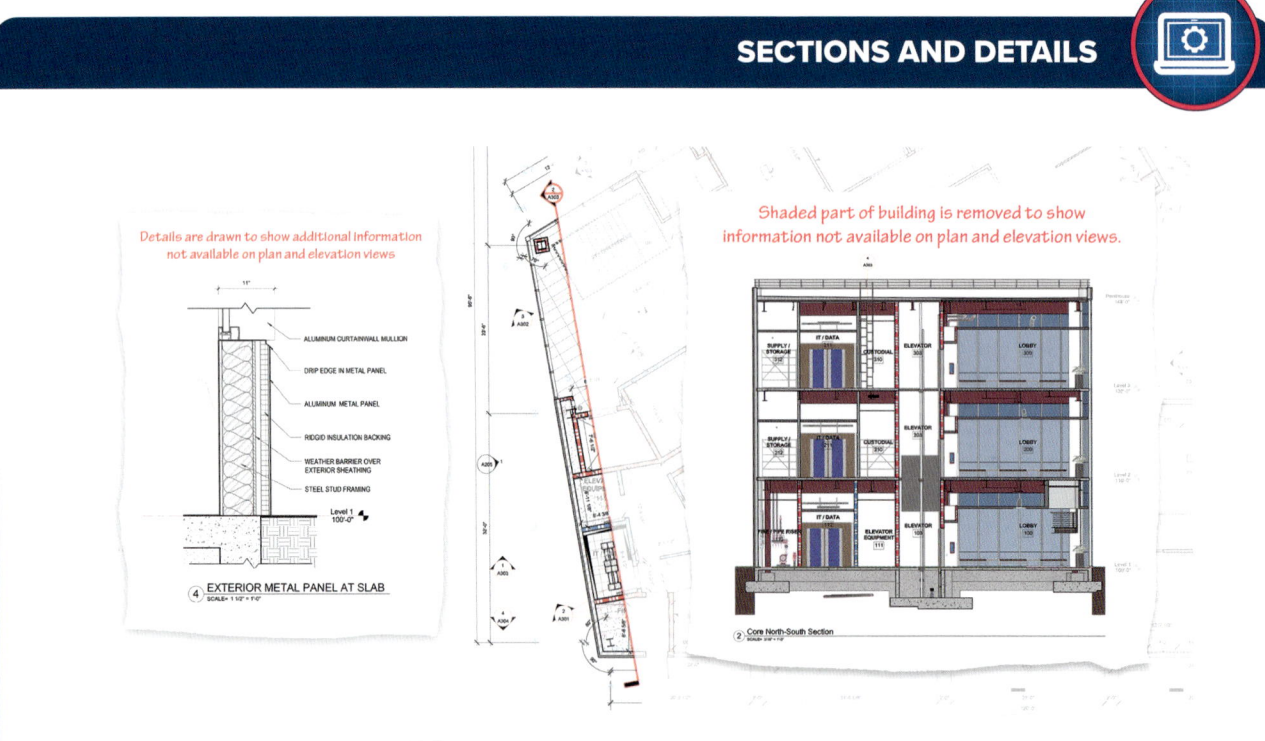

Figure 5-1. *Sections and details show additional information not visible on plan and elevation views.*

COMPARISON OF VARIOUS DRAWINGS

Drawing Type	Scope	Orientation	Use/Purpose	Examples	Typical Scale
Plan	Entire building	Horizontal	View from above to show building shape and space layout	Floor plan Site plan	Small
Elevation	Entire field of view	Vertical	Exterior/interior vertical view	Exterior elevation Interior elevation	Small or large
Detail	Smaller area or feature	Horizontal, vertical, or isometric	Clarity on small area or feature	Area detail Feature detail Wall detail Door detail	Large
Section	Could be small area or entire building	Horizontal or vertical	Building cut by a plane to allow visibility across the plane	Wall section Roof section Foundation section	Small or large

Figure 5-2. Each type of drawing has specific parameters that make it best for certain situations.

DETAIL VIEWS

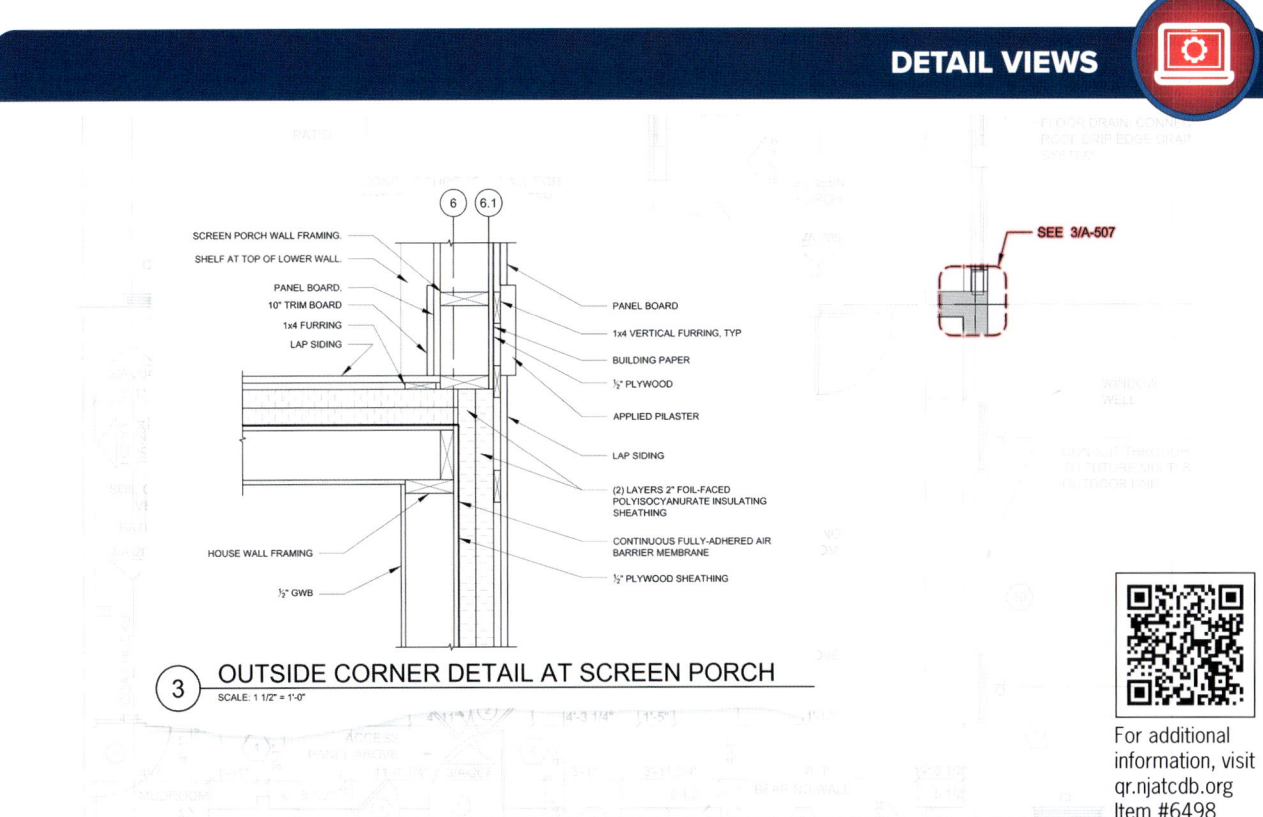

OUTSIDE CORNER DETAIL AT SCREEN PORCH

3   SCALE: 1 1/2" = 1'-0"

For additional information, visit qr.njatcdb.org Item #6498

Figure 5-3. Detail views provide additional information that would not be feasible to show on either a plan or elevation view.

Detail drawings are used for every type of drawing within the set of construction prints. They are commonly used to add greater clarity to civil engineering plans, site plans, structural plans, trade-specific plans, elevations, or almost any other type of drawing. Blueprint drawings must clearly provide all the design criteria, down to the smallest detail, in a manner that will allow the builder to construct a structure as designed.

Because there is no standard for naming detail drawing types, designers use their discretion when naming them. Although drawing names may be interchanged, the drawing title is not the focal point. The information being presented and its clarity are of utmost importance. For example, a vertical detail of an interior feature may be called an elevation, a section, a detail, or a combination of the terms.

Automobile Assembly

An automobile manufacturer cannot build an engine for a new car using only drawings of the exterior of the car (elevation) and a diagram of the engine compartment with the hood open (floor plan). Numerous parts (features) are interconnected to provide the designed operation. It can only happen where engineers provide details that will make construction of the various engine components possible.

The system used by architects to create a building design is no different. The elevations and floor plans alone, while especially important, cannot ensure the finished building meets the vision of the design professionals. Many parts of the building have features that require greater detail than can be shown on the elevation and floor plans.

To summarize, while design professionals have standard guidelines for creating a set of drawings for a building or structure, they also have flexibility in the process. Design team members must place their vision on a set of plans that will convey every detail of their design vision to the construction team members, allowing them to construct the building safely, as designed, and meeting all required codes. Not all plans are created the same.

Detail Drawing Types

Detail drawings are specifically created at a large scale to display a feature to allow the designer to clearly show how it must be built. They can be used to provide enhanced information for features found on other drawing types used in a set of construction documentation. The two major categories of details are plan details (showing a horizontal slice of a building) and section details (showing a vertical slice of the building). **See Figure 5-4.**

Plan Details

The term *plan*, when used in construction drawings, indicates a horizontal cut of a building. Plan details are similar to the top view of an orthographic drawing, and provide construction details of a feature located on a plan view with greater clarity than can be shown on any plan view type. More than one orthographic view may be drawn to show all of the details needed to build the feature. When a plan view's scale is too small, plan details are necessary to provide the required information to construct the component or feature as designed.

An example of a plan detail is the added information necessary to fully understand how a driveway, or approach, is constructed. There would be too much clutter and too little clarity on a site plan; therefore, a detail shows how the feature should be constructed with the designation or a note that the plan detail is typical of the rest of the installation. **See Figure 5-5.**

DETAIL TYPES

Horizontal Details	Vertical Details
Plan details	Elevation details
Site plan details	Framing details
Foundation plan details	Door details
Floor plan detail	Roof details
Reflected ceiling plan details	Section details
Roof plan detail	
Feature details (fireplace, stairs, etc.)	Feature details (fireplace, stairs, etc.)

Figure 5-4. Details are categorized by the direction of the view used in the drawing.

Elevation Details

An elevation detail provides detailed information for specific features shown on an elevation drawing or section view (interior vertical cut). These views are similar to the front, back, or side views of an orthographic drawing. Elevation details can show features located on the exterior or interior of the building, and provide detailed information needed to construct a feature. These elevations are particularly useful where this information is not available on the other drawings.

For example, an exterior elevation of a building incorporating exterior columns will show the external finish of the column and provide an understanding of the shape and physical features. Since there is usually not enough information provided on the elevation drawing to build this feature, an elevation detail may be used to provide the needed information. If the column is structural, how should it be built and how is it attached to the roof structure? These and other questions, including dimensions, can be shown on an elevation detail. **See Figure 5-6.**

PLAN TYPE DETAILS

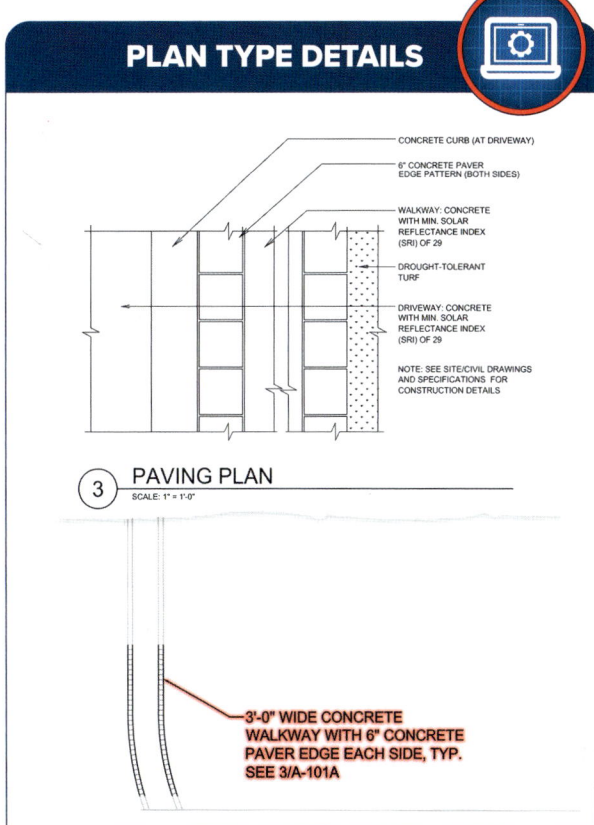

Figure 5-5. Plan type details provide an enlarged look at a building's horizontal feature.

For additional information, visit qr.njatcdb.org Item #6499

ELEVATION TYPE DETAILS

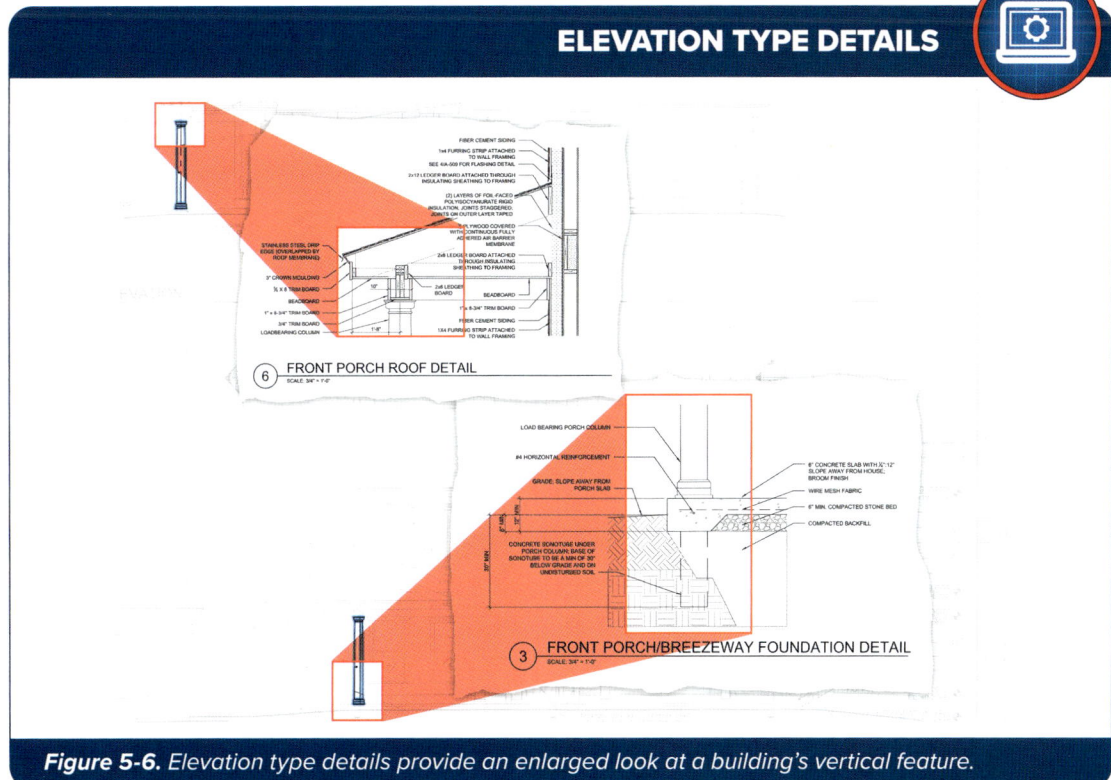

For additional information, visit qr.njatcdb.org Item #6500

Figure 5-6. Elevation type details provide an enlarged look at a building's vertical feature.

Relationship to Other Drawings

Because details are generally conveying information about smaller portions or features of a building, there is a need to provide information about how the information in the detail applies to other drawings. Designers vary in the approach that they use, but they are generally consistent within each set of drawings as to how they show call-outs (or pointers) to details.

Most often they provide call-outs to the details from either a plan or elevation view. In some cases, architects provide a general note with added instructions attached to a specific feature on the drawing. These notes contain detailed information for the feature they refer to and may include the location of a detail or section detail that is needed for its construction. To fully understand the detail, it is helpful to reference either the plan or elevation to better understand the context of the surroundings for the feature being shown. **See Figure 5-7.**

Scale

Generally, every detail drawing has a larger scale that will allow the needed information to be shown clearly. Details are drawn to show precisely how to construct a feature. The detail will include the dimensions needed to ensure the feature is built correctly. Dimensions not shown on the detail can be obtained by using an architectural scale. **See Figure 5-8.**

For additional information, visit qr.njatcdb.org Item #6501

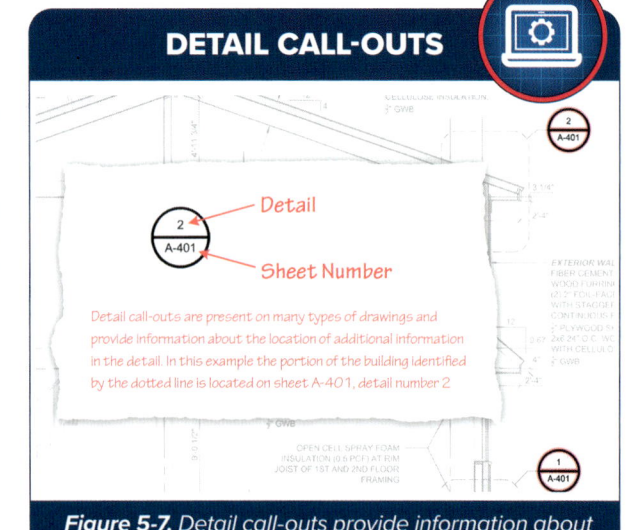

Figure 5-7. Detail call-outs provide information about the location of additional information in the detail.

For additional information, visit qr.njatcdb.org Item #6502

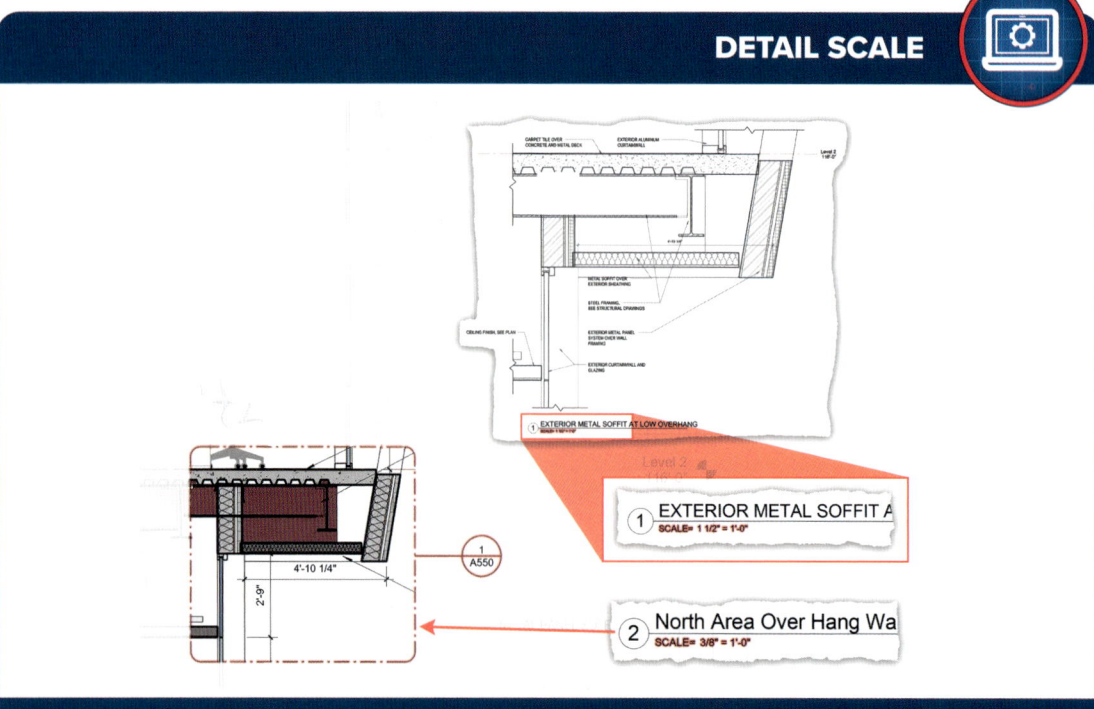

Figure 5-8. Attention must be given to the scale of details, as they are drawn at larger scales than other construction drawings.

Most plan views use a scale of ⅛ inch equals 1 foot, while plan details typically use scales from ¾ inch equals 1 foot to 1 ½ inches equals 1 foot, allowing them to provide greater detail. Larger scales may be used when greater detail is needed.

An example of a feature that usually has a detail is a stairway. Stairway details are typical details that provide a large amount of information and many times show both a horizontal and vertical view. The scale used for these details is dependent on the amount of information to be shown, which could include the type of stairway, attachment methods, and aesthetic considerations, such as ornamental woodwork. **See Figure 5-9.**

Not to Scale

Details intended to provide a better understanding of the assembly of building components are, in some cases, not drawn to scale. Isometric drawings used to illustrate a three-dimensional visualization are often not to scale. Drawing details that are not to scale are usually labeled "NTS." **See Figure 5-10.**

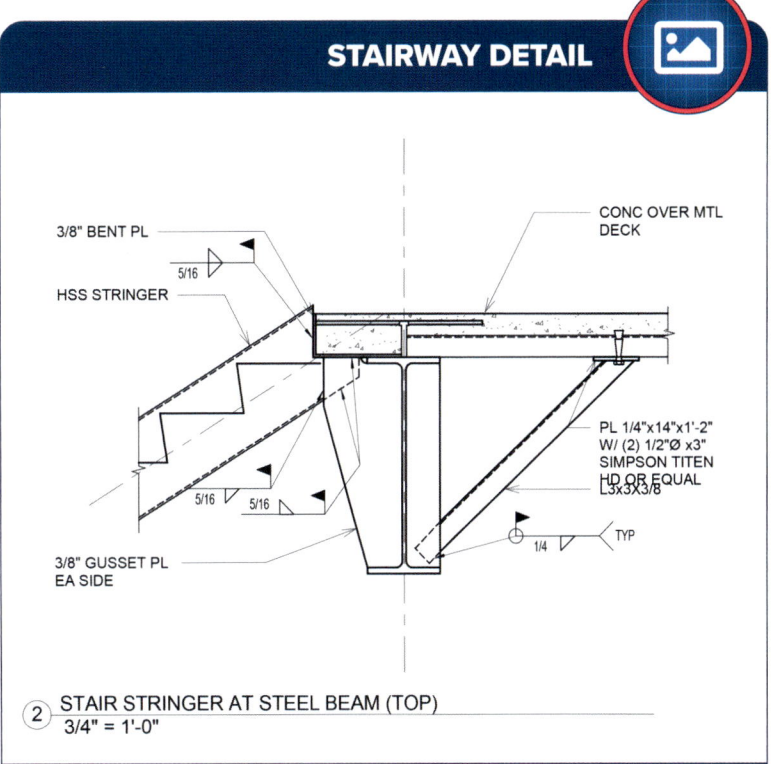

STAIRWAY DETAIL

3/8" BENT PL

5/16

HSS STRINGER

CONC OVER MTL DECK

PL 1/4"x14"x1'-2" W/ (2) 1/2"Ø x3" SIMPSON TITEN HD OR EQUAL L3x3x3/8

5/16   5/16

3/8" GUSSET PL EA SIDE

1/4   TYP

2 STAIR STRINGER AT STEEL BEAM (TOP)
   3/4" = 1'-0"

Figure 5-9. *Stairway details provide information necessary to construct and attach the stair system to the building.*

DETAILS NOT DRAWN TO SCALE

3 SINGLE TOP PLATE AT PARTITION

2 CHASE AT EXTERIOR WALL

1 NON-LOAD BEARING WALL

SEQUENCE NOTES

SEE A-501A FOR 'SEQUENCE NOTES' AND STEPS 1-6.

SEE A-501A FOR 'SEQUENCE NOTES' AND STEPS 1-6, AND A-501B FOR STEPS 7-12.

REQUIRED CONSTRUCTION SEQUENCE - PART A

REQUIRED CONSTRUCTION SEQUENCE - PART

REQUIRED CONSTRUCTION SEQUENCE - PART

Figure 5-10. *Occasionally detail drawings are not drawn to scale to enable an isometric view of the feature.*

For additional information, visit qr.njatcdb.org Item #6503

SECTION VIEWS

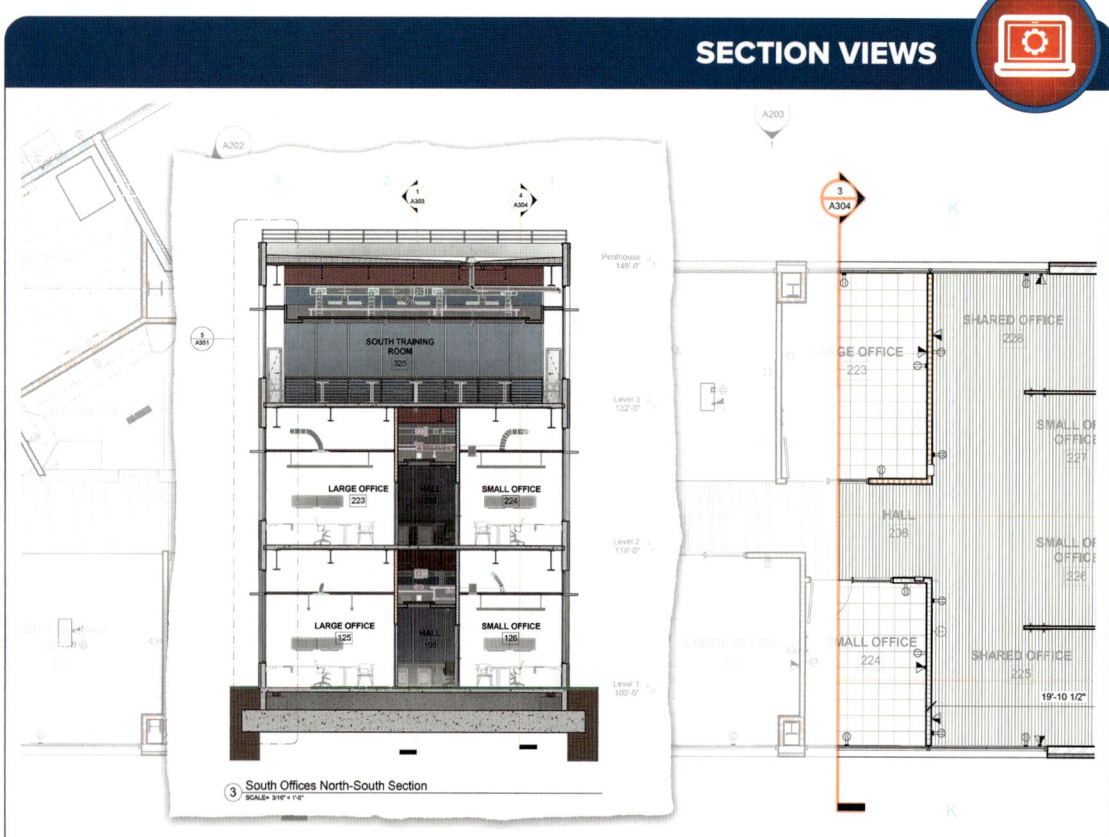

Figure 5-11. *Section views provide additional information created by an imaginary vertical cut through the building at a specific location.*

SECTIONS

A section—also known as section views, sectional drawings, building sections, or a section drawing—is a view that is obtained by cutting through the building along any imaginary vertical plane. These views are similar to the front, or side views, of an orthographic drawing.

Sections are used to provide additional information about the construction and appearance for both exterior and interior features of a building. Sections show this additional information by "slicing the building," which results in the ability to reveal features that are otherwise not visible. **See Figure 5-11.**

Many sets of construction drawings have more than one section contained within the set. The number of sections is relative to the size of the building and the amount of information necessary to properly document the intended final product.

Relationship to Elevations

Sections are similar to elevation views since they are both viewed from a vertical plane. For this reason, some designers refer to both exterior and interior elevations as sections. The most common use of sections, however, is to "cut through" building features to see both what is cut by the plane as well as the surrounding areas.

Scale

Sections are drawn to a scale appropriate for the area of the area of the building that is cut by the vertical plane. Many times they are drawn to a scale of ⅛ inch equals 1 foot or ¼ inch equals 1 foot. Designers may use a scale as large as of ½ inch equals 1 foot for a section, but it may often be called a section detail.

Relationship to Other Drawings

Design professionals use several methods to identify sections using a consistent set of parameters. The parameters include a cutting plane line showing the location of the cut, an arrow indicating the direction of the cutting plane, a number or letter that indicates the specific cumulative section number, and a designator that provides the sheet number where the user can find the section. In cases where there is only one section on a sheet, there may not be a detail number. **See Figure 5-12.**

SECTION DETAILS

In some cases, greater detail is needed than can be ascertained from a section view. In these cases, some designers create increased scale drawings of a portion of a building section. Section details are similar to sections in that they cut through a part of the building to reveal an otherwise unobtainable viewpoint, and they are similar to details in that they show a relatively small area,

For additional information, visit qr.njatcdb.org Item #6505

SECTION CALL-OUTS

Section Number

Sheet Number

1
A-304

The point of the triangle and the rectangle at the opposite end of the cut line indicate the direction of the view.

The cutting plane line shows the point where the building is cut to reveal more information.

Section call-outs are present on many types of drawings and provide information about the direction of the view and location of section view.

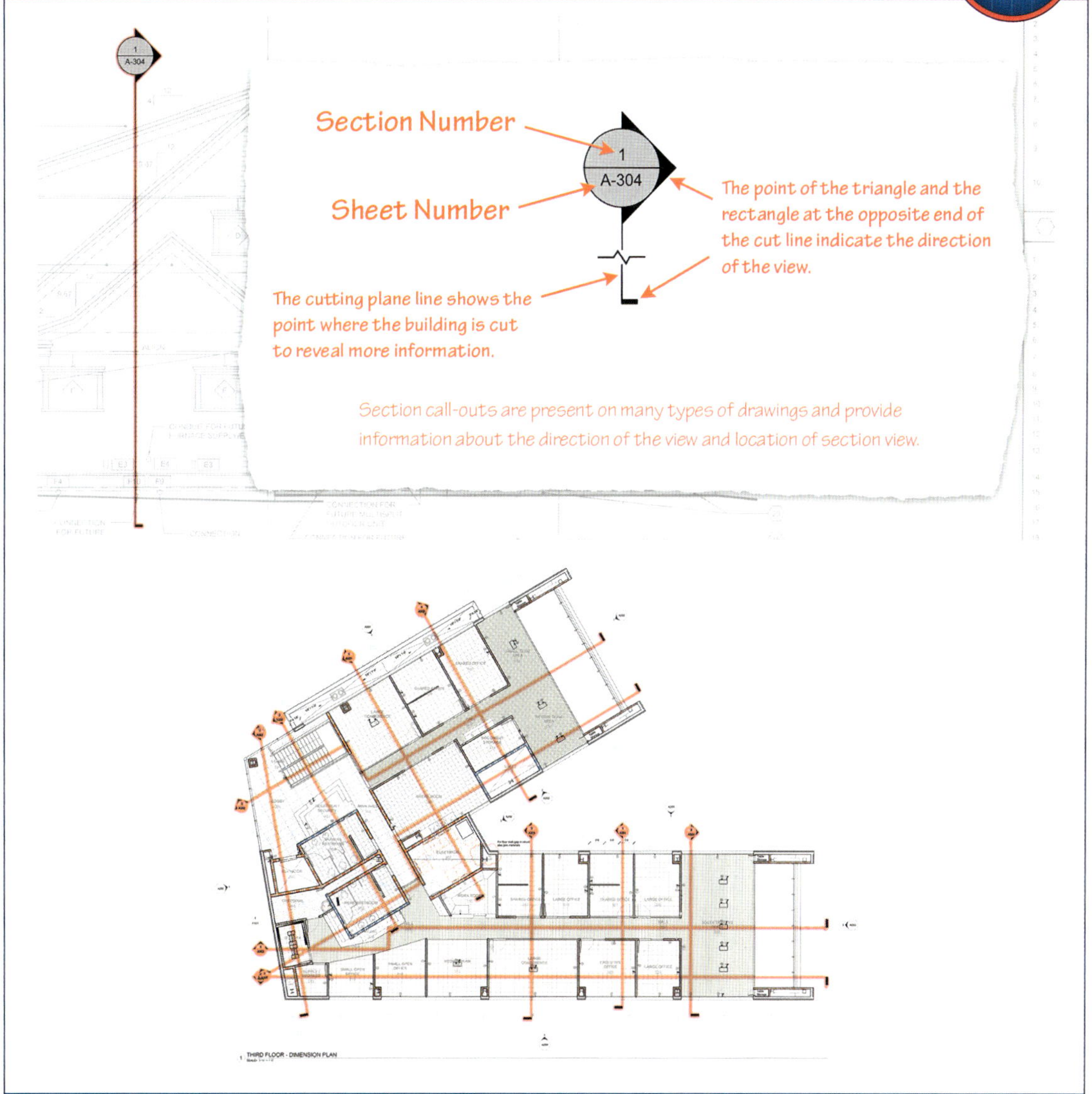

Figure 5-12. *Section call-outs are present on many types of drawings and provide information about the direction of the view and location of section view.*

or feature of the building at an increased scale. Section details may be called sections on some plans, details on others, or a combination of these terms. No matter the name used, the primary purpose of a section detail is to provide construction details that cannot be adequately shown on a section.

A wall section is a typical section detail. Wall sections provide information about the construction of a wall that a plan view cannot show. These sections provide detailed information such as stud size, insulation required within the wall, fire rating of the wall, if any, load-bearing status, and the finish on both sides of the wall. It would be challenging to convey this information without the inclusion of a wall section. **See Figure 5-13.**

Typically, section details are drawn to a scale of 1 ½ inches equals 1 foot or 3 inches equals 1 foot. These scales may be larger or smaller based on the amount of detail the designer feels is needed.

For additional information, visit qr.njatcdb.org Item #6506

SECTION DETAILS

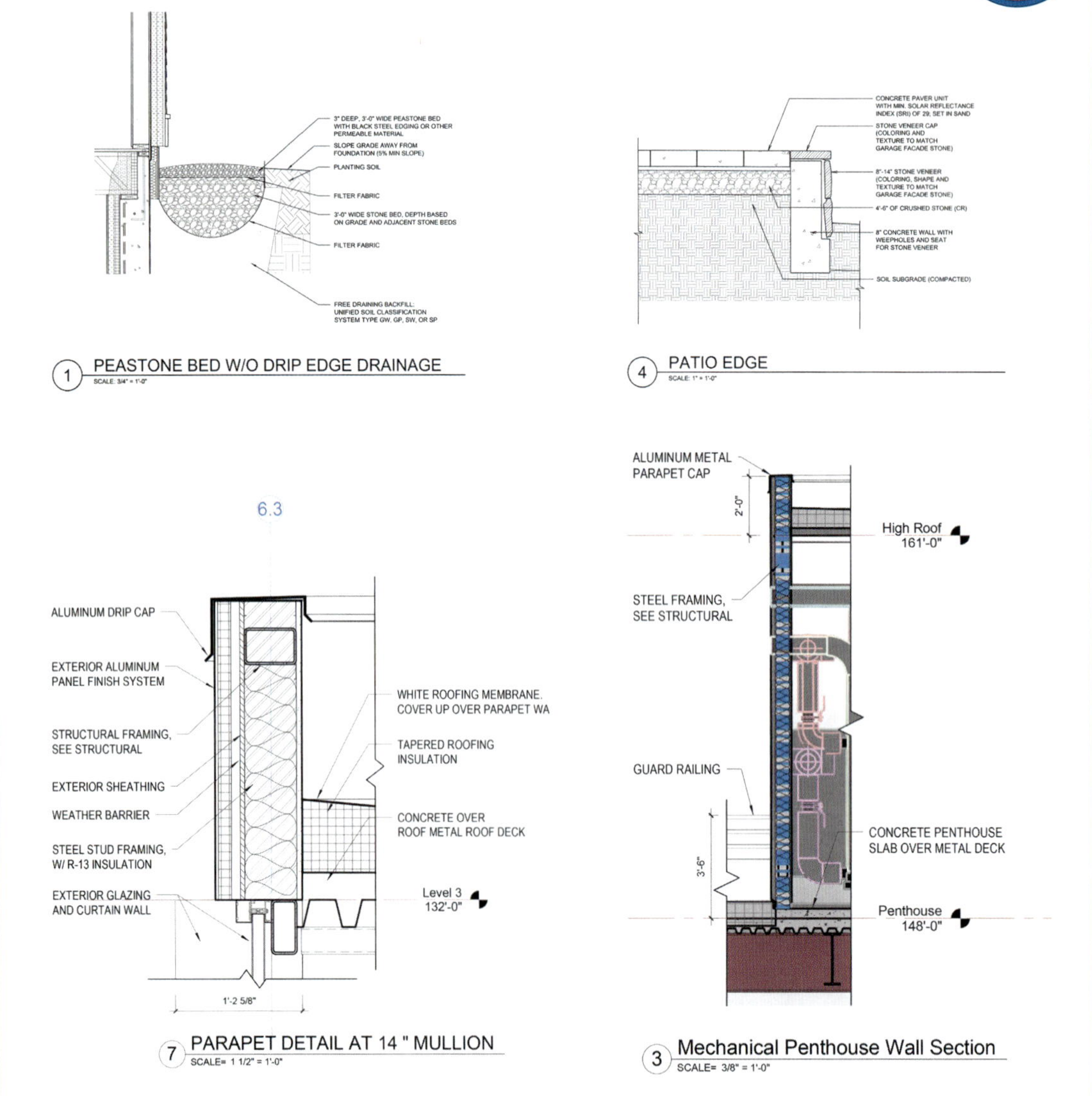

1 PEASTONE BED W/O DRIP EDGE DRAINAGE
SCALE: 3/4" = 1'-0"

- 3" DEEP, 3'-0" WIDE PEASTONE BED WITH BLACK STEEL EDGING OR OTHER PERMEABLE MATERIAL
- SLOPE GRADE AWAY FROM FOUNDATION (5% MIN SLOPE)
- PLANTING SOIL
- FILTER FABRIC
- 3'-0" WIDE STONE BED, DEPTH BASED ON GRADE AND ADJACENT STONE BEDS
- FILTER FABRIC
- FREE DRAINING BACKFILL: UNIFIED SOIL CLASSIFICATION SYSTEM TYPE GW, GP, SW, OR SP

4 PATIO EDGE
SCALE: 1" = 1'-0"

- CONCRETE PAVER UNIT WITH MIN. SOLAR REFLECTANCE INDEX (SRI) OF 29, SET IN SAND
- STONE VENEER CAP (COLORING AND TEXTURE TO MATCH GARAGE FACADE STONE)
- 8"-14" STONE VENEER (COLORING, SHAPE AND TEXTURE TO MATCH GARAGE FACADE STONE)
- 4"-6" OF CRUSHED STONE (CR)
- 8" CONCRETE WALL WITH WEEPHOLES AND SEAT FOR STONE VENEER
- SOIL SUBGRADE (COMPACTED)

6.3

7 PARAPET DETAIL AT 14 " MULLION
SCALE= 1 1/2" = 1'-0"

- ALUMINUM DRIP CAP
- EXTERIOR ALUMINUM PANEL FINISH SYSTEM
- STRUCTURAL FRAMING, SEE STRUCTURAL
- EXTERIOR SHEATHING
- WEATHER BARRIER
- STEEL STUD FRAMING, W/ R-13 INSULATION
- EXTERIOR GLAZING AND CURTAIN WALL
- WHITE ROOFING MEMBRANE. COVER UP OVER PARAPET WA
- TAPERED ROOFING INSULATION
- CONCRETE OVER ROOF METAL ROOF DECK
- Level 3 132'-0"
- 1'-2 5/8"

3 Mechanical Penthouse Wall Section
SCALE= 3/8" = 1'-0"

- ALUMINUM METAL PARAPET CAP
- 2'-0"
- High Roof 161'-0"
- STEEL FRAMING, SEE STRUCTURAL
- GUARD RAILING
- 3'-6"
- CONCRETE PENTHOUSE SLAB OVER METAL DECK
- Penthouse 148'-0"

Figure 5-13. *Section details provide larger scaled views than entire building sections.*

SUMMARY

Details and sections are a big part of understanding how to read blueprints. Although common architectural conventions for sections and details are used, they are not set in stone. There will be minor variations used on plans used throughout an Electrical Worker's experience. Any title variations should not be confusing because no matter what the drawing is named, the goal of all sections and details is to ensure a building to be constructed without problems.

Not many buildings are built alike, and in cases where they are the construction process may not be the same. A successful project lies in the hands of the designers and the construction team. Trade knowledge is one key to being successful; however, it also includes an understanding of the blueprints and applicable codes and standards. Add coordination and cooperation to the process, and job success is on its way. This applies to everyone involved with the project.

For additional information, visit qr.njatcdb.org
Item #6517

REVIEW QUESTIONS

1. Which of the following descriptions are used to describe a detail view? (Choose all that are correct.)

    a. The scope is a smaller area or feature.
    b. The orientation is horizontal, vertical, or isometric.
    c. The building is cut by a plane to allow visibility.
    d. The typical scale is large.

2. The major category/categories of detail views is/are __?__.

    a. feature details
    b. plan details
    c. section details
    d. both b. and c.

3. When an elevation drawing does not provide enough information to build a feature, a(n) __?__ detail may be used to provide the needed information.

    a. plan
    b. section
    c. elevation
    d. none of these

4. Generally, a(n) __?__ is drawn to a larger scale to precisely show how a feature is constructed.

    a. detail
    b. elevation view
    c. plan view
    d. section

5. A section view obtained by cutting through a building on a vertical plane is also known as which of the following? (Choose all that are correct.)

    a. Building section
    b. Section drawing
    c. Sectional drawing
    d. Section view

6. Typically, section details are drawn on a scale of __?__. (Choose all that are correct.)

    a. $\frac{1}{2}$" equals 1'
    b. $\frac{3}{4}$" equals 1'
    c. 1 $\frac{1}{2}$" equal 1'
    d. 3" equal 1'

7. Sections are like elevation views since they are both viewed from a vertical plane.

    a. True   b. False

CHAPTER 6
SCHEDULES AND SPECIFICATIONS

Visual or pictorial drawings are inadequate to provide all of the data necessary to construct a building that matches the design intent of the architect and ultimately the owner of a building. The two main methods of providing additional information are via schedules (most offer information provided in a table format) and specifications, which is a highly structured and detailed statement of requirements for each individual component and building process during construction. Schedules and specifications augment plans, elevations, sections, and details, and act as the glue to hold everything together.

OBJECTIVES

- Identify the role of schedules in relation to construction and the most common applications.
- Identify the role of specifications in relation to construction and the most common applications.
- Demonstrate the ability to locate the needed information from within a set of specifications based on the MasterFormat.

TABLE OF CONTENTS

INTRODUCTION TO SCHEDULES AND SPECIFICATIONS

When a building is designed, it is not feasible to use drawings or illustrations for every bit of needed information. Schedules and specifications convey an added layer of description to construction drawings and documentation to ensure that the design intent of the architects and engineers comes to fruition in the final building.

Schedules and specifications generally take the form of text- and table-based groupings of data. In contrast to blueprints, these items are almost exclusively text and do not contain any type of illustration.

The information provided in schedules includes trade-specific details about building materials and equipment specified for use in the construction process. They give very detailed descriptions of products such as windows, doors, roofing materials, and electrical and plumbing fixtures.

SCHEDULES

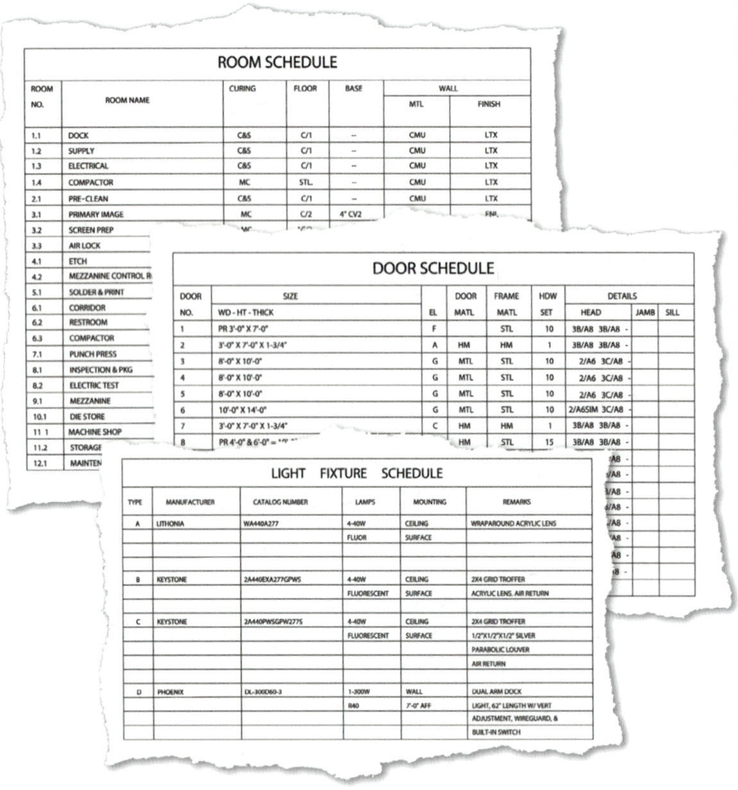

ROOM SCHEDULE

ROOM NO.	ROOM NAME	CURING	FLOOR	BASE	WALL MTL	WALL FINISH
1.1	DOCK	C&S	C/1	–	CMU	LTX
1.2	SUPPLY	C&S	C/1	–	CMU	LTX
1.3	ELECTRICAL	C&S	C/1	–	CMU	LTX
1.4	COMPACTOR	MC	STL.	–	CMU	LTX
2.1	PRE-CLEAN	C&S	C/1	–	CMU	LTX
3.1	PRIMARY IMAGE	MC	C/2	4" CV2		
3.2	SCREEN PREP					
3.3	AIR LOCK					
4.1	ETCH					
4.2	MEZZANINE CONTROL R					
5.1	SOLDER & PRINT					
6.1	CORRIDOR					
6.2	RESTROOM					
6.3	COMPACTOR					
7.1	PUNCH PRESS					
8.1	INSPECTION & PKG					
8.2	ELECTRIC TEST					
9.1	MEZZANINE					
10.1	DIE STORE					
11 1	MACHINE SHOP					
11.2	STORAGE					
12.1	MAINTEN					

DOOR SCHEDULE

DOOR NO.	SIZE WD - HT - THICK	EL	DOOR MATL	FRAME MATL	HDW SET	DETAILS HEAD	JAMB	SILL
1	PR 3'-0" X 7'-0"	F		STL	10	3B/A8 3B/A8 -		
2	3'-0" X 7'-0" X 1-3/4"	A	HM	HM	1	3B/A8 3B/A8 -		
3	8'-0" X 10'-0"	G	MTL	STL	10	2/A6 3C/A8 -		
4	8'-0" X 10'-0"	G	MTL	STL	10	2/A6 3C/A8 -		
5	8'-0" X 10'-0"	G	MTL	STL	10	2/A6 3C/A8 -		
6	10'-0" X 14'-0"	G	MTL	STL	10	2/A6SIM 3C/A8 -		
7	3'-0" X 7'-0" X 1-3/4"	C	HM	HM	1	3B/A8 3B/A8 -		
8	PR 4'-0" & 6'-0" =		HM	STL	15	3B/A8 3B/A8 -		

LIGHT FIXTURE SCHEDULE

TYPE	MANUFACTURER	CATALOG NUMBER	LAMPS	MOUNTING	REMARKS
A	LITHONIA	WA440A277	4-40W	CEILING	WRAPAROUND ACRYLIC LENS
			FLUOR	SURFACE	
B	KEYSTONE	2A440EXA277GPWS	4-40W	CEILING	2X4 GRID TROFFER
			FLUORESCENT	SURFACE	ACRYLIC LENS. AIR RETURN
C	KEYSTONE	2A440PWSGPW277S	4-40W	CEILING	2X4 GRID TROFFER
			FLUORESCENT	SURFACE	1/2"X1/2"X1/2" SILVER
					PARABOLIC LOUVER
					AIR RETURN
D	PHOENIX	DL-300D60-3	1-300W	WALL	DUAL ARM DOCK
			R40	7'-0" AFF	LIGHT, 62" LENGTH W/ VERT
					ADJUSTMENT, WIREGUARD, &
					BUILT-IN SWITCH

Figure 6-1. *Schedules convey a wide range of details about specific components of a building.*

SCHEDULES

Schedules are organized table-like lists of necessary materials and components for a specific job. These documents contain multiple pieces of data about each of the individual categories of items in a building. **See Figure 6-1.** For example, there are several data points about a door that could not be included on a construction drawing, and there are many doors of a particular type on a project. For this reason, information regarding the doors is included in a door schedule.

Schedules are used to organize the many categories of building components used in the construction process. There are many different types of schedules used depending on the type of building components. An example of this is a room schedule. Room schedules, like other schedules, are valuable in estimating, ordering, and organizing the entire construction project.

Window and Door Schedule

Window and door schedules are used on all types of prints, as they are included in nearly every construction project. **See Figure 6-2.** They contain all pertinent information relating to the size, shape, material, and ordering information of doors and windows.

Room Schedule

Room schedules are used primarily on commercial and industrial prints but are sometimes also included in residential drawing sets. These schedules are sometimes referred to by different names, such as *room finish schedules* or *interior finish schedules*, and give pertinent information on the types of finishes to be applied to the walls, ceilings,

Figure 6-2. Door and window schedules contain detailed information about each door or window that would be difficult to display on a drawing or would otherwise clutter the drawing.

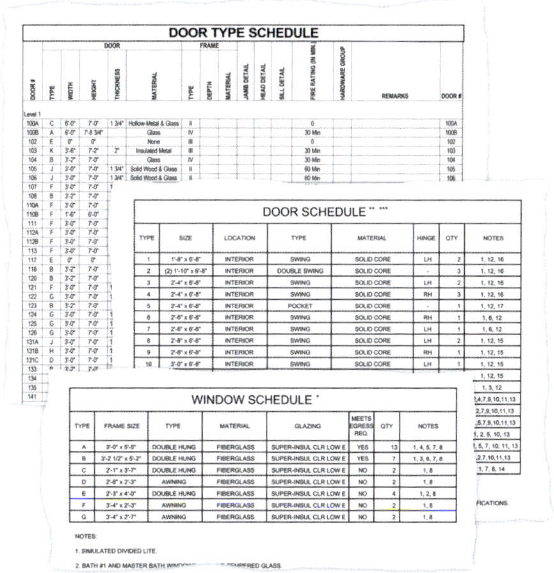

and floors of each room. **See Figure 6-3.** This information is useful to all building trades that must install material in the rooms detailed in the room finish schedule.

TRADE-SPECIFIC SCHEDULE TYPES

Although most schedule types are pertinent to all who work on the construction of a building, some are specific to individual trades to provide trade-specific information about the equipment and materials specified for the scope of work. Examples of trade-specific schedule types are plumbing, heating, ventilation, and air conditioning (HVAC), and electrical.

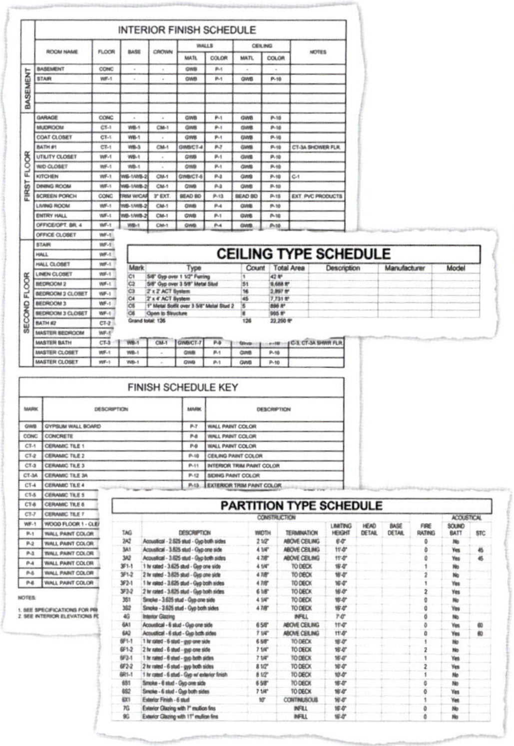

Plumbing

Plumbing schedules provide specific details about plumbing fixtures, risers, and other plumbing details. The plumbing fixture schedule often includes information such as a specific brand or model number, the size and type of the supply, the size of the drain

Figure 6-3. Room schedules provide details about each room such as wall, floor, and ceiling finishes.

PLUMBING SCHEDULES

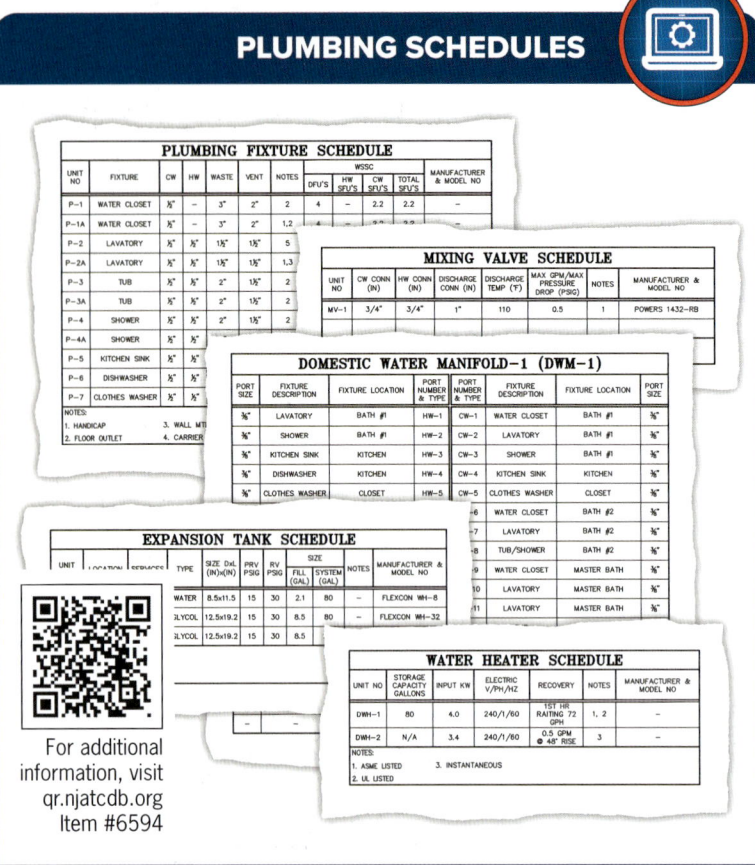

For additional information, visit qr.njatcdb.org Item #6594

Figure 6-4. *Plumbing schedules provide details about individual components of the plumbing system such as fixtures. tanks, and valves.*

lines and vent pipes, and other information that is too detailed and would clutter the plan. **See Figure 6-4.**

HVAC

In a similar manner, HVAC schedules provide information about each of these systems. HVAC schedules include equipment, fans, terminals, variable-air-volume units (VAVs), louvers, and in some cases other systems information, including electrical systems. **See Figure 6-5.**

Electrical

There are a number of schedules that pertain specifically to electrical equipment and installation. These schedules include panelboards, connected loads, lighting fixtures, equipment, and control circuits.

Panelboard Schedules

Panelboard schedules are used on all types of construction to identify and describe the panel. **See Figure 6-6.** They also list current, voltages, and loads, as well as individual branch circuits. There is usually a space left on the panelboard schedule for notes.

HVAC SCHEDULES

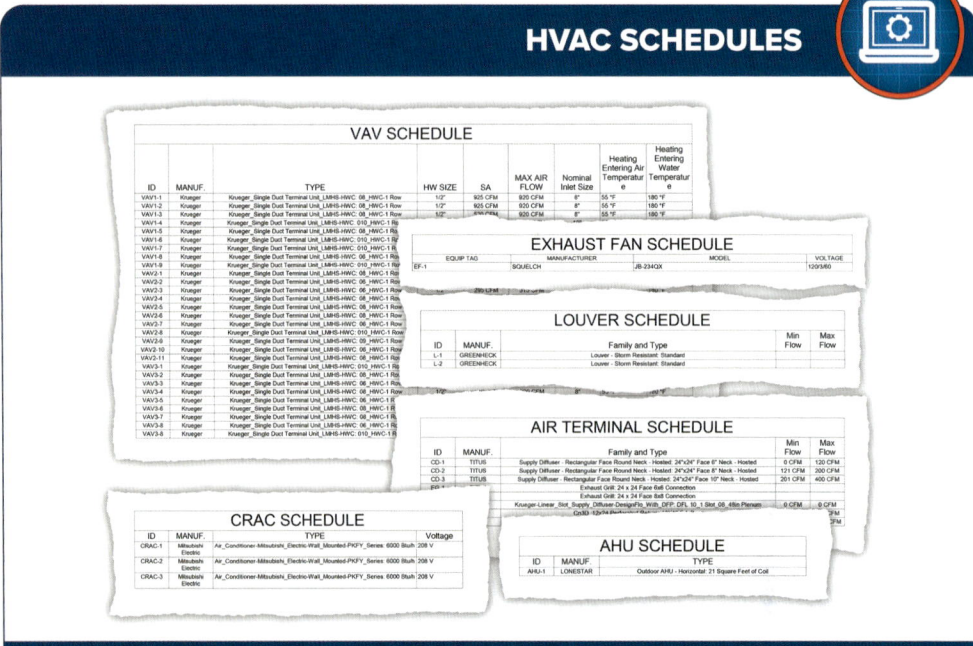

For additional information, visit qr.njatcdb.org Item #6595

Figure 6-5. *HVAC schedules provide details about individual components of the heating, ventilation, and air conditioning system such as air handlers, heat pumps, fans, and other parts of the system.*

PANELBOARD SCHEDULES

For additional information, visit qr.njatcdb.org Item #6596

PANEL: "1LB3"

PANEL: "1LB2"

PANEL: "1LB1"

CKT NO	OCP AMP	POLE	LTG	PWR	CO	DESCRIPTION	A	B	C	DESCRIPTION	CO	PWR	LTG	POLE	AMP	CKT NO
1	20	1	0.0	0.0		SMALL OFFICE	0.0	0.0		SMALL OFFICE	0.0	0.0	0.0	1	20	2
3	20	1	0.0	0.0		SMALL OFFICE		0.0	0.0	EXECUTIVE OFFICE	–	–	–	1	20	4
5	20	1	–			SHARED OFFICE			0.0	0.0	SHARED OFFICE	–	–	–	1	20	6
7	20	1	–			PRINTING SPACE	0.0	0.0		SMALL CONFERENCE	–	–	–	1	20	8
9	20	1	–			BRK ROOM		0.0	0.0	VESTIBULE	–	–	–	1	20	10
11	20	1	–			BRK ROOM FLOOR BOX			0.0	0.0	SPARE	–	–	–	1	20	12
13	20	1	–			MIRCOWAVE	0.0	0.0		SPARE	–	–	–	1	20	14
15	20	1	–			KITCHEN COUNTER		0.0	0.0	SPARE	–	–	–	1	20	16
17	20	1	–			REFRIDGER			0.0	0.0	BRK ROOM FLOOR BOX	–	–	–	1	20	18
19	20	1	–			SPARE	0.0	0.0		BRK ROOM FLOOR BOX	–	–	–	1	20	20
21	20	1	–			SPARE		0.0	0.0	BRK ROOM FLOOR BOX	–	–	–	1	20	22
23	20	1	–			SPARE			0.0	0.0	SPARE	–	–	–	1	20	24
25	20	1	–			SPARE	0.0	0.0		SPARE	–	–	–	1	20	26
27	20	1	–			SPARE		0.0	0.0	SPARE	–	–	–	1	20	28
29	20	1	–			SPARE			0.0	0.0	SPARE	–	–	–	1	20	30
31	20	1	–			SPARE	0.0	0.0		SPARE	–	–	–	1	20	32
33	20	1	–			SPARE		0.0	0.0	SPARE	–	–	–	1	20	34
35	20	1	–			SPARE			0.0	0.0	SPARE	–	–	–	1	20	36
37	50	1	–			SPARE	0.0	0.0		SPARE	–	–	–	3	30	38
39						–		0.0	0.0	–	–	–	–	–	–	40
41	–	–				–			0.0	0.0	–	–	–	–	–	–	42

Figure 6-6. *Panelboard schedules provide details about both the panelboard and the circuits that are connected to it.*

Connected Load Schedules

Connected load schedules provide information on voltage, current, and power requirements, and are used in all types of construction. **See Figure 6-7.** The connected load schedule is used to separate circuits and balance loads when this information is required by local utility companies.

Tech Fact

Many municipalities require electrical code calculations to be provided on the electrical plans. Additionally, the *NEC* requires loads to be balanced.

CONNECTED LOAD SCHEDULES

CONNECTED LOAD:

LIGHTING --------------- 12.2 KW

MISCELLANEOUS ----------- 42.0 KW

WATER HEATING ----------- 7.5 KW

HVAC ------------------- 27.0 KW

TOTAL: 88.7 KW

VOLTAGE 120/208
PHASE 3
WIRE 4

Figure 6-7. *Information about the different types of loads and their sizes is available on connected load schedules.*

LIGHTING FIXTURE SCHEDULES

LIGHTING FIXTURE SCHEDULE

TYPE	MOUNTING	VOLTS	LAMPS NUMBER & TYPE	MANUFACTURER & CAT.#	DESCRIPTION	NOTES
C1	SURFACE	120	LED MIN 180 LUMENS MAX 6 WATTS	ALBEO TECHNOLOGIES TALEA–HP	WHITE UNDER CABINET LED	–
F	SURFACE	120	–	MINKA AIRE F514–ORB	FAN IN LIVING ROOM – BRONZE	–
F/L	SURFACE	120	2–13W	MINKA AIRE F514–ORB	FAN AND LIGHT COMBINATION IN BEDROOMS – BRONZE	–
F/L	SURFACE	120	ENERGY STAR LIGHT KIT	GOSSAMER LIGHTHOUSE	FAN AND LIGHT ON PORCH WITH ENERGY STAR LIGHT KIT – GALVANIZED ALUMINUM	–
W1	SURFACE	120	4–13W	LITHONIA 11534 BN	ANTIQUE BRONZE FOUR LIGHT MASTER BATH VANITY FIXTURE	–
W2	SURFACE	120	2–13W	LITHONIA 11532 BN	ANTIQUE BRONZE TWO LIGHT BATHROOM VANITY FIXTURE	–
W3	SURFACE	120	26W	PROGRESS P7047–20EBWB	ANTIQUE BRONZE WALL SCONCE	–
W4	SURFACE	120	1–18W	THOMAS LIGHTING PL9007–7	MATTE BLACK EXTERIOR LANTERN	–
W5	SURFACE	120	2–13W	PROGRESS P–7093–09EBWB	WHITE BASEMENT STAIR WALL SCONCE	–

REMARKS:
1.   THIS IS A BRAND NAME OR APPROVED EQUAL SCHEDULE. SALIENT FEATURES OF THE SPECIFIED FIXTURE INCLUDE LAMP TYPE AND WATTAGE, ENERGY STAR, QUALITY, STYLE, AND FINISH.

Figure 6-8. Lighting fixture schedules provide information including the type of lamps used, how the fixture is mounted, manufacturer's catalog numbers as well as additional details.

Lighting Fixture Schedule

Lighting fixture schedules are used on all types of prints. **See Figure 6-8.** They identify fixture type (using a given letter that will correspond to a letter on the blueprints), manufacturer, catalog number, lamp number, mounting instructions, and other pertinent information.

The lighting fixture schedule is extremely useful in estimating, ordering, and keeping a running inventory of materials on hand. In some cases, a residential print may not have a lighting fixture schedule. In this case, the architect will give the owner a lighting fixture allowance to select the fixtures at a local lighting center.

Equipment Schedule

Equipment schedules are used to determine the voltage, current, and power requirements for motors and other electrical equipment on construction jobs. **See Figure 6-9.** Equipment schedules also list wire sizes and duty cycle information for the various machinery and equipment used on the project.

Control Circuit Schedule

Control circuit schedules are used most often in commercial and industrial construction. **See Figure 6-10.** Control circuit schedules list lighting or motor control information by room, circuit designation, and contactor or connection details.

EQUIPMENT SCHEDULES

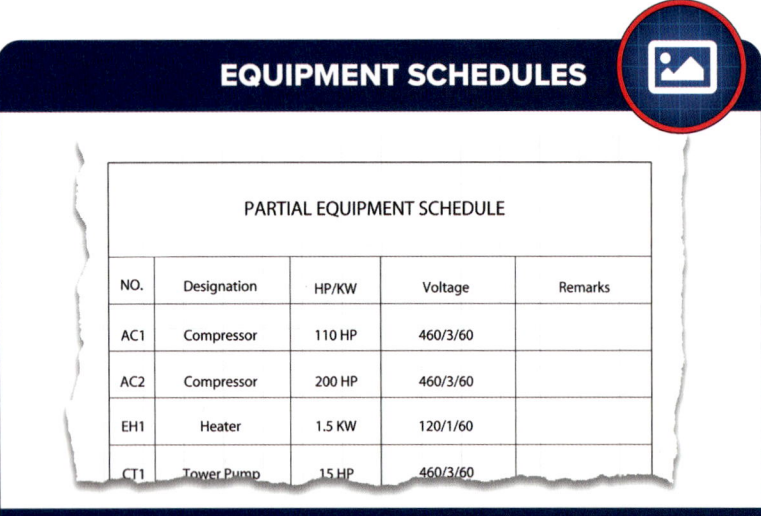

PARTIAL EQUIPMENT SCHEDULE

NO.	Designation	HP/KW	Voltage	Remarks
AC1	Compressor	110 HP	460/3/60	
AC2	Compressor	200 HP	460/3/60	
EH1	Heater	1.5 KW	120/1/60	
CT1	Tower Pump	15 HP	460/3/60	

Figure 6-9. Equipment schedules provide a list of the equipment in a building along with some details about the equipment.

SPECIFICATIONS

When a building is constructed, there is a large amount of information for which it is not feasible to show on a visual type drawing. The specifications are a text-based document that contains many requirements for the job to augment the visual, drawing-based documents. The specifications, in support of the blueprints, are the second half of the design intent created by the architects and engineers for a project. **See Figure 6-11.**

Most jobs, from small residential projects to massive industrial projects, have specifications. Smaller projects, such as residential construction, may detail the specifications within the set of drawings, whereas a large commercial project may contain hundreds of pages of specifications.

CONTROL CIRCUIT SCHEDULES

RELAY PANEL SCHEDULE

RELAY NUMBER	BRANCH CIRCUIT	LOAD SERVED
1	34(RP−BA)	BATH #1 LIGHTS
2	34(RP−BA)	BATH #1 CLOSET LIGHTS
3	34(RP−BA)	KITCHEN LIGHTS WEST WALL
4	34(RP−BA)	KITCHEN LIGHTS NORTH WALL
5	34(RP−BA)	KITCHEN LIGHTS PENINSULA
6	34(RP−BA)	DINING ROOM LIGHTS NORTH WALL
7	34(RP−BA)	DINING ROOM LIGHTS NORTH WALL
8	32(RP−BA)	LIVING ROOM LIGHTS SOUTH WEST WALL
47	10(RP−BA)	GARAGE DISPOSAL NORTH WALL
48	12(RP−BA)	KITCHEN PENINSULA RECEPTACLES
49	8(RP−BB)	KITCHEN PENINSULA INSTRUMENT POWER
50	13(RP−B)	DINING ROOM RECEPTACLES
51	15(RP−B)	ENTRY HALL RECEPTACLES NORTH EAST
52	15(RP−B)	ENTRY HALL RECEPTACLES SOUTH
53	15(RP−BB)	LIVING ROOM INSTRUMENT POWER
54	16(RP−B)	LIVING ROOM RECEPTACLES
55	16(RP−BB)	LIVING ROOM INSTRUMENT POWER
56	12(RP−BB)	OFFICE/OPTIONAL BEDROOM INSTRUMENT POWER
57	14(RP−B)	OFFICE/OPTIONAL BEDROOM INSTRUMENT RECEPTACLES

NOTE: 1. PROVIDE ALL REQUIRED SUB FEED LUGS FOR ADDING FUTURE ADDITIONAL RELAY PANELS.

For additional information, visit qr.njatcdb.org Item #6598

Figure 6-10. *Control circuit schedules provide details about how loads are controlled that is difficult to show on other plans without creating unnecessary clutter.*

SPECIFICATIONS

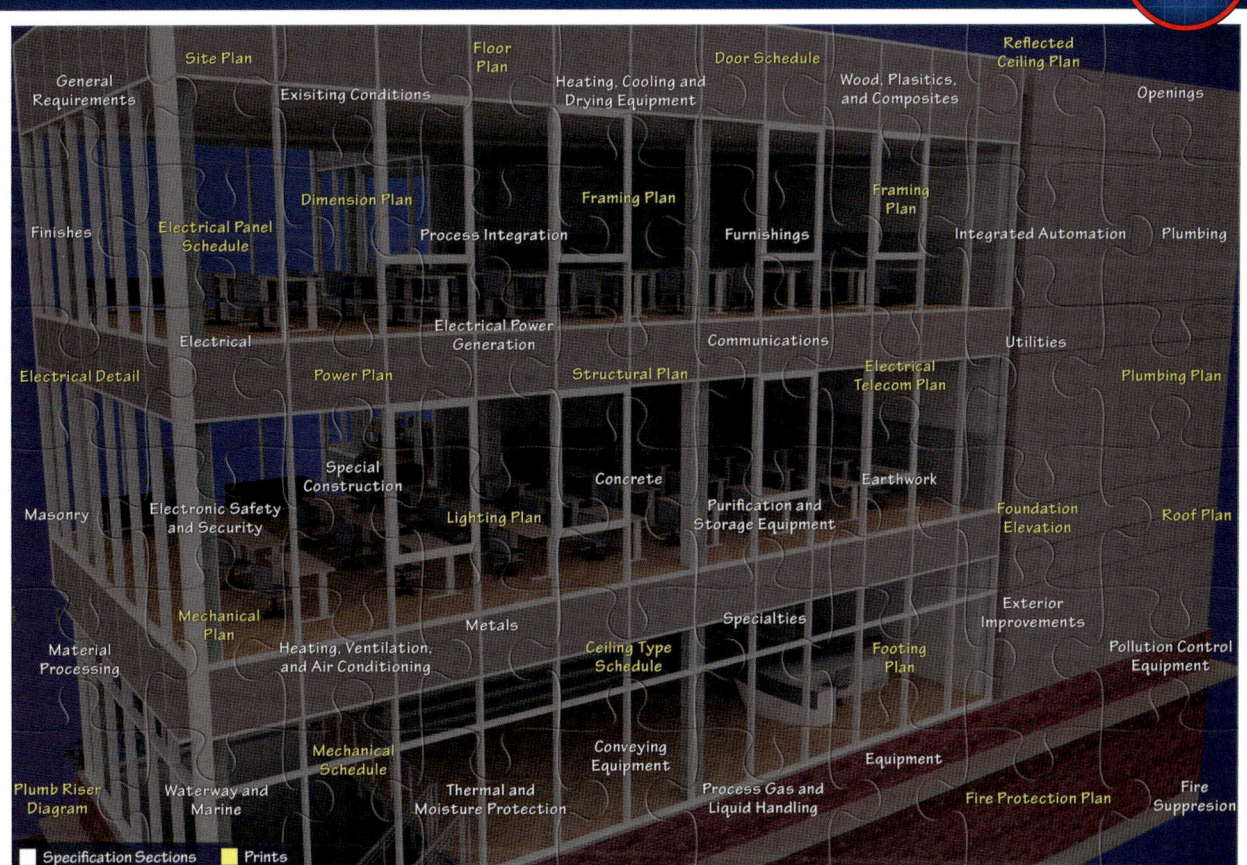

Figure 6-11. *Specifications and drawings fit together like puzzle pieces to provide a clear picture of the final product.*

The Role of Specifications in Construction Documents

The relationship between the specifications and the blueprints can be thought of using the analogy of a movie. **See Figure 6-12.** If a viewer were only able to see the "video" portion of a movie without any audio, it would be similar to viewing the blueprints without any reference to the specifications. The "audio track" in a movie provides a tremendous amount of augmented context to the "video track," without which there would likely be a much different understanding. Similarly, when the blueprints are viewed without reference to the specifications, there could be many different interpretations that would result in a building that differs from the design intent.

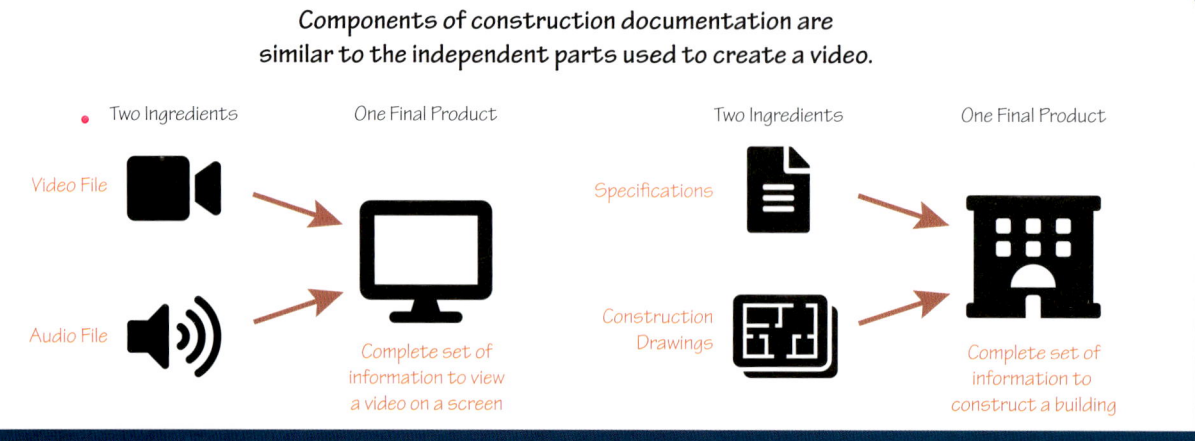

Components of construction documentation are similar to the independent parts used to create a video.

Two Ingredients | One Final Product
Video File
Audio File
Complete set of information to view a video on a screen

Two Ingredients | One Final Product
Specifications
Construction Drawings
Complete set of information to construct a building

Figure 6-12. *Construction drawings do not provide all the information needed to construct a building; specifications provide the additional needed detail.*

For additional information, visit qr.njatcdb.org Item #6599

SPECIFICATIONS PROVIDE PROJECT REQUIREMENTS

1.2   SUMMARY

A.   This Section includes administrative provisions for coordinating construction operations on Project including, but not limited to, the following:

1.   General project coordination procedures.
2.   Conservation.
3.   Coordination Drawings.
4.   Administrative and supervisory personnel.
5.   Project meetings.

B.   Each contractor shall participate in coordination requirements. Certain areas of responsibility will be assigned to a specific contractor.

C.   Related Sections: The following Sections contain requirements that relate to this Section:

1.   Division 1 Section "Construction Progress Documentation" for preparing and submitting the Contractor's Construction Schedule.
2.   Division 1 Section "Execution Requirements" for procedures for coordinating general installation and field-engineering services, including establishment of benchmarks and control points.
3.   Division 1 Section "Closeout Procedures" for coordinating Contract closeout.

SECTION 01 40 00 - QUALITY REQUIREMENTS

A.   This Section includes administrative and procedural requirements for quality assurance and quality control.

SECTION 01 50 00 - TEMPORARY FACILITIES AND CONTROLS

A.   This Section includes requirements for temporary facilities and controls, including temporary utilities, support facilities, and security and protection facilities.

Figure 6-13. *Specifications designate who is responsible to either do a task or provide specific building components.*

The specifications are written requirements describing the work to be performed and how the contract will be administered. They also provide a list of detailed job requirements, under which all work must proceed. In addition to the job requirements, the specifications detail how the job is to be bid and what qualifications requirements the contractor must meet to be able to bid on the job.

Responsibilities and Requirements

The intent of the specifications is to spell out what types of materials must be used on the project and detail various installation procedures, sometimes including how much work experience a person must have to perform a job. **See Figure 6-13.** The specifications will also define the responsibility of the contractor after the job is finished; for example, any warranty that must be provided.

Tech Fact

If a contractor has questions or finds discrepancies on the plans or specifications, this information must be submitted to the architect, engineer, or owner through a structured written request for information (RFI) process. **See Figure 6-14.** RFI process requirements can generally be found in the specifications.

The architect, engineer, or owner will provide a written reply providing the answers to the problem cited in the RFI. Contractors should not proceed with work associated with the RFI until all of their questions are resolved in writing.

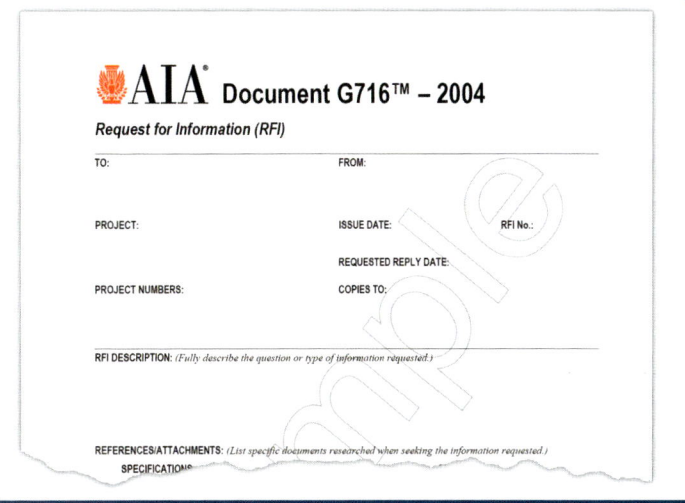

Figure 6-14. When a clarification is needed about the construction drawings or associated documentation is needed, a formal progress called a request for information is utilized.

Bid Documents

All contractors, general or subcontractors, bid jobs based on the conditions detailed in the specifications. **See Figure 6-15.** When jobs are bid, the contractors are held responsible to complete the job as described in both the blueprints and the specifications. If there is a conflict between the prints and the specifications, the project architects, engineers, and/or owner are responsible for providing the needed clarity to alleviate any ambiguity.

Tech Fact

Because of the financial implications, bid documents are very specific.

SPECIFICATIONS PROVIDE BID DETAILS

00 20 00	Instructions for Procurement
00 21 00	Instructions
00 21 13	Instructions to Bidders
00 21 16	Instructions to Proposers
00 22 00	Supplementary Instructions
00 22 13	Supplementary Instructions to Bidders
00 22 16	Supplementary Instructions to Proposers
00 23 00	Procurement Definitions
00 24 00	Procurement Scopes
00 24 13	Scopes of Bids
00 24 13.13	Scopes of Bids (Multiple Contracts)
00 24 13.16	Scopes of Bids (Multiple-Prime Contract)
00 24 16	Scopes of Proposals
00 24 16.13	Scopes of Proposals (Multiple Contracts)
00 24 16.16	Scopes of Proposals (Multiple-Prime Contract)
00 25 00	Procurement Meetings
00 25 13	Pre-Bid Meetings
00 25 16	Pre-Proposal Meetings
00 26 00	Procurement Substitution Procedures

Figure 6-15. Information about the bid process and the responsibilities of all involved are detailed in the specifications.

Construction Process Oversight

Building departments are involved with plans from the very beginning of a project. General contractors or their representatives submit completed blueprints to the building department for review and approval. Separate specifications, if they exist, may or may not be submitted for approval. While specifications are necessary to construct the project, they generally do not contain the information required by plan reviewers to assure code compliance. In most cases, this information is found on the blueprints.

The building department submits the plans to plan reviewers certified in individual disciplines such as structural, electrical, plumbing, HVAC, and fire. Reviewers evaluate the blueprints for compliance with the codes and standards that apply to their discipline. When all required reviewers approve the plans, a permit can be issued.

The responsibility of the building department does not stop here. Approved plans may be on the job, but inspections must be made throughout construction to assure code compliance. It is a good idea for the contractor to meet with the inspector before starting work to determine if there are separate specifications that will be relevant to the inspection. Many building departments do not inspect for compliance with requirements found on a separate set of specifications. The building owner's representative typically enforces the conditions found in the specifications. Additional information, such as local requirements and code interpretations, is essential to discuss in the meeting.

When the construction process begins, it is a good idea for construction personnel to use their knowledge of pertinent codes to ensure that the information on the plans is correct. There is always a chance that a mistake was made during the design or approval process. Using the RFI system to question information on the plans or in the specifications is much better than installing something incorrectly and having to redo the work. Many subcontractor contracts hold the subcontractor responsible for installation errors, even if the error is due to an error on the blueprints. Subcontractors must review all contract documents, including the plans, and report any errors found using the RFI system.

Some of the keys to a successful project are knowledge of the codes relevant to each trade, working knowledge of the blueprints, coordination with other trades, and communication with inspectors, the general contractor, and other trades on the job.

Scope and General Conditions

The scope of what is termed "the work" will be set forth in the specifications. **See Figure 6-16.** The description of the work will be detailed to suit the nature of the job. The specifications can be as simple or complex as the situation demands. The type and quality of materials, equipment, workmanship, and standards required for all trades are spelled out in addition to the necessary work methods and testing requirements. The general conditions are a set of requirements like time and duration of the project, how to deal with conflicts when they arise, and the submittal and records documentation requirements of the project. The general conditions are also contained within the specifications.

Organization

Because there is a large volume of information to be shared pertaining to the construction of the building (commonly the specifications are hundreds of pages in length), there is a need to have a standard organization of this content to ensure that information can be easily found when needed. The Construction Specifications Institute (CSI) creates, maintains, and continually improves upon an industry-accepted method of organization of these jobsite requirements, referred to as specifications. The CSI MasterFormat defines a "master list" numbering for divisions, sections, and subsections used in standard specification sets. **See Figure 6-17.**

PROJECT SCOPE

C.   PROJECT DESCRIPTION

The selected site is located at the northwest corner of the Lands West Development north of Lomas Boulevard and west of the University Boulevard. The five (5) acre site borders the Interstate 25 northbound frontage road on the west. This building will be highly visible to the public. Site utility and road construction is underway. Construction of the UNM Cancer Research and Treatment Center is underway at a site adjacent to this project's site.

This project will construct a five-floor building crowned by a mechanical penthouse and equipment space. The entire building is designed on a 10'-8" wide by 22'-0" deep structural bay module which allows for future flexibility of lab configuration as science and applications evolve. The building floor plan locates all public and receiving functions on the lower two levels.   Administrative and office spaces are positioned to take advantage of daylight and views. An atrium will connect the lower two levels of the building while providing daylight to all adjacent spaces. All three agencies will share a common public entry on the south side of the building block. Public parking is directly adjacent to the entry.

An elevator/stair core is located at the east side of the atrium providing direct access to the reception area, and another elevator core is positioned near the middle of the building. This elevator core will include both passenger elevators and a service elevator which will provide service up to the penthouse level.

The landscape design and site improvements incorporates water-saving native plants, and low maintenance approaches.   The entire landscape will be irrigated by an automatically-controlled, low-water-output, drip system.

Heated building area is 190,000 square feet; Construction Budget is ⬚⬚⬚⬚⬚⬚⬚.

The desire and need for this project is significant. The construction must be completed so that occupancy can start no later than ⬚⬚⬚⬚.

Figure 6-16. *A general description of the project, including its scope and conditions, is included in the specification set.*

STANDARD ORGANIZATION OF SPECIFICATIONS

MasterFormat is the specifications-writing standard for most commercial building design and construction projects in North America. It lists titles and section numbers for organizing data about construction requirements, products, and activities. By standardizing such information, MasterFormat facilitates communication among architects, specifiers, contractors and suppliers, which helps them meet building owners' requirements, timelines and budgets.

The numbers and titles presented here are identical to the numbers and titles contained in the MasterFormat® 2016 publication available for purchase from the Construction Specifications Institute (CSI) and Construction Specifications Canada (CSC).

Contents reflect MasterFormat titles and numbers as of April 2016. Consult http://www.masterformat.com/revisions/ for the most current additions and changes to MasterFormat.

MasterFormat numbers and titles are intentionally structured for anticipated growth and expansion in the future. CSI and CSC encourage all interested parties to provide input using the "Propose a Revision" link on http://www.masterformat.com/revisions/ so that as the built environment evolves so can MasterFormat. Updates to MasterFormat are made annually.

To learn more about MasterFormat training, certification and local chapter information from CSI go to http://www.csinet.org/ or from CSC go to http://www.csc-dcc.ca/. **For information about licensing use of MasterFormat for commercial or educational purposes, contact CSI at http://www.csinet.org/, csi@csinet.org or by calling 800-689-2900.**

For additional information, visit qr.njatcdb.org Item #6600

Figure 6-17. *The CSI maintains the standard for the organization of specification sets.*

The MasterFormat facilitates more effective communication between all parties involved in a construction project including the architects, specifiers, contractors, suppliers, and construction workers.

It is necessary for contractors and field supervisors to be familiar with specification articles that pertain to not only their own work, but also other areas that may directly affect that work. It is also important that a tradesperson review their craft specifications, as well as related specifications. This will help in understanding the overall scope of the job and help prevent costly rework.

Tech Fact

Similar to the filing system used by libraries to easily locate an individual book, the CSI MasterFormat is used to find specific jobsite requirements from within a document that can number well into the hundreds of pages.

MASTERFORMAT ORGANIZATION

The CSI began creating a system to standardize construction contracts in 1963 and published the first standard, which contained 16 divisions. The term *MasterFormat* first appeared in 1975 when a revised standard was published. There were no changes until 1995 when the last 16-division standard was published. The next change would not take place until 2004. In 2004, the Master-Format specifications were further divided from the original 16 divisions. Some divisions are general, and others are specific. General requirements cover areas such as site work and may affect multiple crafts. Specific specifications are given for each craft, such as plumbing, mechanical, or electrical.

At the highest level, the MasterFormat defines two groups: the Procurement and Contracting Requirements Group and the Specifications Group. The Specifications Group consists of five subgroups. **See Figure 6-18.**

1. General Requirements Subgroup
2. Facility Construction Subgroup

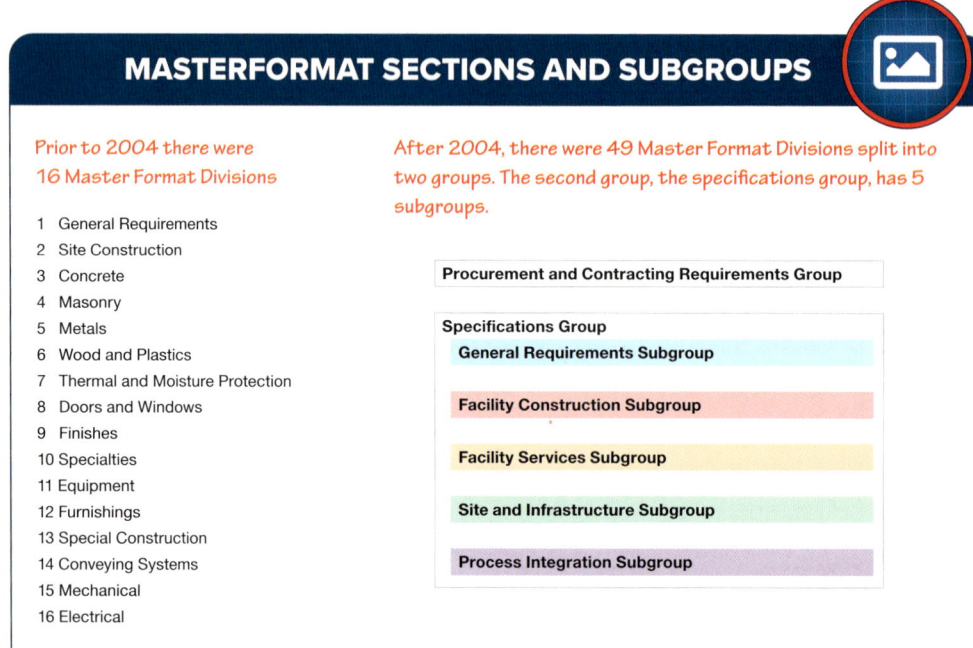

MASTERFORMAT SECTIONS AND SUBGROUPS

Prior to 2004 there were 16 Master Format Divisions

1 General Requirements
2 Site Construction
3 Concrete
4 Masonry
5 Metals
6 Wood and Plastics
7 Thermal and Moisture Protection
8 Doors and Windows
9 Finishes
10 Specialties
11 Equipment
12 Furnishings
13 Special Construction
14 Conveying Systems
15 Mechanical
16 Electrical

After 2004, there were 49 Master Format Divisions split into two groups. The second group, the specifications group, has 5 subgroups.

Procurement and Contracting Requirements Group

Specifications Group
General Requirements Subgroup
Facility Construction Subgroup
Facility Services Subgroup
Site and Infrastructure Subgroup
Process Integration Subgroup

Figure 6-18. *The 2004 MasterFormat revision created groups and subgroups to further aid in organizing the sections of the MasterFormat.*

3. Facility Services Subgroup
4. Site and Infrastructure Subgroup
5. Process Equipment Subgroup

2004 MasterFormat

The 2004 revision of the MasterFormat made a significant change to address the ever-growing complexity of buildings and the construction process. This edition expanded the number of divisions from 16 to 49 and increased the classification numbering system for sections from five to six digits.

Some key differences in the 2004 MasterFormat include:

1. The revised system can cover commercial, industrial, and process specifications.
2. There is room for growth built into the system, allowing for emerging technologies, change, and expansion.
3. The revision makes it easier to locate information. For example, Divisions 20 through 29 (with Division 20 and 29 reserved for future expansion) cover and expand the information formerly found in Divisions 15 and 16. The new format created several new divisions where electricians can look to find information. **See Figure 6-19.**

MasterFormat Numbering System

CSI's MasterFormat has changed over its history and continues to adapt to the needs of the construction industry. Although there have been multiple revisions since 1995, the most prevalent version of the MasterFormat is the 2014 publication; however, some owners and designers still use the more simplified 1995 version of the MasterFormat. A detailed listing of each of the changes that have occurred in the MasterFormat can be viewed in a change log on CSI's website.

The construction industry has been historically slow to adopt new ideas, which is the reason that several versions of the MasterFormat exist, and why construction professionals should

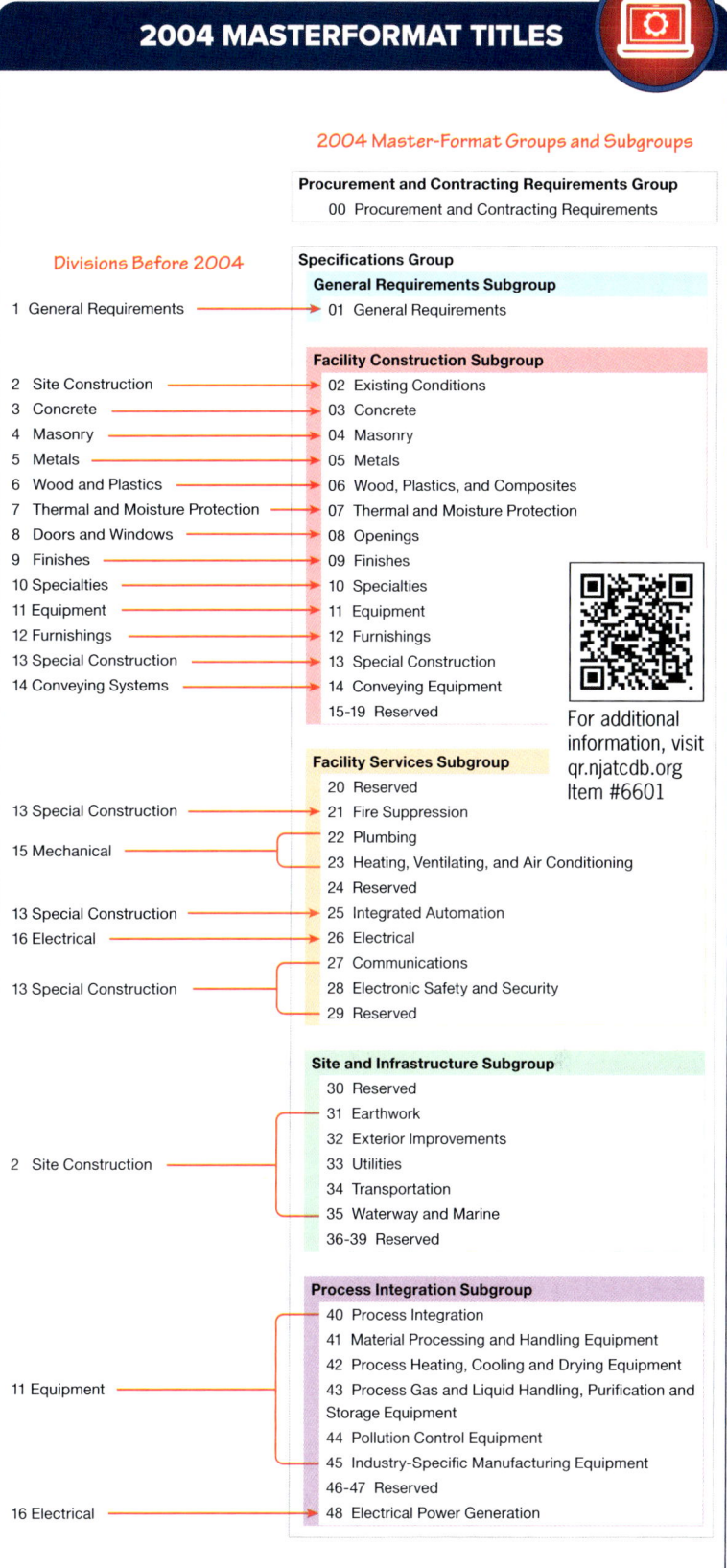

2004 MASTERFORMAT TITLES

2004 Master-Format Groups and Subgroups

Procurement and Contracting Requirements Group
  00 Procurement and Contracting Requirements

Divisions Before 2004

Specifications Group
  General Requirements Subgroup
1 General Requirements → 01 General Requirements

  Facility Construction Subgroup
2 Site Construction → 02 Existing Conditions
3 Concrete → 03 Concrete
4 Masonry → 04 Masonry
5 Metals → 05 Metals
6 Wood and Plastics → 06 Wood, Plastics, and Composites
7 Thermal and Moisture Protection → 07 Thermal and Moisture Protection
8 Doors and Windows → 08 Openings
9 Finishes → 09 Finishes
10 Specialties → 10 Specialties
11 Equipment → 11 Equipment
12 Furnishings → 12 Furnishings
13 Special Construction → 13 Special Construction
14 Conveying Systems → 14 Conveying Equipment
  15-19 Reserved

  Facility Services Subgroup
  20 Reserved
13 Special Construction → 21 Fire Suppression
  22 Plumbing
15 Mechanical → 23 Heating, Ventilating, and Air Conditioning
  24 Reserved
13 Special Construction → 25 Integrated Automation
16 Electrical → 26 Electrical
  27 Communications
13 Special Construction → 28 Electronic Safety and Security
  29 Reserved

  Site and Infrastructure Subgroup
  30 Reserved
  31 Earthwork
  32 Exterior Improvements
2 Site Construction → 33 Utilities
  34 Transportation
  35 Waterway and Marine
  36-39 Reserved

  Process Integration Subgroup
  40 Process Integration
  41 Material Processing and Handling Equipment
  42 Process Heating, Cooling and Drying Equipment
11 Equipment → 43 Process Gas and Liquid Handling, Purification and Storage Equipment
  44 Pollution Control Equipment
  45 Industry-Specific Manufacturing Equipment
  46-47 Reserved
16 Electrical → 48 Electrical Power Generation

For additional information, visit qr.njatcdb.org Item #6601

Figure 6-19. *The movement from 16 to 49 divisions in the 2004 MasterFormat allowed for more granularity in each of the sections.*

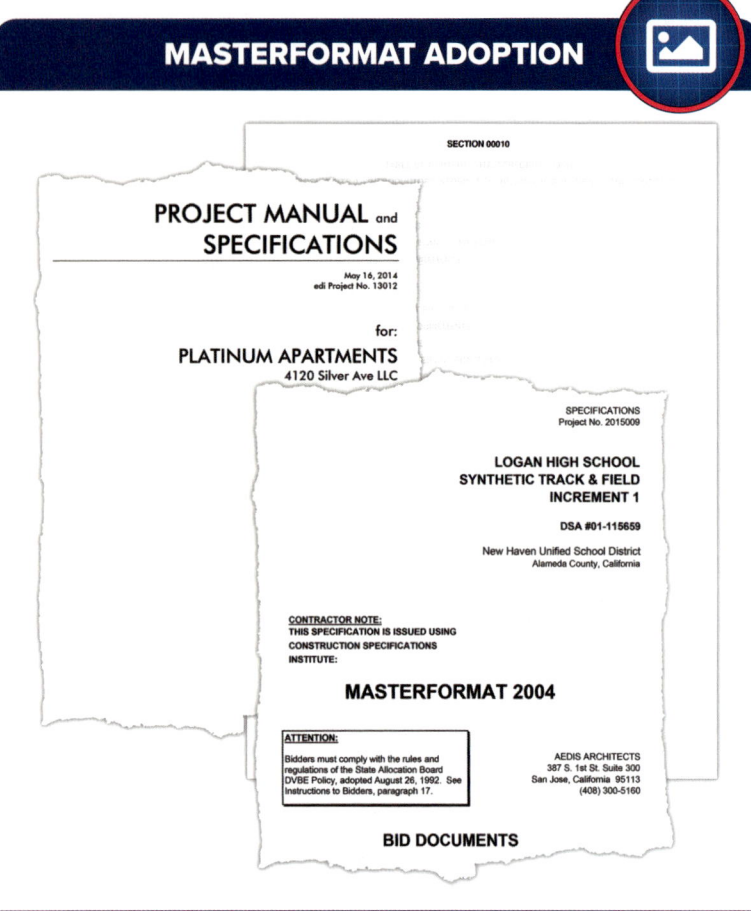

MASTERFORMAT ADOPTION

SECTION 00010

PROJECT MANUAL and
SPECIFICATIONS

May 16, 2014
edi Project No. 13012

for:

PLATINUM APARTMENTS
4120 Silver Ave LLC

SPECIFICATIONS
Project No. 2015009

LOGAN HIGH SCHOOL
SYNTHETIC TRACK & FIELD
INCREMENT 1

DSA #01-115659

New Haven Unified School District
Alameda County, California

CONTRACTOR NOTE:
THIS SPECIFICATION IS ISSUED USING
CONSTRUCTION SPECIFICATIONS
INSTITUTE:

MASTERFORMAT 2004

ATTENTION:
Bidders must comply with the rules and
regulations of the State Allocation Board
DVBE Policy, adopted August 26, 1992. See
Instructions to Bidders, paragraph 17.

AEDIS ARCHITECTS
387 S. 1st St. Suite 300
San Jose, California 95113
(408) 300-5160

BID DOCUMENTS

Figure 6-20. Construction professionals need to be able to work in either the earlier 16-section version or the 49-section version of the MasterFormat because both are still in use.

be versed in several versions. **See Figure 6-20.**

A discussion of MasterFormat revisions requires the understanding that no particular revision date is mandated; the design team chooses which version of the construction project documents it will employ. The milestone to remember is 2004, when there were significant changes to the MasterFormat structure; more minor revisions were made between 2004 and 2014. Changes during this period were generally new subdivisions, deleted subdivisions, and renumbered subdivisions.

Design teams generally choose a format based on their preference of a 16-division format or a 49-division format. If the choice is 16 divisions, the 1975 format is used. If they choose 49 divisions, one of the newest formats, which have at least minor revisions every two years, are used.

The new numbering systems have the following advantages:

1. The ability to address the ever-growing complexity of buildings and the construction process. The 49 divisions and a 6-digit numbering system made it possible for the system to provide additional

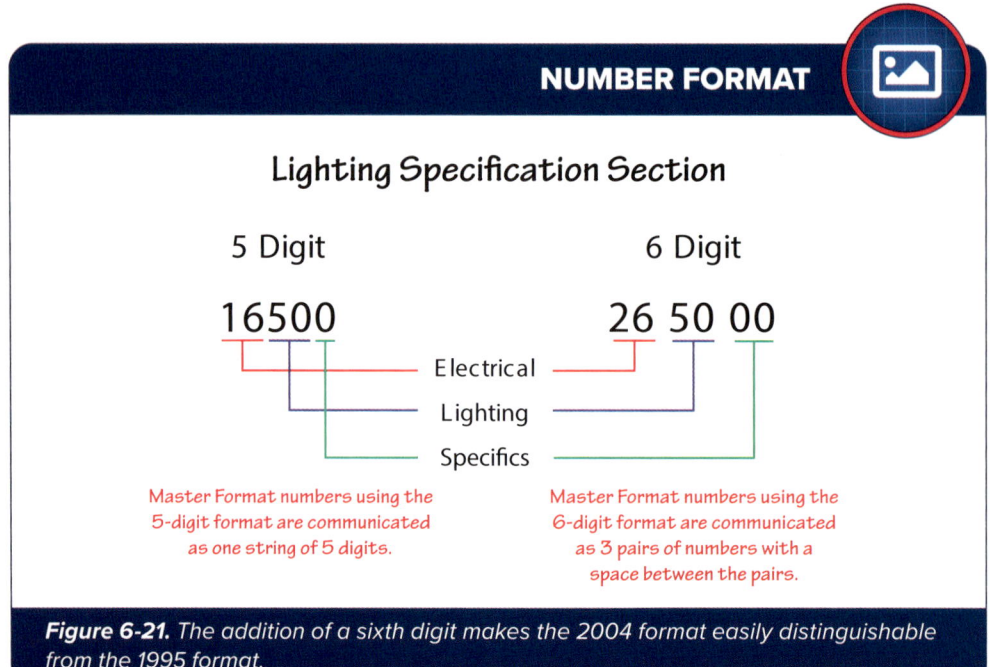

NUMBER FORMAT

Lighting Specification Section

5 Digit

16500

6 Digit

26 50 00

Electrical
Lighting
Specifics

Master Format numbers using the 5-digit format are communicated as one string of 5 digits.

Master Format numbers using the 6-digit format are communicated as 3 pairs of numbers with a space between the pairs.

Figure 6-21. The addition of a sixth digit makes the 2004 format easily distinguishable from the 1995 format.

detail, new technologies, construction processes, the use of database tools, and the ability to address project life-cycle issues. **See Figure 6-21.**

2. The format change in 2004 kept Divisions 1 through 14 almost intact, with few minor changes. Divisions 15 and 16 became Divisions 21 through 28.

3. The revision also provided for future expansion by reserving sections of the numbering system for definition and utilization as needed.

4. Each of the four levels of detail in the MasterFormat allow for additional detail than was possible in the 1995 publication of MasterFormat. **See Figure 6-22.**

5. It provides a level of detail where necessary for user-defined information. **See Figure 6-23.**

A detailed exploration of the expanded numbering system reveals that it is systematically arranged with finer levels of detail nested within higher-level topics, much in the same manner as an outline. The levels created in the

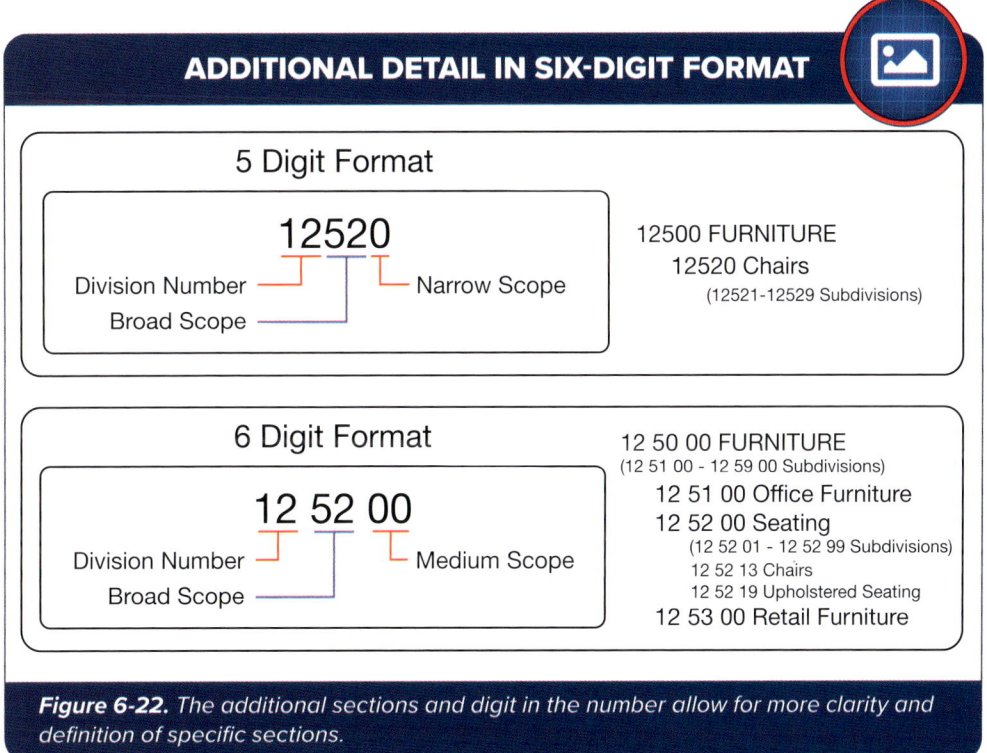

Figure 6-22. *The additional sections and digit in the number allow for more clarity and definition of specific sections.*

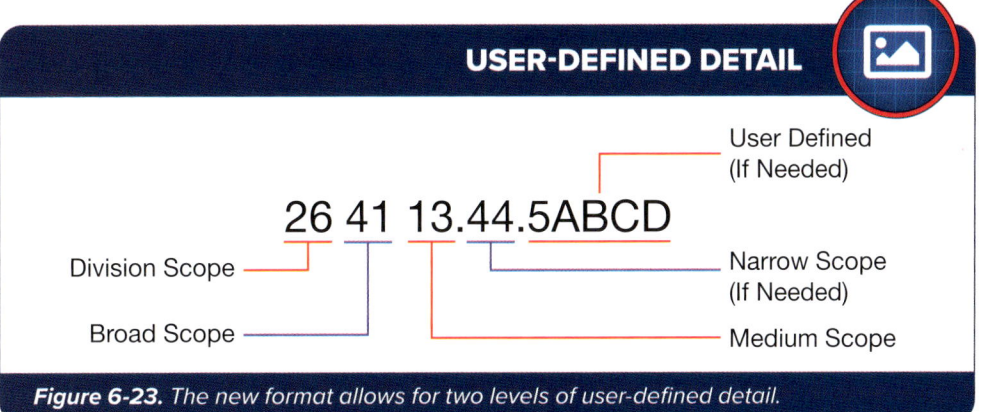

Figure 6-23. *The new format allows for two levels of user-defined detail.*

new number system include groups, subgroups, divisions, and sections.

Each section of the 2004 MasterFormat consists of specifics about the material or process that is being described. Each subgroup is further broken down using a standard format for divisions. This format employs a standard number system with three sets of two-digit numbers each separated by a space. The new format also made the standard more user friendly by adding consistency to the numbering of second-level subsections. Second-level subsections located under two or more sections and that have duplicate information have consistent second-level subsection numbers. For example, the subsections *Operations and Maintenance*, *Common Work Results*, *Schedules*, and *Commissioning* are numbered using the parallel system. **See Figure 6-24.**

PARALLEL NUMBERING

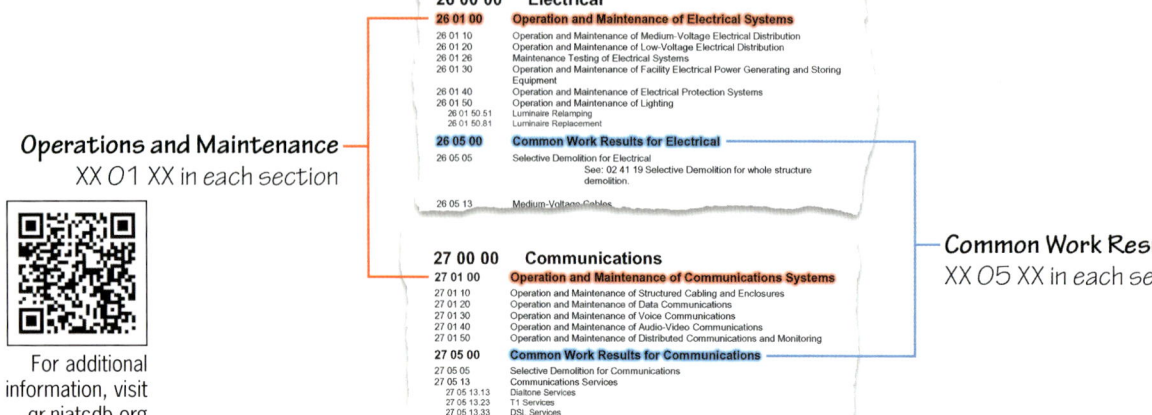

Operations and Maintenance —
XX 01 XX in each section

For additional information, visit qr.njatcdb.org Item #6602

Common Work Results
XX 05 XX in each section

Parallel Numbering
XX 01 00 Operations and Maintenance
XX 05 00 Common Work Results
XX 06 00 Schedules and Automation
XX 08 00 Commissioning

Additional Examples in the Divisions and Facilities Subgroups
2X 07 00 XXX Insulation
2X 09 00 Instrumentation and Control for XXX

Figure 6-24. *Parallel numbering of sections and divisions aid in the usage of the MasterFormat since common topics across sections have similar numbers.*

Specification Variability

Specifications using the MasterFormat may vary depending on the design professional. A set of specifications will often not contain all of the sections provided in the MasterFormat regardless of the edition implemented. Its use, however, does provide consistency.

For example, if a contractor wanted to know the requirements for construction facilities on a project where the specifications were created using MasterFormat, they will be found in Section 01 52 00.

SUMMARY

The additional content provided in the schedules and specifications ensures that the final product created with a complete set of construction drawings is exactly what was intended at the project inception. Without table-based details about components that vary by usage and location and a detailed list of requirements, the construction drawings would either end up cluttered, making them hard to utilize, or there would be ambiguity that would result in various interpretations of design intent. Both would result in a less than satisfied building owner.

For additional information, visit qr.njatcdb.org Item #6603

REVIEW QUESTIONS

1. The information provided in schedules includes trade-specific details about __?__ specified for use in the construction process. (Select all that are correct.)

   a. equipment
   b. materials
   c. responsibilities
   d. tools

2. Schedules contain single pieces of data about each of the individual categories of items in a building.

   a. True   b. False

3. Room schedules are used primarily on commercial and industrial prints but are sometimes also included in residential drawing sets.

   a. True   b. False

4. Control circuit schedules would usually be found on the __?__ drawings.

   a. architectural
   b. electrical
   c. mechanical
   d. plumbing

5. The specifications, in support of the blueprints, are the __?__ of the design intent created by the architects and engineers of a project.

   a. final part
   b. first part
   c. second half
   d. third part

6. The specifications provide a list of detailed job requirements, under which all work may proceed.

   a. True   b. False

7. The __?__ of the specifications are a set of requirements like time and duration of the project, how to deal with conflicts when they arise, and the submittal and records documentation requirements of the project.

   a. facility construction subgroup
   b. facility services subgroup
   c. general conditions
   d. project scope

8. Although there have been multiple revisions since 1995, the most prevalent version of the MasterFormat is the __?__ publication.

   a. 1995
   b. 2004
   c. 2012
   d. 2014

APPENDIX A
ABBREVIATIONS

NOTE: This section contains a list of common abbreviations used by Electrical Workers and in the construction trades. There are specific abbreviations for switches, outlets, wire types, and square and round box notes. These abbreviations are found in this text and in electrical handbooks.

A or amp	amperes		A/C	air conditioner
AB	anchor bolt		B or BA	bathroom
AC	above counter		BALC	balcony
AC	air conditioning		BASM	basement
AC	alternating current		BATT	batten
AFF	above finished floor		BC	broom closet
AGGR	aggregate		BD	board
AHU	air-handling unit		BG	below grade
AL	aluminum		BL	building
ALT	alternate		BLDG	building
ALUM	aluminum		BLK	black
ANSI	American National Standards Institute		BLK	block
			BLKG	blocking
ANT	antenna		BLT-IN	built in
AP	access panel		BLU	blue
APPROX	approximate		BLO	blower
ASB	asbestos		BM	beam
ASPH	asphalt		BM	benchmark
ASTM	American Society for Testing and Materials		BP	blueprint
			BR	bedroom
AUTO	automatic		BRG	bearing
AWG	American wire gauge		BRK	brick

BRKR	breaker	COL	column
BRN	brown	COM	common
BSMT	basement	COMB	combination
BTU	British thermal unit	CONC	concrete
BTM	bottom	COND	conductor
BX	flexible armored cable	CONST	construction
C	common	CONTR	contractor
C to C	center-to-center	COP	copper
CA	cold air	CORR	corridor
CAB	cabinet	COV	cutoff valve
CALK	caulking	CSI	Construction Standards Institute
CB	catch basin		
CB	circuit breaker	CSK	countersink
CEIL JST	ceiling joist	CSP	central switch panel
CEM	cement	CT	current transformer
CER	ceramic	CTL	central
CF	cement floor	CTR	center
CI	circuit interrupter	CU	copper
CJ	control joint	CU	cubic
CKT	circuit	CV	check valve
CL	ceiling joist	CW	cold water
CL	center line	D	disposal
CLG	ceiling	D	drain
CLO	closet	D	dryer
CLR	clear	DB	decibel
CMU	concrete masonry unit	DC	direct current
CND	conduit	DCP	dimmer control panel

DEG	degree		F	Fahrenheit
DET	detail		F	fluorescent
DF	drinking fountain		FAB	fabricate
DIA	diameter		FAM RM	family room
DIM	dimension		FB	fuse block
DIM	dimmer		FBRK	firebrick
DIF	diffuser		FC	foot candle
DISP	disposal		FC	furred ceiling
DK	decking		FD	floor drain
DMR	dimmer		FIN	finished
DN	down		FIN FLR	finished floor
DNG RM	dining room		FIN GR	finished grade
DP	double pole		FIX	fixture
DPR	damper		FL	flashing
DPDT	double pole, double throw		FL JST	floor joist
DPST	double pole, single throw		FLEX	flexible
DR	dining room		FLAM	flammable
DS	downspout		FLR	floor
DSC	disconnect		FLUR	fluorescent
DT	double throw		FLUOR	fluorescent
DW	dishwasher		FMC	flexible metal conduit
DW	drywall		FND	foundation
E	east		FO	finished opening
E	voltage		FOS	face of studs
EG	earth ground		FOUND	foundation
ELEC	electric or electrical		FP	fireplace
ELEV	elevation		FP	fireproof
ELV	elevation		FPRF	fireproof
EMT	electrical metallic tubing		FS	flow switch
ENT	entrance		FS	full size
ENT	electrical nonmetallic tubing		FSBL	fusible
EP	electrical panel		FSC	full scale
EP	explosion proof		FT	feet
EST	estimate		FU	fuse
EWC	electric water cooler		FUBX	fuse box
EXC	excavate		FUR	furnace
EXH	exhaust		FURN	furnace
EXHV	exhaust vent		FXTY	fixture
EXP JT	expansion joint		G	gas
EXPO	exposed		GA	gauge
EXT	exterior		GALV	galvanized
EXT GR	exterior grade		GAR	garage
EXTN	extension		GD	ground

GFCI	ground fault circuit interrupter		KIT	kitchen
GFI	ground fault interrupter		KO	knockout
GIRD	girder		KVA	kilovolt ampere
GL	glass		KW	kilowatt
GL	grade line		L	inductor
GND	ground		L CL	linen closet
GR	grade		LAU	laundry
GRD	grade		LAU	laundry room
GRN	green		LAV	lavatory
GRY	gray		LB	pound
GWB	gypsum wallboard		LDG	landing
GVL	gravel		LED	light-emitting diode
GYP	gypsum		LEV	level
GYP BD	gypsum board		LFMC	liquid-tight flexible metal conduit
HA	hot air		LFNM	liquid-tight flexible nonmetallic conduit
HB	hose bib			
HDR	header		LH	left hand
HGT	height		LIB	library
HORIZ	horizontal		LIN	linen
HP	horsepower		LIV	living room
HT	heater		LR	living room
HT	height		LT	light
HTG	heating		LTS	lights
HTR	heater		LV	louver
HVAC	heating ventilating and air conditioning		LUM	lumber
			M	meter
HW	hot water		M	motor
HWH	hot water heater		M-G	motor generator
Hz or cps	hertz (cycles)		MANUF	manufacturer
I	current		MAS	masonry
ID	inside diameter		MAT	material
ILLUM	illuminate		MAX	maximum
IMC	intermediate metal conduit		MC	medicine cabinet
IN	inches		MCM	thousand (milli) circular mils
INCAND	incandescent		MD	medium
INS	insulation		MDP	main distribution panel
INST	install		MECH	mechanical
INSUL	insulation		MEMB	membrane
INT	interior		MH	manhole
J-BOX	junction box		MIN	minimum
JCT	junction		MIRR	mirror
JST	joist		MN	main
JT	joint			

MOT	motor	PLS BD	plaster board
MRB	marble	PLY	plywood
MTL	metal	PLYWD	plywood
N	north	PNL	panel
NA	not applicable	PREFAB	prefabricated
NAT	natural	PRCST	precast
NAT GR	natural grade	PROP	property
NEC	*National Electrical Code*	PT	part
NEG	negative	PT	pressure-treated (lumber)
NELA	National Electric Light Association	PTD	painted
		PVC	polyvinyl chloride
NFPA	National Fire Prevention Association	PVMT	pavement
		PWR	power
NG	natural grade	QTY	quality
NIC	not in contract	QTY	quantity
NO	number	R	radius
NOM	nominal	R	range
NTS	not to scale	R	recessed
N/C	normally closed	R	resistance
N/O	normally open	RAD	radiator
O	overload contactor	RAD	radius
OC	on center	RCPT	receptacle
OC	over current	RD	roof drain
OD	outside diameter	RD	round
OH	overhead	REBAR	reinforcing bar
OPG	opening	REC	recessed
OPP	opposite	RECP	receptacle
OSB	oriented strand board	REF	reference
OUT	outlet	REF	refrigerator
OVHD	overhead	REFR	refrigerator
P	power	REINF	reinforced
PAR	parallel	REG	register
PART	partition	RET	return
PB	push button	RFG	roofing
PC	pull chain	RGH	rough
PERM	permanent	RH	right hand
PERP	perpendicular	RIS	riser
PH	phase	RM	room
PL	plate	RMC	rigid metal conduit
PLAS	plastic	RNC	rigid nonmetallic conduit
PLAT	platform	RO	rough opening
PLMG	plumbing	ROW	right of way
PLS	plaster		

S	south
S	switch
SAN	sanitary
SC	solid core
SCR	silicon-controlled rectifier
SCR	screw
SCRN	screen
SD	smoke detector
SD	storm drain
SDG	siding
SECT	section
SERV	service
SEW	sewer
SHTG	sheathing
SIM	similar
SL	sliding
SLT	skylight
SP	single pole
SPDT	single pole, double throw
SPECS	specifications
SPST	single pole, single throw
SST	stainless steel
STAT	thermostat
STO	storage
STL	steel
STR	structural
SUB	substitute
SUS CLG	suspended ceiling
SW	switch
T	thermostat
T & G	tar and gravel
T & G	tongue and groove
TC	temperature control
TC	terra-cotta
TEL	telephone
TELE	telephone
TEMP	temperature
THK	thick
TR	tread
TS	terminal strip
TV	television
TW	top of wall

TUB	tubing
TYP	typical
TZ	terrazo
U	underground
UBC	Uniform Building Code
UF	underground feeder
UGND	underground
UL	Underwriters Laboratories
UNFIN	unfinished
UR	urinal
USE	underground service entrance
UTIL	utility
UTY	utility
V	valve
V	volts or voltage
VA	volt-amp
VAN	vanity
VB	vapor barrier
VB	vinyl base
VD	voltage drop
VENT	ventilation
VIN	vinyl
VOL	volume
VP	vent pipe
VT	vinyl tile
W	watt
W	west
W/	with
W/O	without
WC	water closet
WD	wood
WH	water heater
WH	weep hole
WIC	walk in closet
WM	washing machine
WP	waterproof
WS	waste stack
WT	weight
WTHPRF or WP	weatherproof
WV	wall vent
XP	explosion proof
YD	yard

HOW TO READ A TAPE MEASURE

Measurements used in construction are either provided on a drawing or taken in the field. These measurements are usually in feet, inches, and fractions of an inch. The Electrical Worker must be able to locate the measurements on a rule or tape measure. In some cases, the measurements must be added or subtracted to achieve the desired results.

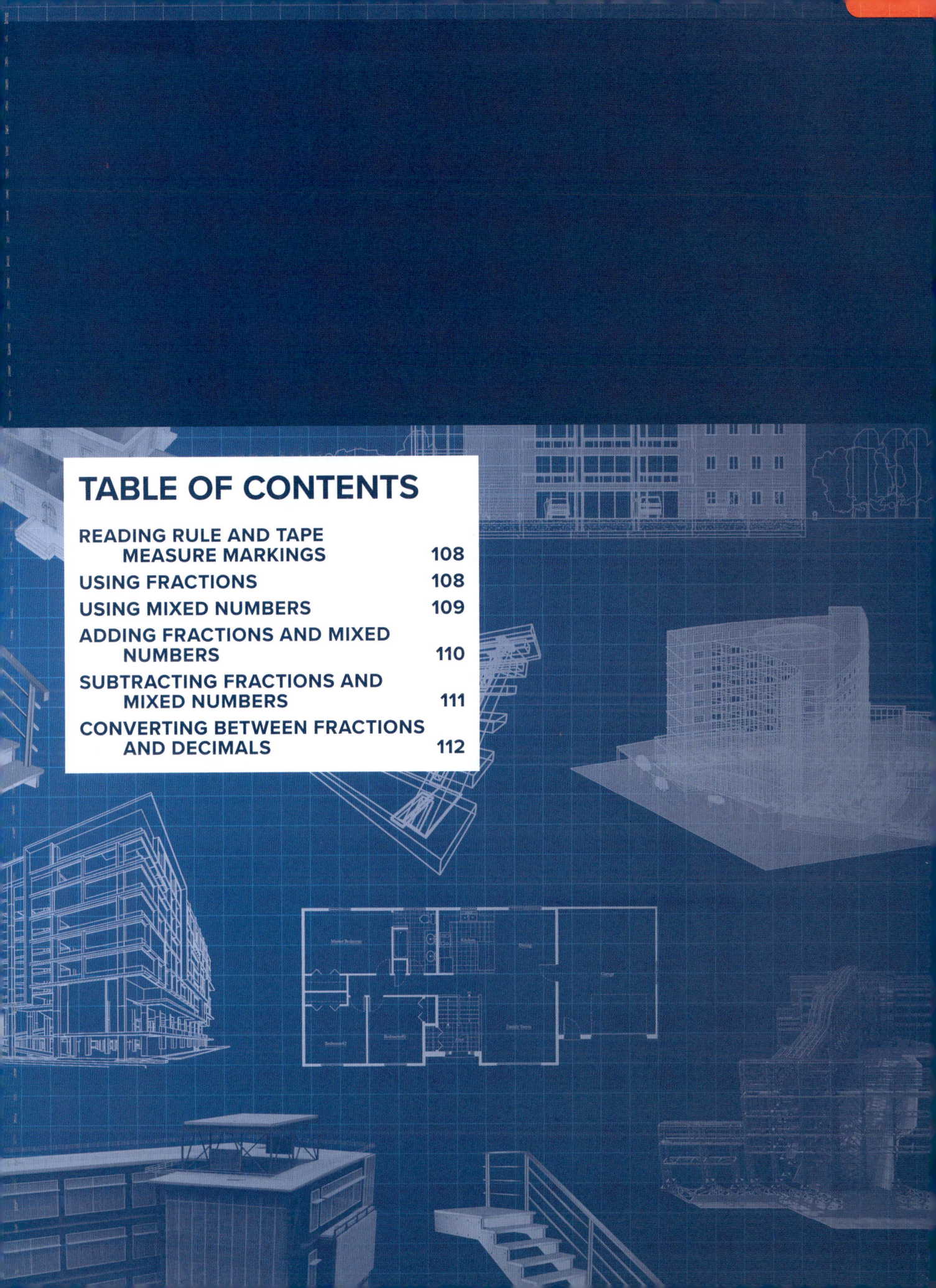

TABLE OF CONTENTS

READING RULE AND TAPE MEASURE MARKINGS

There are different types of markings on different measuring tools. However, all rules and tape measures have several markings in common.

The most prominent markings on a tape measure are the large numbers at every inch, located next to the long lines. **See Figure B-1.** These long lines usually extend all the way across the tape. The numbers designate the number of inches from the end. Every 12" there is another number, which represents the number of feet from the end. In addition, there are smaller markings between the inch lines. These markings represent fractions of an inch.

Each inch is divided into 16 equal divisions. Each division represents $\frac{1}{16}$". Between the inch lines, the longest marks represent halves of an inch and the next longest marks after that represent quarters of an inch. After that, the marks continue to get smaller for eighths and sixteenths of an inch.

Some measuring tools may have markings representing other divisions. For example, some tools have markings every $\frac{1}{32}$" for the first foot and every $\frac{1}{16}$" after that. Some tools have additional markings at other intervals for carpentry applications, such as every 16" for locating studs. Others have standard inch and foot measurements along one edge and metric measurements along the other edge. These extra markings can usually be ignored in construction applications.

USING FRACTIONS

Fractions of an inch are expressed with a numerator and a denominator. The numerator and denominator are separated by a horizontal or inclined fraction bar. The denominator is the lower number of the fraction. For example, in the fraction $\frac{5}{16}$", 16 is the denominator. The denominator indicates the number of equal divisions of the inch. A greater number of divisions indicates a greater degree of precision.

The numerator is the upper number in the fraction. The numerator shows the number of actual divisions that make up a given length of measurement. For example, $\frac{5}{16}$" indicates an inch that has been divided into 16 equal parts (the denominator), of which the actual length of measurement is equal to 5 of those parts (the numerator).

The distance between the smallest marks on a tape measure represents a length of $\frac{1}{16}$". For example, the distance from the 12" mark to the next small mark is $\frac{1}{16}$". **See Figure B-2.** A distance of two marks is $\frac{2}{16}$", representing 2 parts of the 16 equal parts of an inch.

The numerator of a fraction is normally an odd number. If the numerator is an even number, these fractional values are converted to simpler equivalent fractions. For example, $\frac{2}{16}$" is equal to $\frac{1}{8}$". Some values can be further simplified. The fraction $\frac{8}{16}$" is equal to $\frac{4}{8}$", $\frac{2}{4}$", and $\frac{1}{2}$". This simplification is used when adding and subtracting fractions of an inch.

TAPE MEASURE MARKINGS

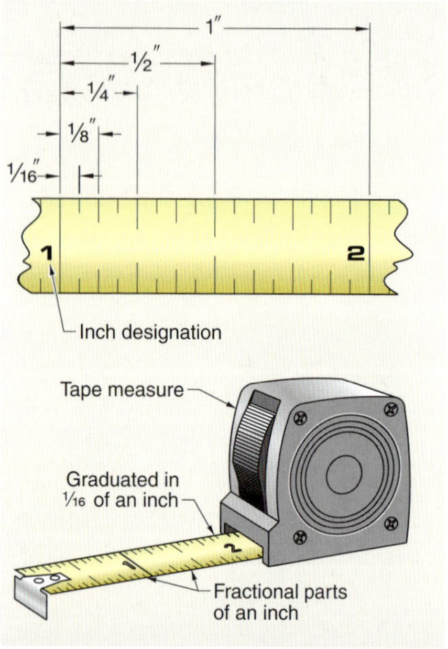

Figure B-1. A tape measure or rule has markings to indicate the inches and fractions of an inch.

EQUIVALENT FRACTIONS

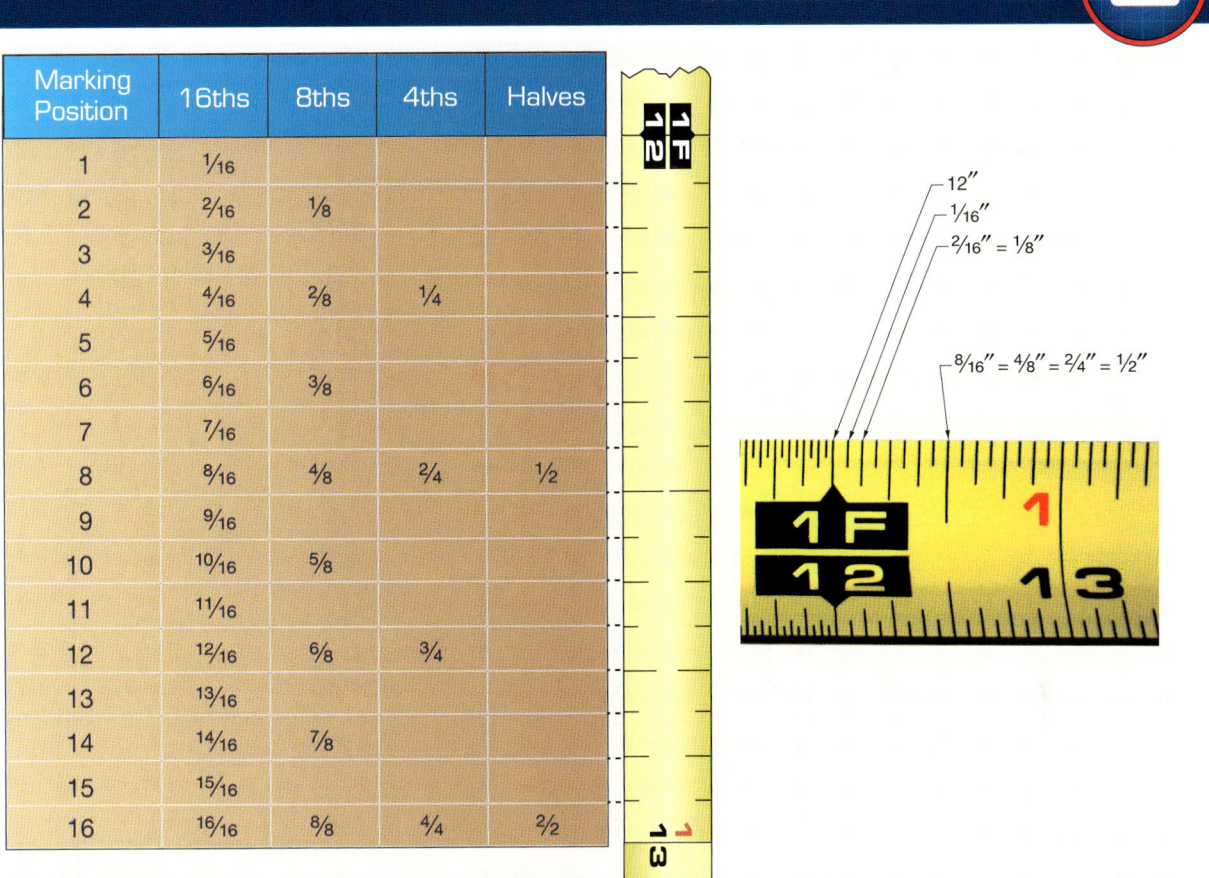

Marking Position	16ths	8ths	4ths	Halves
1	1/16			
2	2/16	1/8		
3	3/16			
4	4/16	2/8	1/4	
5	5/16			
6	6/16	3/8		
7	7/16			
8	8/16	4/8	2/4	1/2
9	9/16			
10	10/16	5/8		
11	11/16			
12	12/16	6/8	3/4	
13	13/16			
14	14/16	7/8		
15	15/16			
16	16/16	8/8	4/4	2/2

Figure B-2. *Many fractions are equivalent to other fractions. These equivalent fractions should be memorized.*

USING MIXED NUMBERS

A mixed number is a combination of a whole number and a fraction. For example, a distance measurement of 12 5/16" is a mixed number that is a combination of the number 12, representing 12", and the fraction 5/16, representing 5/16". The number and the fraction are added to represent the total distance. **See Figure B-3.**

An improper fraction, such as 15/12", has a numerator larger than its denominator. An improper fraction is normally reduced to a mixed number. The numerator is divided by the denominator, and the remainder is kept as a fraction. For example, 15 is divisible by 12 only 1 time with a remainder of 3. Therefore, 15/12" is equal to 1 3/12", or 1 1/4".

MIXED NUMBERS

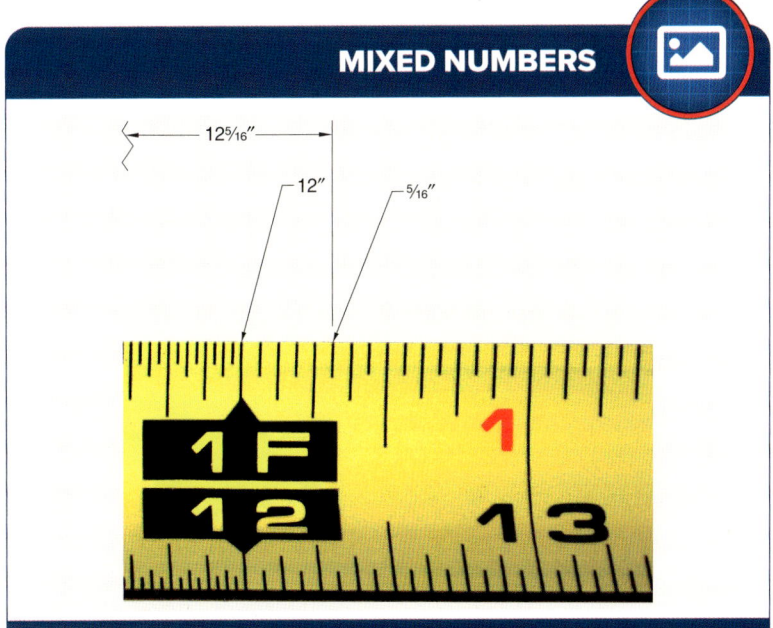

Figure B-3. *A mixed number is a combination of a whole number and a fraction.*

A measurement in feet and inches is treated in a similar manner to a measurement in inches and fractions of an inch. An inch represents $\frac{1}{12}$ of a foot. For example, a measurement of 5" represents a distance of $\frac{5}{12}$'. A distance of 15" represents a distance of $\frac{15}{12}$', or 1 $\frac{3}{12}$', or 1'-3". Similarly, a measurement of 2'-7 $\frac{1}{4}$" represents a measurement of 2' plus 7" plus $\frac{1}{4}$".

A measurement in feet can be converted to its equivalent measurement in inches by multiplying it by 12. For example, a measurement of 1' is equal to 12" ($1 \times 12 = 12$), and a measurement of 4' is equal to 48" ($4 \times 12 = 48$).

There are many situations where a measurement in feet and inches must be converted to inches. To accomplish this, the number of feet in the measurement are multiplied by 12 and added to the inch part of the measurement. For example, a measurement of 1'-1" is equal to 13" ($1 \times 12 + 1 = 13$), and 4'-3" is equal to 51" ($4 \times 12 + 3 = 51$).

ADDING FRACTIONS AND MIXED NUMBERS

In the field, dimensions on prints as well as other foot and inch measurements will need to be added together. Calculations involving feet are simple. Calculations involving inches are more complex because inches are based on 12 equal divisions of a foot, and fractions of an inch are based on 16 equal divisions.

Since the foot, inch, and fraction systems are based on different divisions, foot, inch, and fraction calculations must be performed separately and then combined. In order to add fractions, both fractions must have the same denominator, called a common denominator.

To add two fractions, the numerator and denominator of the fraction with the smaller denominator are multiplied by a factor so that the denominator equals the larger number denominator. Once the common denominator is determined, the numerators are added. For example, when adding $\frac{1}{4}$" and $\frac{5}{8}$", both the numerator and denominator of $\frac{1}{4}$" are multiplied by a factor of 2 to change the fraction to $\frac{2}{8}$". **See Figure B-4.** (It may be necessary to multiply the numerators and denominators of both fractions by a factor in order for the denominators to be equal.)

With a common denominator of 8, $\frac{2}{8}$" and $\frac{5}{8}$" are added for a total $\frac{7}{8}$" ($\frac{2}{8} + \frac{5}{8} = \frac{7}{8}$). When adding $\frac{1}{2}$" and $\frac{5}{16}$", both the numerator and denominator of $\frac{1}{2}$ are multiplied by a factor of 8 to change the fraction to $\frac{8}{16}$. With a common denominator of 16, $\frac{8}{16}$" and $\frac{5}{16}$" are added for a total of $\frac{13}{16}$" ($\frac{8}{16} + \frac{5}{16} = \frac{13}{16}$).

When the sum of two fractions is more than 1, the sum must be converted to a mixed number. For example, when adding $\frac{3}{4}$" and $\frac{7}{8}$", both the numerator and denominator of $\frac{3}{4}$" are multiplied by 2 to change the fraction to $\frac{6}{8}$". With a common denominator of 8, $\frac{6}{8}$" and $\frac{7}{8}$" are added for a total $1\frac{3}{8}$" ($\frac{6}{8} + \frac{7}{8} = \frac{13}{8}$). This fraction must be converted to a mixed number. The

ADDING FRACTIONS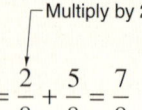

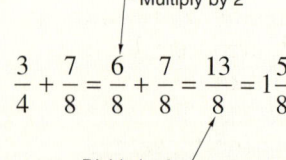

Figure B-4. *Fractions can be added by using a common denominator.*

ADDING MIXED NUMBERS

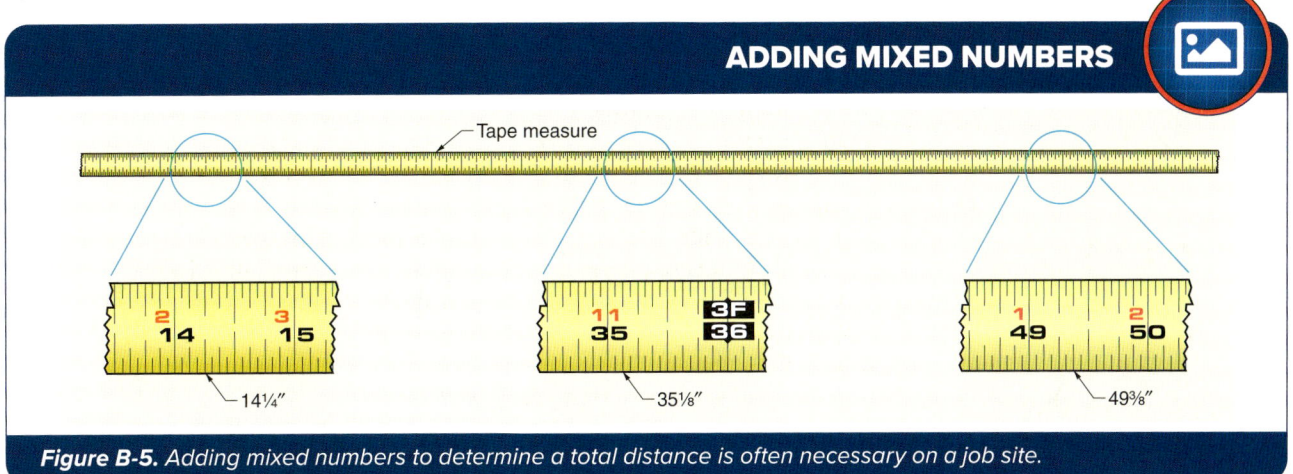

Figure B-5. *Adding mixed numbers to determine a total distance is often necessary on a job site.*

numerator is divided by the denominator and the remainder is kept as a fraction. For example, 13 is divisible by 8 only 1 time with a remainder of 5. Therefore, $^{13}\!/_8$" is equal to 1 $^5\!/_8$".

Length measurements are often given as mixed numbers. For example, a length is measured at 14 $^1\!/_4$", and another length is measured as 35 $^1\!/_8$". **See Figure B-5.** The whole inch part and the fraction part of the mixed numbers must be added separately, and the common denominator for the fraction part must be found first. In this case, the measurement of 14 $^1\!/_4$" is equal to 14 $^2\!/_8$". The sum of these two lengths is calculated as follows:

$$\begin{array}{r} 14\ ^2\!/_8" \\ +\ 35\ ^1\!/_8" \\ \hline 49\ ^3\!/_8" \end{array}$$

In some cases, the sum of the fraction part is more than 1. For example, a length is measured at 35 $^7\!/_8$" and another length is measured as 14 $^1\!/_4$". Again, the inch part and the fraction part of the mixed numbers are added separately, and the common denominator for the fraction part is found first. In this case, the measurement of 14 $^1\!/_4$" is equal to 14 $^2\!/_8$". The sum of these two lengths is calculated as follows:

$$\begin{array}{r} 35\ ^7\!/_8" \\ +\ 14\ ^2\!/_8" \\ \hline 49\ ^9\!/_8" \end{array}$$

The fraction part is an improper fraction that must be converted to a mixed number. The fraction $^9\!/_8$ is equivalent to 1 $^1\!/_8$. Therefore, the sum of 35 $^7\!/_8$" and 14 $^1\!/_4$" is 50 $^1\!/_8$".

Tech Fact

Fractions need to be converted to decimal numbers before being added on a calculator.

SUBTRACTING FRACTIONS AND MIXED NUMBERS

Foot and inch measurements on job sites or dimensions on prints may need to be subtracted from each other. Subtracting fractions is very similar to adding fractions. The fractions must be converted to fractions with a common denominator. The numerator and denominator of the fraction with the smaller denominator is multiplied by a factor so that the denominator equals the larger denominator. (It may be necessary to multiply the numerators and denominators of both fractions by a factor in order for the denominators to be equal.)

Once the common denominator is determined, the numerators are subtracted. For example, when subtracting $^1\!/_4$" from $^5\!/_8$", both the numerator and denominator of $^1\!/_4$" are multiplied by a factor of 2 to change the fraction to $^2\!/_8$".

SUBTRACTING FRACTIONS

Multiply by 2

$$\frac{5}{8} - \frac{1}{4} = \frac{5}{8} - \frac{2}{8} = \frac{3}{8}$$

Multiply by 8

$$\frac{1}{2} - \frac{5}{16} = \frac{8}{16} - \frac{5}{16} = \frac{3}{16}$$

Multiply by 2

$$37\frac{3}{4} - 5\frac{1}{2} = 37\frac{3}{4} - 5\frac{2}{4} = 32\frac{1}{4}$$

Figure B-6. *Mixed numbers can be subtracted by using a common denominator.*

See Figure B-6. With a common denominator of 8, ²⁄₈" is subtracted from ⅝" for a difference of ⅜" (⅝ − ²⁄₈ = ⅜).

When subtracting ⁵⁄₁₆" from ½", both the numerator and denominator of ½ are multiplied by a factor of 8 to change the fraction to ⁸⁄₁₆. With a common denominator of 16, ⁵⁄₁₆" is subtracted from ⁸⁄₁₆" for a difference of ³⁄₁₆" (⁸⁄₁₆ − ⁵⁄₁₆ = ³⁄₁₆).

There are situations where mixed numbers must be subtracted. Just like with addition, the inch part and the fraction part are subtracted separately. The common denominator for the fraction part must be found first. For example, a distance is measured at 37 ¾". A length of 5 ½" must be subtracted from the measurement. The numerator and denominator of the ½ must be multiplied by a factor of 2 to give ²⁄₄. The calculation is completed as follows:

$$\begin{array}{r} 37\ ¾" \\ -\ 5\ ²⁄₄" \\ \hline 32\ ¼" \end{array}$$

CONVERTING BETWEEN FRACTIONS AND DECIMALS

It is very useful to be able to convert between fractions of an inch and their decimal equivalents. Many calculations involving fractions are done on calculators. The fractions must be converted to decimal numbers so that they can be entered into the calculator. After the calculations are completed, the decimal number needs to be converted back to a fraction in order to use a tape measure.

The simplest method for converting between decimals and fractions is to use a conversion table. **See Figure B-7.** To convert from a fraction to a decimal, the fraction is located in the table and the equivalent decimal is found by following the line across in the table. To convert from a decimal to a fraction, the decimal number is found and the line followed back to its equivalent fraction.

For example, from the table the fraction ⁵⁄₁₆ is equal to 0.3125. Similarly, if the result of a calculation is 0.625, then the equivalent fraction is ⅝. If the decimal number is not in the table, the value in the table that is nearest to a decimal should be selected. For example, if the result of a calculation is 0.6, the nearest decimal in the table is 0.625 and the equivalent fraction is ⅝.

If a calculator is available, any fraction can be converted to a decimal by dividing the numbers. For example, the fraction ¾ can be converted to a decimal by dividing the numerator, 3, by the denominator, 4, resulting in 0.75. Similarly, the fraction ⁵⁄₁₆ can be converted to a decimal by dividing the 5 by the 16, resulting in 0.3125.

A calculator can also be used to convert a decimal number to a fraction. Simply multiply the decimal number by 16. This gives the number of 16ths in the fraction. For example, the decimal number 0.62 multiplied by 16 gives 9.92, or approximately 10. Therefore, the decimal number 0.62 is approximately equal to ¹⁰⁄₁₆, or ⅝. **See Figure B-8.**

FRACTION AND DECIMAL CONVERSION TABLES

Fraction	Decimal
$\frac{1}{16}$	0.0625
$\frac{2}{16}$, $\frac{1}{8}$	0.125
$\frac{3}{16}$	0.1875
$\frac{4}{16}$, $\frac{2}{8}$, $\frac{1}{4}$	0.25
$\frac{5}{16}$	0.3125
$\frac{6}{16}$, $\frac{3}{8}$	0.375
$\frac{7}{16}$	0.4375
$\frac{8}{16}$, $\frac{4}{8}$, $\frac{3}{4}$, $\frac{1}{2}$	0.5
$\frac{9}{16}$	0.5625
$\frac{10}{16}$, $\frac{5}{8}$	0.625
$\frac{11}{16}$	0.6875
$\frac{12}{16}$, $\frac{6}{8}$, $\frac{3}{4}$	0.75
$\frac{13}{16}$	0.8125
$\frac{14}{16}$, $\frac{7}{8}$	0.875
$\frac{15}{16}$	0.9375
$\frac{16}{16}$	1

Figure B-7. *It is often necessary to convert a number from a fraction to a decimal or from a decimal to a fraction. These conversions should be memorized.*

For mixed numbers, care must be taken to multiply only the decimal part by 16. Multiplying the entire mixed number by 16 gives the wrong results. Only the part to the right of the decimal point is multiplied by 16. If a calculation result of 20.80" is multiplied by 16, the result is 332.8, which has no meaning. If the part to the right of the decimal point, 0.80, is multiplied by 16, the result is 12.8, or about 13. This means that 20.80" is approximately equal to 20 $\frac{13}{16}$".

CALCULATOR CONVERSIONS

CONVERT 0.62 TO A FRACTION

$0.62 \times 16 = 9.92$

$0.62 = \dfrac{10}{16}$ *(approximately)*

CONVERT 20.80 TO A FRACTION

$20.80 \times 16 = 332.8$ *(no meaning)*

$0.80 \times 16 = 12.8$

$0.80 = \dfrac{13}{16}$ *(approximately)*

$20.80 = 20\dfrac{13}{16}$

Figure B-8. *A calculator can be used to convert decimals to fractions.*